THE AMERICAN RENAISSANCE RECONSIDERED

The American Renaissance
Reconsidered

Edited by Walter Benn Michaels and Donald E. Pease

THE JOHNS HOPKINS UNIVERSITY PRESS
BALTIMORE AND LONDON

Originally published in 1985 as Selected Papers from the English Institute,
1982–83, New Series, no. 9
Johns Hopkins Paperbacks edition, 1989

The Johns Hopkins University Press, 701 West 40th Street,
Baltimore, Maryland 21211
The Johns Hopkins Press Ltd., London

Library of Congress Cataloging-in-Publication Data may
be found on the last printed page of this book.

Contents

Introduction

The term *American Renaissance* designates a moment in the nation's history when the "classics," works "original" enough to lay claim to an "authentic" beginning for America's literary history, appeared. Once designated as the *locus classicus* for America's literary history, however, the American Renaissance does not remain located within the nation's secular history so much as it marks the occasion of a rebirth from it. Independent of the time kept by secular history, the American Renaissance keeps what we could call global renaissance time—the sacred time a nation claims to renew when it claims its cultural place as a great nation existing within a world of great nations. Providing each nation with the terms for cultural greatness denied to secular history, the "renaissance" is an occasion occurring not so much within any specific historical time or place as a moment of cultural achievement that repeatedly provokes rebirth.

The English Institute session entitled "The American Renaissance Reconsidered" met not so much to reconsider this demand for rebirth as to reconsider the terms of the demand. Or, rather, it reconsidered the terms other than those ordained by the American Renaissance. Consequent to this reconsideration, the demand for rebirth was met, but this time the American Renaissance was reborn not *without* but within America's secular history.

As Eric Sundquist reminds us in "Slavery, Revolution, and the American Renaissance," being reborn within an American past did not necessarily entail a recovery of secular history. Sanctioned by a sense of progressive revolution, events in America became historical out of their ability to recall America's revolutionary past. This revolutionary past was a return to lost principles (of the Glorious Revolution of 1689) rather than a rebellion against them. The American Revolution, in other words, ceased to be a historical event and instead partook of the same sacred time in demand of renewal at work in the "renaissance" formation in literary history. For Sundquist, the "renaissance" moment in our classic antebellum literature coincided with a crisis in the power of the "revolutionary moment" to keep the peace. Both proponents and opponents of slavery invoked the American Revolution as the authority for their charged positions: opponents called for a true revolution (a return to the Spirit of 1776), whereas proponents focused on the Union established by the founding fathers and warned against a war of rebellion (a separation from the principles of a people united by revolution).

In relocating the moment of literary renaissance within an anxious historical meditation over the authority to father a nation, Sundquist oversees the "rebirth" of many more figures than the American Renaissance usually legitimizes. In this essay Martin Delany's *Blake,* Harriet Beecher Stowe's *Uncle Tom's Cabin,* and Frederick Douglass's *My Bondage and My Freedom* occupy the same literary space as Melville's *Benito Cereno.* But they do not undermine Melville's authority; instead, they reinvest his narrative with the power to do more than literary justice to the terms of the historical crisis they share.

If Sundquist opens up space in the American Renaissance by relocating texts from secular history within its boundaries, Jane Tompkins recalls an "other" American Renaissance, forgotten or repressed by the values informing the authoritative Renaissance period. In the scenario implicit in the rebirth metaphor, the works of this other American Renaissance constituted the popular world of sentiment.

In affiliating this "other" American Renaissance with the revivalist movements of the time, Tompkins discusses the domestic novel and specifically Susan Warner's *The Wide Wide World* in terms other than those used to sanction Melville's *Moby Dick* published in the same year. She restores the assumptions that the sanctioning authorities of *the* American Renaissance ruled out of discussion. As it turns out, the sentimental narratives in the *other* American Renaissance convert powerlessness into a "future" power by reinterpreting submission as a discovery of the power to master one's inner nature as well as the world. As the "revival" of the "nature" that the cultivation of the American Renaissance apparently left behind, this "other" American Renaissance discloses the uncanny at work in the equation of a cultural origin with a "renaissance" moment. Despite the "excluding" progression from nature to culture in the critical romance, both nature and culture, secular history and sacred time are prone to be reborn within the American Renaissance.

In "Romance and Real Estate" Walter Benn Michaels exploits this uncanny effect. He does so moreover by entangling one of the key terms used to confirm the cultural power of the Renaissance, "Romance," within the subtle legal fictions of nineteenth-century property law. As a term "romance" corroborated the "renaissance" claim to be a world apart from the merely secular. In treating this claim as an assertion of a "personal" relation to property, "a clear and unobstructed title," Michaels redesignates romance not only as a space wherein that claim can be disputed (by the other claimants in say Sundquist's or Tompkins's renaissance) but also as the locus for the individual's efforts to come to terms with his "inalienable," hence "free," self.

Michaels does not inscribe the American Renaissance within either a strictly secular history or a literary history. Instead he suggests that one of the key figures within the American Renaissance, Nathaniel Hawthorne, invoked one of the key literary terms used to sanction the canonicity of the Renaissance, that is, romance, in order to work through the relation of individuality to certain aspects of American property law. In Michaels's essay the American Renaissance notions of freedom, revolution, romance, and even selfhood underwriting Sundquist's and Tompkins's essays turn out to be epiphenomena of legal as opposed to literary fiction.

If the "American Renaissance Reconsidered" culminated in an implicit questioning of the grounds for that title to continue legally to buy claim to that literary property, the papers delivered at the Second English Institute session, "The 'Other' American Renaissance," attempted to focus the strictly literary claims in that title. In the first session, Tompkins and Sundquist located within the period called the American Renaissance figures (like Warner, Delany, Douglass) who had been excluded from the Renaissance canon; and the second session addressed explicitly the powers of the Renaissance to include or exclude. In Sundquist's and Tompkins's essays F. O. Matthiessen in his canonical work *American Renaissance: Art and Expression in the Age of Emerson and Whitman* had emerged as a tutelary presence whose powers were evoked implicitly and on occasion explicitly to account for the exculsion of certain work and certain themes from the American canon. So the session entitled "The 'Other' American Renaissance" attempted to provide that presence with a kind of self-consciousness.

This program began with Louis A. Renza's essay on a figure Matthiessen excluded from his canon but who, as a result of his incorporation within the French tradition (as well as the post structuralist methodology sanctioned by that tradition) has returned to America. In Renza's analysis, the Poe whom Matthiessen excluded returns from the unconscious literary canon with all the power derived from having been repressed. Renza's Poe has buried himself alive within his text as the only subject capable of possessing the text. Renza argues that Poe always reclaims possession of his text from readers because he anticipated and trumped their readings in order to become aware of the secret self that emerges as what remains unread (and unwritten) but that can only appear as the unconscious reserve that writing and reading releases.

Renza reads Matthiessen's exclusion of Poe from the American Renaissance as a premature burial anticipated by Poe in his fiction, but Jonathan Arac discloses what Matthiessen had to repress (if not quite bury) in order to authorize the canon. In Arac's reading, Matthiessen achieves the masterful sense of unity in his canonizing operation at the expense of finding some of his most cherished values misrepresented. In attending to the discrepancy between the values he cherished and the masterwork of American literature he produced, Arac discovers another American Renaissance. He insists on an international as opposed to a strictly nationalistic approach to literature, representing the values of "all the people" rather than those of exclusively Renaissance figures and making possible experience rather than constraining all experience within Matthiessen's symbol structure of an organicist aesthetic.

In "Moby Dick and the Cold War," Donald E. Pease suggests that Matthiessen repressed the other American Renaissance because of the political demands of World War II. Affiliating canon-formation with a kind of national consensus-formation, Pease suggests that Matthiessen's work of canon-formation silences both his own powers of dissent as well as the "dissenting" views of such canonical figures as Melville. Pease locates *Moby Dick* within what he calls two scenes of cultural persuasion—that at work in the oratory of Melville's time and that at work in Cold War rhetoric—and releases *Moby Dick* from the key terms of persuasion at work in both scenes.

Allen Grossman ended the session with a meditation on the relationship between polity implicit in Whitman's poetics and the art implicit in Lincoln's national polity. If Michaels ended the first session by reinscribing the American Renaissance within the fictions informing the history of property, Grossman ended the second session by representing the literary (Whitman) and the secular (Lincoln) claims of the American Renaissance, bringing the foundations for the nation's laws, the Constitution and the Declaration of Independence, up for an accounting.

Grossman attends to the contradiction between the principles of sociability and justice exemplified by Lincoln and Whitman and the institutions through which these principles could become national polity, and discloses the limits of both these Renaissance men to confer freedom and justice. Most importantly, Grossman's provocative meditation observes that the American Renaissance— the creation of a real world consistent with American principles both of order and value—is unfinished. Hence it demands our continued reconsideration.

DONALD E. PEASE
Dartmouth College

THE AMERICAN RENAISSANCE RECONSIDERED

Eric J. Sundquist

Slavery, Revolution, and the American Renaissance

On the first anniversary of the *Liberator* in 1832 William Lloyd Garrison invoked the "Spirit of Liberty" that was "thundering at castle-gates and prison-doors" throughout the world. Rather than celebrate the fires of democratic revolution that had spread from the America of 1776, Garrison dwelled on the significant failure of the American Revolution—the problem of slavery. When liberty "gets the mastery over its enemy," Garrison asked rhetorically, "will not its retaliation be terrible?" Only "timely repentance" could save the American "nation of blind, unrelenting, haughty, cruel, heaven-daring oppressors" from the fate of foreign despots and aristocracies. Because repentance on a national scale did not seem likely, Garrison introduced a paradoxical possibility: in order to avoid having to join in defending the South against slave insurrection, the North ought to dissolve the Union; were this threat to "break the chain which binds [the South] to the Union" actualized, however, Garrison predicted that "the scenes of St. Domingo would be witnessed throughout her borders."[1]

Garrison was no doubt thinking of the Nat Turner rebellion of the previous year, America's largest and most successful slave rebellion (which became, as Thomas Wentworth Higginson put it some thirty years later, "a memory of terror, a symbol of wild retribution"), and he thus drew back from such outright "treachery to the people of the south" and paused simply to reflect that, as a nation condoning slavery, "we are guilty—all guilty—horribly guilty." But the "double rebellion" Garrison found stirring in 1832—the rebellion of the South against the United States government, and of slaves against masters—was nonetheless prophetic. It defined the crisis of civil war that would engulf the nation thirty years hence, just as the guilt Garrison sought here to expunge can only be understood to have increased over that period. Surely it

1

had increased by 1844, when Garrison, on behalf of the American Anti-Slavery Society, announced their policy of "No Union with Slaveholders" and raised the "banner of revolution." Declaring that "the Union which grinds [slaves] to the dust rests upon us" as well, that "their shackles are fastened to our limbs," Garrison called for "bloodless strife, excepting *our* blood be shed."[2]

Although he spoke radically in advocating the dissolution of the Union, Garrison's nonviolent passion suggests in its hesitation to act, or to act violently, the ambivalence that pre–Civil War generations felt and expressed toward the legacy of the founding fathers. In defining a relation to the recent past, the new generations embraced conflicting impulses and contradictions of the kind that appear boldly in the literary work of the period. Just as the political and social documents of the antebellum period constitute some of its greatest and most imaginative writing, so the literary work in its most powerful forms is infused with directly engaged social and political issues. In both cases, the problem of slavery impinged upon all others, producing a national ideology riddled with ambiguities and tension, and year by year distorting the course of American democracy. Before examining in more detail the major events and ideas that united the complex problem of slavery with the principles of the Revolution, and the significant literature that the slavery crisis produced, we might first glance at representative responses of two of the period's great politicians and orators, Webster and Lincoln.

I

The character of the generations between the wars has been described variously—as a grand fete of nationalism, an exercise in imperial aggression, a time during which the new nation darkened with unredeemed sins. The simultaneous truth of these descriptions, and the psychological development that may be said to accompany them, are exemplified in the career of Webster. In 1825 Webster chose a popular rhetorical figure (later echoed to different effect by Emerson in the opening of *Nature*) in order to celebrate the laying of the cornerstone of the Bunker Hill Monument. As a race of "children" standing "among the sepulchres of our fathers," Webster counseled, Americans should be thankful that the "great wheel of political revolution," which began in America but soon spread "conflagration and terror" around the world, issued here in tranquillity and prosperity. In the spirit of nationalism with which they are blessed, the American children should accept as their great duty the "defence and preservation" of the fathers' creation, the cultivation of "a true spirit of union and harmony." When the monument was completed in 1843, its "foundations in soil which drank deep of early Revolutionary blood," Webster again commemorated the fathers, especially Washington, but spoke ominously against the day when the American Union "should be broken up and destroyed" and "faction and dismemberment obliterate for ever all the hopes of the founders of our republic and the great inheritance of their children." By 1850, anxious to preserve the Union at the cost of conciliating slave interests, Webster would dedicate his famous speech of March 7 in defense of the Compromise of 1850 to Massachusetts, and further suggest in a following speech that Massachusetts, "so early to take her part in the great contest of the Revolution," and by "a law imposed upon her by the recollections of the past," would again be among the first "to offer the outpouring of her blood and treasure" in defense of the Union. At this point, however, Emerson asserted that Webster had become "the head of the slavery party" in the United States.[3]

   Although Webster sought to ward off a sectional crisis, not to precipitate one, his fall from political grace became part of an unfolding drama of ideals sacrificed and redeemed. Contemptuously alluding to Webster's "noble words" at Bunker Hill, "the spot so reddened with the blood of our fathers," Theodore Parker replied to Webster that "the question is, not if slavery is to cease, and soon to cease, but shall it end as it ended in Massachusetts, in New Hampshire, in Pennsylvania, in New York, or shall it end as in St. Domingo? Follow the counsel of Mr. Webster—it will end in fire and blood." In courting the attacks of Emerson, Parker, and

others, Webster illustrated the crisis that convulsed the Union—in
the very name of "union"—and made appeals to the spirit of the
Revolution ironic, if not, as Emerson said of the Fugitive Slave
Law that accompanied the Compromise, "suicidal." Perhaps,
though, the vision of the fathers and the suicide of the sons were
entangled; perhaps, Lincoln warned in his 1838 Lyceum Address,
"as a nation of freemen we must live through all time, or die by
suicide." Setting the context for his ostensible subject, "the per-
petuation of our political institutions," Lincoln spoke against the
kind of mob violence that took the life of abolitionist editor
Elijah Lovejoy (an event that Edward Beecher that same year described as not simply the murder of a "father" but the slaying of
the laws and liberties of a "nation"), and he chose as another example the lynching of "Negroes suspected of conspiring to raise an
insurrection."[4] The decades that followed, in which Lincoln would
in the eyes of many become the heroic savior of his country,
proved the examples less significant than the fundamental question
they raised: how, in "a nation of freemen," did the Revolution
speak to the issue of slavery?

Lincoln's address, often seen to desecrate the fathers and to
betray a monumental desire for personal power, marks his initial
turn away from the mesmerizing power of the Revolutionary past.
Twenty years later he broke free from the awe of previous generations at the same time he broke free from the nonviolence of conservative antislavery. In saving the Union while abolishing slavery,
he thus stood between Garrison and Webster. He was able to do so
because the scenes of the Revolution, as he argued in his early address, had grown "dim by the lapse of time." The "forest of giant
oaks" had been swept over, leaving only "here and there a lonely
trunk," with "mutilated limbs," "despoiled of its verdure." The
relationship between Lincoln and the Revolutionary generation
can be gauged symbolically by noting that his image of the fathers
as declining giant oaks had been anticipated by Thomas Paine,
who warned in *Common Sense* that in "the seedtime of continental
union" the least fracture would be "like a name engraved with

the point of a pin on the tender rind of a young oak; the wound would enlarge with the tree, and posterity read it in full-grown characters."[5] The name engraved in the oak was slavery; only the further violence of domestic rebellion and fraternal war would heal the wound.

The New Testament figure of a "house divided against itself" that Paine had used to characterize the struggle of king against people in the American colonies would likewise reappear in Lincoln's famous House Divided speech of 1858. On this occasion, as he did even after the Civil War was a reality, Lincoln continued to speak for union—in the name of the fathers' tacit, limited protection of slavery; but the internal divisions between free soil and proslavery, recast by abolitionists and Republicans to show the South as a stronghold of despotism equal to any European monarchy, were nevertheless present in Lincoln's allusion to a secret conspiracy to extend slavery by means of the Nebraska doctrine and the recent Dred Scott decision. Like much of the nation, that is to say, Lincoln himself was divided. As the values and intent of the Revolution became less and less vivid as doctrine, yet more and more compelling as symbols that could be seized with equal insistence by either side, a further division in the "house"—between the Revolutionary past and the nationalistic present—complicated the issues of democratic freedom and sectional power. As George Forgie has argued, the anxiety of the "post-heroic generations" in the face of the inimitable achievements of the Revolutionary fathers left them at once unable to act with originality and unwilling obediently to follow the example set by the fathers. They were rebellious and conservative at the same time, on no issue more so than slavery. The failure to abolish slavery in the late eighteenth century left succeeding generations stymied, imprisoned by the Constitution's apparent protection of slavery, yet conscious of the implicit attack on it in the Declaration of Independence. The post-Revolutionary sons, it could be said, harbored the sins of the past until the accumulated pressure—of territorial acquisition, of political dissension, of guilt—became too great. In the violence of

internal reblleion and civil war the post-Revolutionary generations
became, as Jefferson had feared in the wake of San Domingo, "the
murderers of our own children."[6]

II

The "rebirth" our classic literature is said to constitute occurred
precisely in an era—from the 1830s through the Civil War—in which
the authority of the fathers had become the subject of anxious
meditation and in which the national crisis over slavery's limits
compelled a return to the fraternally divisive energies of revolution. Though duplicitous attitudes toward America's own recent
birth and her course of empire increased in cultural and political
thought over that period, they had been nonetheless present from
the beginning. The Civil War restored union and may therefore be
seen as essentially conservative or redemptive, much as the Revolution itself was seen by many of its participants to be a return—a
revolution, rather than a *rebellion*—to lost principles on the model
of the Glorious Revolution of 1689. In this respect, the Civil War
itself might be seen as restoring those freedoms suppressed in 1776,
or intended but never actualized: that is, it became a *revolution*
rather than the "war of the rebellion" it seemed at the outset. The
irony of the 1689 model lies in the great wave of slave imports
into the North American colonies that occurred at nearly the same
moment; at a more contemporary level, the irony appears in the
notion of continuing, progressive revolution that Sacvan Bercovitch
has demonstrated to constitute the tradition of the jeremiad in
America and to provide the basis for a "national consensus" in
which the providential design of the country was constantly reaf-
firmed and revolutionary radicalism "socialized into an affirmation of order." By the time of the war, Lincoln and others would
have no trouble appropriating the fiery vision of the Revolutionary
fathers to their own regenerative purposes; but Lincoln's initial
desire to punish the South and redeem the fathers *without* abolish-

ing slavery betrays a problem that the national consensus served as well to conceal as to express.[7]

It was a question to which Hawthorne, a man otherwise attentive to the ambiguities of freedom and the fraternal complexities of the Revolution, was strangely blind, except, characteristically, as he recognized the elementary doubleness of America's political origins. Although he understood that "the children of the Puritans" were connected to the Africans of Virginia in a singular way, since the "fated womb" of the Mayflower "sent forth a brood of Pilgrims on Plymouth Rock" in her first voyage, and in a subsequent one "spawned slaves upon the Southern soil," Hawthorne's apprehension of this "monstrous birth," recorded in 1862, did not prevent him from satirizing Lincoln and envisioning a group of escaped slaves "akin to the fawns and rustic deities of olden times." The symbolic connection Hawthorne noted between pilgrims and slaves in a larger sense forms one of the central paradoxes of American history. The rise of liberty and the rise of slavery in America took place simultaneously from the seventeenth to the nineteenth centuries. In Virginia especially, as Edmund Morgan has demonstrated, slavery made free white society more homogeneous, allowed the flourishing of commonwealth ideas about taxation, property, and representation, and thus brought Virginians into the political tradition of New England. The links between liberty and slavery were all the more complicated in view of the rhetoric of enslavement that American colonists employed during the Revolution. A famous suppressed clause of the Declaration of Independence charged George III with "violating the most sacred rights of life and liberty" in the practice of the slave trade and, moreover, with instigating rebellion among American slaves, "thus paying off former crimes committed against the *liberties* of one people, with crimes he urges them to commit against the *lives* of another." Revolutionary pamphlets often cast Americans as slaves of king and parliament, suggesting at times that chattel slavery was but an extreme form of a more pervasive political oppression. As attempts to abolish slavery during and after the

Revolution foundered on the questions of (human) property rights, vital economy, fear of insurrection and amalgamation, and the legacy of the fathers, the tentative identification between colonists and slaves collapsed. The very fact that some of the most influential founding fathers—among them Jefferson and Washington—were slaveholders enhanced the doubleness at the heart of the American experiment and in the long run invited the two-edged sarcasm of Theodore Parker: "The most valuable export of Virginia, is her Slaves, enriched by 'the best blood of the old dominion;' the 'Mother of Presidents' is also the great Slave Breeder of America. Since she ceased to import bondsmen from Africa, her Slaves [have] become continually paler in the face; it is the 'effect of the climate'—and Democratic Institutions."[8]

The increasing distance from the Revolution allowed later generations to focus the contradiction between liberty and slavery in the question of "perpetual union," a question that, despite the great power of Washington's Farewell Address in 1796, did not—perhaps, could not—become a vital issue until the generation of the fathers was dead. At that point Americans opposed to slavery had to balance the harmony of union against the principle of freedom; they not only *could* entertain a contradiction in sentiments, but virtually *had* to, unless they were willing to follow radicals like Garrison in calling for the dissolution of the Union. Lincoln himself, even though he sought a new "field of glory" equivalent to that enjoyed by the "once hardy, brave, and patriotic, but now lamented and departed, race of ancestors, demanded in the Lyceum address of 1838 that "every lover of liberty ... swear by the blood of the Revolution" never to violate the laws of the country embodied in the Constitution, and remember that to do so "is to trample on the blood of his father, and to tear the charter of his own and his children's liberty."[9]

Lincoln's magically ambivalent speech, juggling the concept of union as precariously as Jefferson had juggled the concept of liberty in framing the Declaration of Independence, is one of the initiating documents of the impending national trauma and the explosive literature that accompanied it. It forecasts Lincoln's reluctance to contravene the fathers' protection of slavery, and it finely illuminates what David Brion Davis has described as the "widening chasm of time between the transcendent moment of rebirth—when the 'Word of Liberty' created a nation—and the recurring rediscoveries of America's unredeemed sin."[10] The sense of "continuing Revolutionary time" that kept the chasm from swallowing up the nation could not be extended indefinitely. Though it was prolonged for close to a century, one may date the first serious fractures, the recurring rediscoveries of sin, most vividly from the early 1830s. A time of new revolutions in Europe, it was in America a time during which the national memory of the Revolution took on a particularly fragile cast and during which the forces of social and sexual reform, an accelerating market economy, and the crisis over territorial acquisition and the extension of slavery that were to produce the major issues for the writers of the American Renaissance first became tangible.

III

The year of Garrison's anniversary editorial, 1832, also saw the publication of his *Thoughts on African Colonization*, which argued vigorously that the colonization of American blacks was a futile project and became instrumental in turning antislavery attention to the real question of black freedom *in America*. The year 1832 was also the widely celebrated centennial of Washington's birth, a fact that brings into special relief the significant events that surround it. Hawthorne that year published his two great tales of revolutionary anxiety, "My Kinsman, Major Molineux" and "Roger Malvin's Burial" (both responding to the glimmering memory of Washington himself and the generations of fathers that had passed away with the mystical deaths of Adam and Jefferson on the Fourth of July, 1826), and John Pendleton Kennedy brought forth *Swallow Barn*, the first significant fictional defense of slavery. At the same time, the Virginia House of Delegates undertook the most serious debate in its history on the

question of slave emancipation. In the wake of Nat Turner's bloody
Virginia rebellion and another threatening uprising of slaves in
British Jamaica in 1831, the delegates were almost exactly split on
the possibility of abolishing slavery in its American place of birth.
After this date the southern stance in defense of slavery prevailed
and rigidified, and was characterized with fierce precision by
Thomas R. Dew, whose classic 1832 essay, "Abolition of Negro
Slavery" (later expanded as *Review of the Debate in the Virginia
Legislature of 1831-1832*), argued against both colonization and
emancipation. Pointing to the example of continued turmoil in
Haiti and comparing potentially freed slaves to a Frankenstein
monster incapable of coping with liberty, Dew belittled analogies
between the cause of American slaves and contemporary revolutions in Poland and France; the "right of revolution" does not
exist, he said, for persons "totally unfit for freedom and self-
government" and certain to bring "ruin and degradation," "relent-
less carnage and massacre" upon all.[11] Dew on one side and
Garrison on the other defined the extreme form polemics for and
against slavery would take for the next thirty years.

The early 1830s, still transported by the enthusiastic nationalism of the previous decade, also witnessed the initial signs of dissent over a problem that would bring to a crisis the issue of
slavery—the problem of territorial acquisition and America's sense
of democratic mission. Celebrating the centennial of Washington's
birth, Webster reminded his audience that Washington regarded
nothing of greater importance than the "integrity of the Union"
and warned that "disunion and dismemberment" would "sweep
away, not only what we possess, but all our powers of regaining
lost, or acquiring new possessions." The following year, 1833,
Lydia Maria Child from a rather different point of view lamented
the fact that Washington's farewell advice about the necessity of
union no longer "operated like a spell upon the hearts and con-
sciences of his countrymen." She noted that southern threats of
secession had diminished the public's reverence for union; and
fearing the extension of slavery into new territories (but thankful,
at this point, that Mexico placed a barrier against the acquisition

of Texas), she derided the government's refusal to recognize Haitian independence. By the 1850s, appeals to the fathers on this score seemed more than ever to summon up an illusion. In his 1853 inauguration speech, alluding to the "manifest and beneficient [sic] Providence" that guided "our fathers," Franklin Pierce praised the Compromise of 1850 and predicted the acquisition of Cuba ("certain possessions not within our jurisdiction eminently important for our protection"), proslavery positions voiced, as Pierce said, "within reach of the tomb of Washington, with all the cherished memories of the past gathered around me like so many eloquent voices from heaven."[12]

The legacy of the fathers provided for manifest destiny, which increased fears of the extension of slavery and slave power, which in turn destroyed the integrity of the Union and the legacy of the fathers. A belief in the divine mission of America could sanction antislavery but it could just as easily compel devotion to union in the service of slavery and its expansion. The spirit of American mission that legitimized war with Mexico and prompted self-congratulation that 1776 was the source of current "democratic" revolutions in Europe in 1848 also prompted patriotic defenses of moderation, even fire-eating, on the question of slavery. Thus Hawthorne, in his campaign biography of Pierce, celebrated Pierce's bodily descent from a renowned Revolutionary father; he repeatedly emphasized the necessary link between Revolutionary glory and the concept of union; he dwelled on Pierce's "heroic" role in the war with Mexico, which "struck an hereditary root in his breast" and linked him to the vision of the fathers; and he argued, with respect to Pierce's support of the Compromise of 1850, that as an "unshaken advocate of Union," Pierce saw that "merely human wisdom and human efforts cannot subvert [slavery], except by tearing to pieces the Constitution . . . and severing into distracted fragments that common country which Providence brought into one nation, through a continued miracle of almost two hundred years, from the first settlement of the American wilderness until the Revolution."[13]

Hawthorne's *Life* of Pierce may be his most neglected romance.

It is a primary document in the nationalistic Young America movement, and it exemplifies Hawthorne's need (one he shared with
Simms and Cooper) to ground the value of contemporary accomplishments in the bedrock of a highly conservative Revolutionary tradition. Yoking together union and slavery, sentimental
politics and American expansion, the *Life* allows Hawthorne the
widely shared fantasy that slavery is "one of those evils which
divine Providence does not leave to be remedied by human con-
trivances" but one day, "by some means impossible to be anticipated," will cause "to vanish like a dream." His argument, like the
typological patterns of his tales, locates the providential origin of
union well in advance of 1776. As the American Revolution is for
Hawthorne a return to the strength of betrayed Puritan principles
in which the rebellious patriot shadows forth the grim features of
his forefathers, so manifest destiny is here part of the "continued
miracle" of America, and union the state of grace ordained by the
sacred document, the Constitution. This aspect of American civil
religion was endorsed by Pierce in his acceptance of the nomina-
tion when he called upon "a Power superior to human might"
that "from the first gun of the Revolution, in every crisis through
which we have passed," has brought "out of darkness the rainbow
of promise." But the power Pierce relied upon, abolitionists feared,
was a godless, aggrandizing "Slave Power," which sought to extend
its political influence, along with the institution of slavery, by
"revolutionizing" new territories in the name of democratic freedom. Casting back to the common ground of colonial revolt,
abolitionists saw a Slave Power conspiracy that resembled and
reanimated old fears of a conspiracy of king and parliament against
their subjects. By "reenacting the primal resistance to subversion"
that had prevailed in "popular conceptualizations of the American Revolution" as a combat of conspiratorial British plots against
existing liberties, antislavery forces could affirm their kinship with
the founding fathers and finish the incomplete Revolution.[14]

Who, though, were the subversives in this case? As they built
upon the pattern of paranoia about subversion that had characterized American popular politics since the earliest incidents of

revolution, abolitionists on the one hand and proslavery forces on the other displayed the double face of American liberty. Antislavery appeared as a conspiracy of Jacobins, British sympathizers, and religious fanatics to renounce the Constitution and to create slave rebellion and revenge; the Slave Power appeared a means of imperial expansion that in its very nature would destroy the liberties first generated by 1776.

IV

The distilled symbolic representation of this doubleness in the legacy of the American Revolution from the 1790s forward was the slave revolution in San Domingo. Replete with ironies, as W. E. B. Du Bois sensed, San Domingo caught the fire of the French Revolution in 1791; it bolstered the antislavery movement in England and accelerated the suppression of the slave trade; it became a primary point of reference for both proslavery and antislavery forces in America; and it ended Napoleon's vision of American empire, leading thus to the Louisiana Purchase and, eventually, the crisis question of slavery in the territories. Following the first flight of terrified planter refugees to the United States in the early 1790s, and again in the wake of Turner's balked rebellion in Southampton, Virginia, San Domingo was summoned up in arguments over the possibility of slave or free black insurrection. Like a prism, it reflected all sides and shades of the question, paradoxical or not, and appears throughout the literature of the antebellum period. For example, a southern abolitionist, Angelina Grimke, argued that the worst bloodshed in San Domingo took place not because of black revolution and emancipation but because of France's attempt to reimpose slavery in 1802; while a northern moderate, Catherine Beecher, replied to Grimke in 1837 that radical abolitionism, by evoking such examples and making slavery more severe in reaction, was raising "the paean song of liberty and human rights" among slaves and preparing the way for the "terrors of insurrection" and catastrophic civil war. From either point of view, however, the presiding threat of San Domingo to the United States was a form of historical revenge. It threatened to spread what Winthrop Jordan has called "the cancer of revolution" throughout the slaveholding empires and held forth the promise, as the black novelist and political activist William Wells Brown wrote in 1855, that "the revolution that was commenced in 1776 would . . . be finished, and the glorious sentiments of the Declaration of Independence" realized. Having "shed their [own] blood in the American revolutionary war," Brown argued, slaves were now "only waiting the opportunity of wiping out their wrongs in the blood of their oppressors."[15]

Here Brown turned on its head the frequent warnings against slave insurrection and echoed a pamphleteer who had written in the wake of Denmark Vesey's 1822 conspiracy that "our NEGROES are truly the *Jacobins* of the country . . . the *anarchists* and the *domestic* enemy." Surely, Brown and others suggested, there was a Toussaint waiting to rise in revolt against the southern states, a "black Cromwell," as Parker wrote, ready to annihilate slavery just as theocracy, monarchy, and aristocracy had been (or were being) annihilated in Europe. It seemed not. The closest American slaves had and would come to San Domingo was Turner's 1831 rebellion. Turner originally planned the rebellion to occur, appropriately, on the Fourth of July. To the extent that Fourth of July orations served in the decades preceding the Civil War to give ritual form to America's progressive revolution, Turner's plot—like Garrison's burning of the Constitution on the Fourth of July, 1854, following Pierce's enforcement of the Fugitive Slave Law in Boston with federal troops—made the theatrical aspects of American politics more apparent. "What to the American slave," asked Frederick Douglass in a famous 1852 address, "is your Fourth of July?"—what but "a thin veil to cover up crimes which would disgrace a nation of savages." The Fourth's ritual importance was itself thus double: what does it more resemble, with respect to white America, than one of those holidays of which Douglass wrote in his autobiography, designed to keep down "the spirit of insurrection among the slaves" and provide a "safety valve to carry off the

explosive elements inseparable from the human mind, when reduced to the condition of slavery.''[16] But as Turner's plot and
other evidence suggests, holidays, especially the Fourth, could
not only defuse insurrection but also conceal and promote it. Like
the idea of union, the spirit of the Fourth of July wore a special
mask of political vengeance; its annual celebrations and oratory
defined freedom restrictively, of course, but did so with increasirg
tension and ambiguity.

Turner may have embodied the spirit of the age of revolution,
but the most intriguing thing about the record of Turner's own intentions we have, Thomas Gray's *Confessions* (1831), is that the
ideas of rebellion and freedom are hardly in evidence; instead, the
emphasis lies, in Turner's purported confessions, on his messianic
visions and, in Gray's editorial commentary, on the derangement
of Turner and his "dreadful conspiracy" of "diabolical actors." By
staging Turner as a "gloomy fanatic" lost "in the recesses of his
own dark, bewildered, and overwrought mind" as he plotted his
apocalyptic drama and carried it out in methodical, cold-blooded
fashion, Gray reduced this "first instance in our history of an
open rebellion of the slaves" (as he deceptively termed it) to a
unique example of deviation from the normally good-willed, safe
relationship of master and slave. As it embodied the central
paradox of southern representations of slaveholding—that the
institution was one of affectionate paternalism *but* that bloody
insurrection could break forth at the least relaxation of vigilance—
the *Confessions* served thus to sound an alarm but also to suppress
the violent justness of Turner's plot and to disguise its motives.[17]

Contrary to this picture of an isolated madman, Toussaint, by
all accounts one of the great leaders of the age of revolution, considered himself the "father" of his new country's "children." In
warning the Directory in 1797 of a reactionary move in the legislature to restore slavery, he cautioned that the slaveholding interests were "unable to conceive how many sacrifices a true love of
country can support in a better father than they." Compared by
Wendell Phillips to Lafayette, Washington, Napoleon, Cromwell,
and John Brown in a famous address of 1861 (the more startling

because the black general had "no drop of white blood in his veins"), Toussaint invited the withering comparison to the father of America that William Wells Brown provided several years earlier:

> Each was the leader of an oppressed and outraged people, each had a powerful enemy to contend with, and each succeeded in founding a government in the New World. Toussaint's government made liberty its watchword, incorporated it in its constitution, abolished the slave-trade, and made freedom universal amongst the people. Washington's government incorporated slavery and the slave-trade, and enacted laws by which chains were fastened upon the limbs of millions of people. Toussaint liberated his countrymen; Washington enslaved a portion of his, and aided in giving strength and vitality to an institution that will one day rend assunder the UNION that he helped to form. Already the slave in his chains in the rice fields of Carolina and the cotton fields of Mississippi, burns for revenge.

Brown, author of a novel in which the reputed slave mistress and children of Jefferson figure in a story that includes the Turner revolt (*Clotel*, 1853), was thus ready to deliver the "scorching irony" that Douglass called for in his Fourth of July address.[18] Nat Turner, as presented by Gray, could be afforded no such irony: a maniac, self-styled martyr, perhaps, but hardly the "father" of a new nation. Still, Gray's version of Turner's revolt commands special attention because it contains at once the contradictory aspects of slave heroism that would soon appear in two of the central fictional treatments of the question of slave resistance, Stowe's *Uncle Tom's Cabin* and Delany's *Blake*.

V

Not surprisingly, the messianic, suffering Turner was precisely the one embraced by such vocal abolitionists as Higginson, Garrison, and Stowe. The ambivalence about Turner is nowhere clearer than in Stowe's novel *Dred* (1856), which modeled its title character on Turner (she appended a copy of the *Confessions* to the novel) and portrayed him as the son of Denmark Vesey; made him appear even more insane than Gray had; and killed him off before anything decisive could come of his plots. For Stowe, of course, violent revolution was no answer, and her sentimental racialism prevented her from imagining fully the need for, and the effects of, such insurrection. Rebellion, as it appears in Uncle Tom's Cabin, is an apocalyptic issue: obviously in the Christ-like martyr-dom of Tom; or, more revealingly, in the gothic intrigues of Cassy, the demented tragic mulatto who follows Tom's advice to escape "without blood-guiltiness" but does so in a way that acts out the psychic trauma of racial liberation with which the novel, Stowe herself, and the nation were struggling. When Cassy effects her final escape by terrorizing Legree in the "ghostly garments" of his mother's shroud, she enacts the revenge of feminine power on which Stowe's entire novel draws. Legree's decaying mansion, reminiscent of the house of Usher, is the House Divided in ex-tremity, the home of both domestic (sexual) and political (racial) perversions of the family. Whatever "lurid shadows of a coming retribution" the destruction of Legree might anticipate, how-ever, one may be cautious about the novel's commitment to liber-ation.[19]

Stowe's colonizationist impulses were less racist than those of many abolitionists; yet they remain one sign of the disturbing problem of political union that pervades her novel in the form of gothic sentimentalism. An additional sign appears in St. Clare's assertion that only the "sons of white fathers" among the slaves, only those with Anglo-Saxon blood "burning in their veins," can bring forth "the San Domingo hour" and "raise with them their mother's race." The belief in dominant Anglo-Saxon blood, wide-spread enough to be echoed even by Brown in Clotel, compromises the invocation of the founding fathers by George Harris and threatens to undermine the power of Stowe's comparison between fugitive slaves and the "heroic" fugitives from the failed Hungarian revolution, eagerly received and honored by Americans. Whatever its intention, the book's stated assumption that pure blacks are naturally docile comes close to implying that slaves were incapable of revolution and unsuited even for the European "millennium of . . . greasy masses" that St. Clare's brother invokes in ridicule of the worldwide extension of democratic rights. Once America's missionary spirit and its enthusiasm for the European revolutions of 1848 waned, moreover, the effectiveness of comparisons between American slaves and European rebels was reduced and in large part reversed as Southerners once again emphatically invoked the possibility of a slave "reign of terror."[20]

In advocating the elevation of the race of slave "mothers" but denying the possibility of rebellion among *black* slaves, Stowe codified the matrix of women, slaves, and children that the cult of domesticity had generated in the decades before the war. Stowe perfected an imagistic rhetoric of sentiment that derived from the eighteenth-century ideal of benevolence, in part a Rousseauian belief that man was everywhere "in chains" and in part a result of a rising evangelical Protestantism. Although antislavery and other campaigns of reform had employed the rhetoric of sentiment for years with sporadic success, Stowe may have captured the welling emotions of a guilty nation poised for cathartic release. *Uncle Tom's Cabin* strengthened political resolve in some quarters, North and South, but more immediately it produced a flood of melodrama, graveyard poetry, popular songs, dioramas, engravings, gift books, card games, printed tippets and scarves, china busts and figurines, gold and silver spoons, commemorative plates, needlepoint, and similar artifacts that gave conventional expression to subversion and thereby contained and controlled it. Sentiment, not antislavery, made the book popular and its black hero an exemplary suffering heroine; Tom's access of feminine power and his pious sacrifice, in explicit contrast to Legree's inexorable lust and cruelty, marks the fantasy Stowe's audience eagerly adopted— that slavery was the culture's extreme revelation of lust and the South an arena of erotic dissipation "where the repressed came out of hiding." Stowe thus focused the often invisible and passive politics of domesticity and gave them a readily assimilable set of scenes calculated to incite an internal cultural revolution. Stepping beyond the restricted "women's sphere" of feminine involvement with the politics of slavery advocated by Catherine Beecher and others, Stowe insisted that the power of sentiment, a rebellion of the emotions, of heart over head, would crush the masculine tyranny of American institutions and the law of the "fathers."[21]

But as her depiction of Tom suggests, nothing in American culture was more infused with the doubleness at the heart of slavery than the sentimental ideal of domesticity and no "home" more threatened by violent dissension than the House of political union. A short sketch Stowe wrote in 1851 depicts "The Two Altars"— the "Altar of Liberty, or 1776," in which a Revolutionary family sacrifices its domestic comforts to support the struggle against a despotic British government that would make Americans "slaves of a foreign power"; and the "Altar of ——, or 1850," in which a fugitive slave is returned to bondage, "sacrificed on the altar of the Union." The obvious contrast of the tales obscures the fact that conservative abolition only with difficulty broke free from the domestic ideal sanctioned by the Revolutionary past. As in the case of San Domingo, the ideal of the "family was claimed on both sides as a justification of its ideology. In rejecting American participation in the 1826 Panama Congress, where black delegates from Haiti were certain to discuss their revolution, for instance, Robert Hayne warned that the South considered slavery a "domestic question" concerning "our most sacred rights" that could be meddled with only at the risk of "the safety of our families, our altars, and our firesides." In addition to making the usual arguments that northern wage labor was more exploitative than chattel slavery, that slavery was authorized by the Bible, and that the Constitution sanctioned slavery, the numerous novelistic replies to *Uncle Tom's Cabin* joined more respected polemicists like William Gilmore Simms and George Fitzhugh in claiming that antislavery was a misguided attack on the twin paternalistic ideals of family authority and political union.[22]

In her treatment of black character and her implicit challenge to the paternal ideal of the Revolutionary past, then, Stowe's novel embraces the very tensions that divided the nation. Her merger of slavery and sexual mastery, her moving exploration of "deep-laid patterns of escape, bondage, and rebellion" (in the several senses Constance Rourke refers to), draws upon the tangled guilt that Garrison's "No Union" policy sought to expunge but could only etch more boldly. The romance of sentimental domesticity that lends her novel its great emotional power might free the slaves and crucify them at the same time. The apocalyptic suffering that activates *Uncle Tom's Cabin* arises not only from repressed Calvanistic fears of Negro "blackness" but also from a crisis of purification in which Revolutionary sentiment and the will of God struggled antagonistically to become united against slavery. As the issue of union became increasingly tied to sentimental images of home, tranquillity, and moral virtue located in the heroic age of the founding fathers, it exacerbated the paradox that antislavery offered a divine stage for the redemption of America's national sins at the same time it invited regressive capitulation to the authority (and chastisement) of the civil fathers. Our "fear of dissolving the Union," Lydia Maria Child had written twenty years earlier of this "siamese question," is the strongest reason for "our supineness of the subject of slavery."[23] The double impulses of defiance and obedience Child identified, so infusing Lincoln's political vision, also lie behind Stowe's association of gothic terror and domesticity. The gothic was preeminently the genre of revolution and psychological upheaval, and domesticity had become the image of America's successful revolution and its stymied incompletion. Sentiment, because it turned the idea of *black* revolutionary violence inward and internalized suffering as imminent heavenly wrath, made it possible to conceive of the revolutionary destruction of slavery without violence.

Calling instead for human wrath and externalized revolutionary force, Martin Delany replied to Stowe in his novel *Blake; Or, the Huts of America*, written in the early- to mid-1850s and published serially in part in 1859 and probably in full in 1861 and 1862. Though it is not artfully crafted and lacks the visionary powers of *Uncle Tom's Cabin*, *Blake* advocates slave revolution and depicts a leader, Henry Blake, who combines the vision of Nat Turner and the commanding intelligence and authority of Toussaint. Identifying divine deliverance with violent revolution and associating the plotted insurrections of Gabriel Prosser,

Denmark Vesey, and Nat Turner with the spirit of the American Revolution, Blake, a free man, spreads a plot for "terrible insurrection" throughout the South after his wife, a slave who rejects the attentions of her owner-father, is sold to a planter in Cuba. Blake then follows her trail to Cuba, buys her freedom, and becomes the leader of the "Army of Emancipation" that will free the slaves of Cuba and, presumably, spread the fire of revolution to the United States.[24] The novel, as it survives, breaks off appropriately in an unresolved state of tension, on the brink of black revolution.

The portion of the novel set in Cuba is significant in several respects, not least because it carries the action to a country that the South, on the example of Texas, had hoped for years to annex either by purchase or outright seizure. Throughout the filibustering of the 1840s and '50s it was argued that the United States had a providential right to Cuba, as well as Haiti, Mexico, and Latin America at large; moreover, it was believed that freedom for blacks in those regions posed a genuine threat to white life and institutions in the South. Purported conspiracies between Britain and Spain for the "Africanization of Cuba," combined with countering southern designs on Caribbean and Latin American territories, made Cuba significant in symbolic as well as actual terms. The same year that *Blake* first appeared, the *Democratic Review*, long an organ for the most extraordinary claims of manifest destiny, published a lead essay promoting the acquisition of Cuba that invoked the spirit and blood baptism of 1776, implored the government to "rescue" Cuba from likely European despotism, and anticipated the continued onward movement of "the ark of the Democratic covenant." Slavery, of course, would be protected and extended.[25]

The ironies of such patriotic designs upon Cuba are used to careful effect by Delany. Throughout the novel Cuba appears as a representative object of the increase of Slave Power; in Cuba itself the American residents term themselves "patriots" and "rebels" who engineer false alarms of black rebellion against planters in order to increase their political power with the Spanish and to set the stage for American annexation. One such alarm occurs on King's Day, a festival of African celebration that Delany suggests might well conceal the "rage" of "wild animals" and one day make "the streets of Havana run with blood." Delany had advised as early as 1849 in the *North Star* that the annexation of Cuba "should be the signal for simultaneous rebellion of all the slaves in the Southern States and throughout the island"; and the ominous conclusion to the novel as it survives—"Woe be unto those devils of whites, I say!"—leaves little doubt that Delany's vision of insurrection was meant explicitly to answer Stowe's nonviolence and to counter plots of annexation by proslavery forces in the United States. Those forces, relying on a familiar rhetoric, as did Buchanan and the other authors of the notorious Ostend Manifesto in late 1854, sensed impending treason against "our gallant forefathers" and posterity if the flames of a Cuban slave rebellion, "a second St. Domingo," were allowed to "consume the fair fabric of our Union." They advocated imperial seizure of Cuba on "the very same principle that would justify an individual in tearing down the burning house of his neighbor if there were no other means of preventing the flames from destroying his own home."[26] Domesticity and manifest destiny, union *and* slavery, were here linked indissoluably; the threat of slave rebellion became, paradoxically, a mask for the spread of slavery. Delany's novel, unlike *Uncle Tom's Cabin,* tore sentiment and slavery apart by envisioning the suppressed power of the age of revolution ushered in by the America of 1776: the power to end slavery throughout the western world, certainly in the Americas, most of all in the United States.

A free man and a professional physician (despite being forced out of Harvard Medical School when white students protested the presence of blacks and women in their class), Delany became a fierce emigrationist, and thus joins Stowe on one critical issue. Yet his vision of black colonization, first articulated in *The Political Destiny of the Colored Race on the American Continent* (1854), attacks the premise of Anglo-Saxon manifest destiny and anticipates twentieth-century arguments in predicting that the colored two-thirds of the world population will not forever "passively submit to the universal domination" of the white third. Delany also participated in John Brown's 1858 Chatham convention (but was in Liberia during Harper's Ferry), and if his emigration schemes were evidence that black "alienation had crystallized into a sweeping ideology that transcended national identity,"[27] *Blake* is meant to suggest, as Higginson warned, that every slave family concealed a Nat Turner—perhaps even a Toussaint—and that alienation would lead to violent resistance before it led to escape.

VI

For whom, though, did Stowe and Delany speak? And who, in fact, spoke most eloquently for black freedom in the decades before the war? One might ask Judge Joseph Mills, who had an appointment with Lincoln in 1864. Mr. President, Mills told Lincoln,

> I was in your reception room today. It was dark. I suppose that clouds & darkness necessarily surround the secrets of state. There in the corner I saw a man quietly reading who possessed a remarkably physiognomy. I was rivetted to the spot. I stood and stared at him. He raised his flashing eyes & caught me in the act. I was compelled to speak. Said I, Are you the President? No, replied the stranger, I am Frederick Douglass.[28]

Mills's confusion was appropriate since Douglass, long before Lincoln, saw no contradiction between the principles of the American Revolution and freedom from slavery. Falling here ideologically and chronologically between Stowe and Delany, Douglass offers what neither of them can—a firsthand account of the rise from slavery. Although it sacrifices some of the immediacy and visceral simplicity of the *Narrative of the Life of Frederick Douglass,* which appeared in 1845, the expanded 1855 version entitled *My Bondage and My Freedom* develops a philosophical frame and psychological depth for Douglass's moving autobiography and is a classic text of the American Renaissance—not least because of the literal rebirth into freedom it records and the rebirth, the reawakening, of revolutionary principles it advocates. Because it can carry

Douglass's life forward to his alliance with Garrison and his break with him over the disunion issue, *My Bondage and My Freedom* is able to describe the new dilemmas of freedom faced by an escaped slave.

A man of subtle paradoxes, Douglass was once shocked to discover that he needed to "talk like a slave, look like a slave, [and] act like a slave" in order to find a willing audience for his story, but he later rebelled against the leading abolitionist ranks and avowed his belief in the "more perfect union"—without slavery—he thought sanctioned by the Constitution. Douglass's faith in union also finds sanction in the rhetoric of revolution employed in the autobiography. Like those of Stowe and Delany, Douglass's story is grounded in the sentiment of family, and in this case as in others its argument combines the powers of each, enacting both the display of eroticized cruelty destructive of families that *Uncle Tom's Cabin* portrays and the reasoned progress toward violent resistance on behalf of families that *Blake* depicts. "Slavery does away with fathers, as it does away with families," Douglass wrote. The barbarous separation of husbands, wives, and children, along with the usurpation of sexual privileges by white masters (as, possibly, in the case of Douglass's own father-master), forms a part of "the grand aim of slavery" to obliterate "from the mind and heart of the slave, all just ideas of the sacredness of *the family,* as an institution." It is in this context that Douglass's growing sentiments of rebellion—against his different masters and against the slave-breaker Covey—acquire their great persuasive force and remind him that a slave who "kills his master . . . imitates the heroes of the revolution."[29] Precisely because the fathers to be killed might in this instance be literal fathers, and precisely because their charade of paternalistic concern was often transparently a lie, the appeal to the founding fathers drew on the emotion of lost or threatened union in a doubly powerful and relevant way.

The unsettling irony infusing that appeal to the Revolutionary past arises as well in Douglass's 1853 story "The Heroic Slave," a fictional treatment of the slave rebellion aboard the *Creole* in 1841. Like the revolt of slaves aboard the Cuban *Amistad* in 1838, the *Creole* revolt attracted international attention; whereas the *Amistad* raised the question of the North's guarantee of freedom for illegally transported slaves (the Supreme Court, against the wishes of President Van Buren and to the diplomatic outrage of Cuba and Spain, upheld that freedom), the case of the *Creole* involved American slaves who seized their ship, sailed to Nassau, and were freed by British authorities (despite protests from American officials that contradicted the findings in the *Amistad* case). Douglass's treatment of the revolt, however, focuses on Madison Washington, the leader of the revolt, and an Ohio man named Listwell, who is converted to antislavery through several encounters with Washington. In Douglass's version of the revolt, Listwell supplies the files that allow Washington and his comrades to escape their chains; but the emphasis in the final part of the story lies clearly on the slaves' determination to strike for liberty: "We have done that which you applaud your fathers for doing," Washington tells the ship's first mate, "and if we are murderers, *so were they.*" As the mate later recognizes, the slaves were acting on "the principles of 1776," and the entire story, from its exploitation of the birth in Virginia of a *black* hero named Washington to its interlocutory narrative technique aimed at the conversion of a white audience, intends to show that slaves have both the right and the ability to rebel.[30]

Even in 1855, however, the year of Melville's *Benito Cereno,* Douglass was wary of revealing the various "incendiary" sentiments likely to arise in the minds of slaves. But he warned in one of several passages in his autobiography devoted to the idea of rebellion that "the slaveholder, kind or cruel," every hour violates the "inalienable rights of man" and is "every hour silently whetting the knife of vengeance for his own throat. He never lisps a syllable in commendation of the fathers of this republic, nor denounces any attempted oppression of himself, without inviting the knife to his own throat, and asserting the rights of rebellion for his slaves." Benito Cereno, mimicking the prototypical image of a languid slaveowner, glimpses the significance of this fatal lesson; Captain Delano, racist New Englander in the age of revolution,

only *imagines* revenge in the theatrical pantomime of decapitation
played out in the notorious shaving scene aboard the *San Domin-
ick.* Unable to see past an enchanting domestic vision of slavery as
"naked nature," a relationship of paternal care and affection,
Delano fails to understand the meaning of the very rebellion that
he helps to suppress.[31]

More than any of his earlier long works, which struggle indirectly
with the question of slavery through treatments of territorial
acquisition and America's national mission, Melville's short tale
comprehends the complex history and knotted contemporary
issues of black bondage in America. The setting—on board a
Spanish ship off the coast of Chile in the late 1790s—displaces the
question of domestic slave insurrection. But it does so by casting
back to the Spanish initiation of the New World slave trade
through the first importation of slaves into San Domingo (under
the auspices of Dominican priests) and by alluding to the United
States' continued fear of Caribbean revolution and its projected
acquisition of Central and South American territories. As a response to the Compromise of 1850, which in part defined policy
on slavery in the territory acquired in the Mexican War, *Benito
Cereno* exploits the collision of domestic and international interests that had previously arisen in the cases of revolt aboard the
Amistad and the *Creole,* but which were now given more urgency
by expansionist calls to "revolutionize" Cuba and all of Mexico.
Far from dwelling on an eccentric incident, then, Melville envi-
sioned a conflict between Anglo-Saxon and Spanish of the kind
Theodore Parker had spoken of in his 1854 speech on 'The
Nebraska Question." As the "children of a decomposing State,
time-worn and debauched," said Parker, Spanish colonies in America were doomed to corruption and failure. They inherited super-
stition and tyranny, rather than arts, letters, and liberty; founded
on slavery and despotism, the Spanish empire in its entirety tended
toward the fate of Mexico: "Where the carcass of a nation rots
there will the fillibusters be gathered together. Every raven in the
hungry flock of American politicians looks that way, wipes his
greedy beak, prunes his wings, and screams 'Manifest Destiny.'"

The Puritan spirit, diligent and liberty-loving, has a history counter to that of the Spanish, Parker argued, but still the worldwide march of mankind toward freedom, "every step a Revolution," must overcome the monstrous iniquity of slavery, and America, if it is to lead the march, must first destroy slavery within its own borders.[32]

Parker's speech, without the trenchant ironies of Melville's tale, leaves the resolution of this crisis untold, though its version of progressive revolt, in apocalyptic purification, leads closer to the actuality of the Civil War. Melville's version is the story of a minor rebellion that, in historical fact, did occur. Yet the enervating suspense of Melville's prose, intimating but suppressing revolt in nearly every phrase, as in the masquerade of terror between Benito Cereno and Babo staged for the sanguine Delano, defines a crisis that would not arise: despite Turner's example, American slaves would not mount a great insurrection. Rather, the South would rebel against the North, and in putting down this "parricidal rebellion" against "the Constitution, the Union, and the Flag" (as Lincoln called it), the North would appeal to the example of the Revolutionary fathers and the sustained ideal of union. The value and, indeed, the price of union haunts Melville's tale from beginning to end, not least because in Delano Melville seems to pillory his own father-in-law, Lemuel Shaw, who presided in the trial and return to slavery of Thomas Sims, declaring the Fugitive Slave Law constitutional; and also to pillory Webster, whose support of the Compromise and the Sims decision became notorious. When Delano invokes the blue sea, blue sky, and sunshine that Benito Cereno, overcome by the shadow of "the negro," cannot appreciate, he echoes Webster, who spoke similarly in the wake of Sims's trial. "A long and violent convulsion of the elements has just passed away, and the heavens, the skies, smile upon us," said Webster of the struggle over the Compromise and the Fugitive Slave Law. Drawing this "analogy between the occurrences in the natural, and occurrences in the moral and political world," Webster praised the ideal of union once again and assured his Boston audience that "the rich blessings which we have inherited from our fathers will endure, will be perpetual, will be immortal."[33]

Perhaps they would, but not without the national violence Webster hoped to avoid, the violence Melville's tale holds at a point of agonized restraint. Like the compromise with the spirit of freedom it refers to, *Benito Cereno* simply postpones the final crisis and its potential vengeance. Whereas Douglass and Delany sought to release the image of just human revenge in the name of the Revolutionary fathers, Melville, like Delano and like the American government through the 1850s, cagily suppresses that image and, retreating into the resolute silence of legal documentation, returns the question to the courts. In doing so, he incorporates every tangled aspect of the crisis over slavery articulated in the decades before the war, and displays in a tableau of painfully frozen gestures the failure of America to act against slavery. Like so many works on slavery and revolution during the American Renaissance, Melville's story speaks still with particular power and forecasts a volatile problem that reaches beyond the victory for union and abolition in 1865, a problem, without doubt, that has continued for over another century slowly to clarify the meaning of the Revolutionary tradition in America.

NOTES

1. William Lloyd Garrison, *The Liberator,* 7 January 1832, rpt. in *William Lloyd Garrison,* ed. George M. Frederickson (Englewood Cliffs, N.J.: Prentice-Hall, 1968), pp. 27–29.

2. Thomas Wentworth Higginson, "Nat Turner's Insurrection," *Atlantic Monthly* 8 (1861), rpt. in *Travellers and Outlaws: Episodes in American History* (Boston: Lee & Shepard, 1889), p. 326; Garrison, the *Liberator,* 7 January 1832 and 31 May 1844, in *Garrison,* ed. Frederickson, pp. 29–30, 51–53.

3. Daniel Webster, *The Works of Daniel Webster,* 5 vols. (Boston: Little, Brown, 1851), 1:59–60, 72–73, 77–78, 81, 89–90; 5:435–38; Ralph Waldo Emerson, "The Fugitive Slave Law" (Concord, Mass., 3 May 1851), *The*

Complete Writings of Ralph Waldo Emerson (New York: William H. Wise, 1929), p. 1155.

4. Theodore Parker, "Reply to Webster," speech of 25 March 1853, *The Slave Power,* ed. James K. Hosmer (n.d.; rpt. New York: Arno Press, 1969), pp. 246–47; Emerson, *Complete Writings,* p. 1156; Abraham Lincoln, *The Collected Works of Abraham Lincoln,* ed. Roy P. Basler, 8 vols. (New Brunswick, N.J.: Rutgers University Press, 1953), 1:109, 111; Edward Beecher, *Narrative of Riots at Alton* (1838; rpt. Miami: Mnemosyne, 1969), p. 155.

5. Lincoln, *Collected Works,* 1:114–15; Thomas Paine, *Common Sense and Other Political Writings,* ed. Nelson F. Adkins (Indianapolis: Bobbs-Merrill, 1953), p. 19.

6. Paine, *Common Sense,* p. 8; Lincoln, *Collected Works,* 2:461–69; George B. Forgie, *Patricide in the House Divided: A Psychological Interpretation of Lincoln and His Age* (New York: W.W. Norton, 1979), pp. 13–53; 89–122; Jefferson, letter of 28 August 1797, quoted in Winthrop Jordan, *White over Black: American Attitudes toward the Negro, 1550–1812* (1968; rpt. New York: W. W. Norton, 1977), p. 386.

7. See, for example, Garry Wills, *Inventing America: Jefferson's Declaration of Independence* (New York: Random House, 1978), pp. 49–64 and Hannah Arendt, *On Revolution* (1963; rpt. New York: Penguin Books, 1977), pp. 41–47; Eugene D. Genovese, *From Rebellion to Revolution: Afro-American Slave Revolts in the Making of the New World* (1979; rpt. New York: Random House, Vintage Books, 1981), p. xvii; Sacvan Bercovitch, *The American Jeremiad* (Madison: University of Wisconsin Press, 1978), pp. 132–75, quote on p. 134; on the revival of Revolutionary rhetoric, see George M. Frederickson, *The Inner Civil War: Northern Intellectuals and the Crisis of the Union* (New York: Harper & Row, 1965), pp. 36–65, and Daniel Aaron, *The Unwritten War: American Writers and the Civil War* (1973; rpt. New York: Oxford University Press, 1975), pp. 1–38.

8. Nathaniel Hawthorne, "Chiefly about War Matters," *Atlantic Monthly* (July 1862), in *The Complete Works of Nathaniel Hawthorne,* 13 vols. (Boston: Houghton, Mifflin, 1909), 12:319; cf. Allen Flint, "Hawthorne and the Slavery Crisis," *New England Quarterly* 41, no. 3 (September 1968):393–408; Edmund S. Morgan, "Slavery and Freedom: The American Paradox," in *The Challenge of the American Revolution* (New York: W.W.Norton, 1976), pp. 171–72; Jefferson, "Declaration of Independence," quoted in David Brion Davis, *The Problem of Slavery in the Age of Revolution, 1770–1823* (Ithaca: Cornell University Press, 1975), p. 273;Parker, "The Nebraska Question" (1854), *Additional Speeches, Addresses, and Occasional Sermons,* 2 vols. (Boston: Little, Brown, 1855), 1:362–63; on slavery during and after the Revolution, see also Bernard Bailyn, *The Ideological Origins of the*

American Revolution (Cambridge: Harvard University Press, 1967), pp. 232–46; Duncan J. MacLeod, *Slavery, Race and the American Revolution* (Cambridge University Press, 1974); and Davis, *The Problem of Slavery in the Age of Revolution, 1770–1823,* esp. pp. 255–342.

9. On "perpetual union" in early national literature and political thought, see R. A. Yoder, "The First Romantics and the Last Revolution," *Studies in Romanticism* 15, no. 4 (Fall 1976):493–529, David M. Potter, *The Impending Crisis, 1848–1861* (New York: Harper & Row, 1976), pp. 44–48, and Kenneth M. Stampp, "The Concept of a Perpetual Union," in *The Imperiled Union: Essays on the Background of the Civil War* (New York: Oxford University Press, 1980), pp. 3–36; Lincoln, *Collected Works,* 1:108, 112–13.

10. Davis, *The Problem of Slavery in the Age of Revolution,* pp. 307–8.

11. Thomas R. Dew, "Abolition of Negro Slavery," in Drew Gilpin Faust, ed., *The Ideology of Slavery: Proslavery Thought in the Antebellum South, 1830–1860* (Baton Rouge: Louisiana State University Press, 1981), pp. 56–60.

12. Webster, *Works,* 1:230–31; Lydia Maria Child, *An Appeal in Favor of that Class of Americans Called Africans* (New York: John S. Taylor, 1836), pp. 119–21; Franklin Pierce, Inaugural Address, 4 March 1853, rpt. in *Franklin Pierce, 1804–1868,* ed. Irving J. Sloan (Dobbs Ferry, N.Y.: Oceana, 1968), pp. 17–24.

13. Nathaniel Hawthorne, *Life of Franklin Pierce,* in *Complete Works,* 12:352–54, 361, 372, 412–13, 415; on manifest destiny see Frederick Merk, *Manifest Destiny and Mission in American History* (New York: Random House, 1963); Ernest Lee Tuveson, *Redeemer Nation: The Idea of America's Millennial Role* (Chicago: University of Chicago Press, 1968), pp. 91–136; and Potter, *The Impending Crisis,* pp. 1–198.

14. Hawthorne, *Life of Franklin Pierce,* and Pierce, quoted therein, *Complete Works,* 12:417, 435; David Brion Davis, *The Slave Power Conspiracy and the Paranoid Style* (Baton Rouge: Louisiana State University Press, 1969), pp. 10–12.

15. W. E. B. DuBois, *The Suppression of the African Slave-Trade to the United States of America, 1638–1870* (1898; rpt. New York: Russell & Russell, 1965), p. 70; Genovese, *From Rebellion to Revolution,* pp. 49, 93, 95, 134; Davis, *The Problem of Slavery in the Age of Revolution,* pp. 392 ff.; Angeina Emily Grimke, *Appeal to the Christian Women of the South* (1835; rpt. New York: Arno Press, 1969), pp. 34–35; Catherine Beecher, *An Essay on Slavery and Abolitionism* (Philadelphia: Henry Perkins, 1837), pp. 88–95; Jordan, *White over Black,* pp. 375–403; William Wells Brown, *St. Domingo: Its Revolutions and Its Patriots* (Boston: Bela Marsh, 1855), pp. 38, 32–33.

16. Edwin C. Holland, quoted in MacLeod, *Slavery, Race and Revolution,* p. 157; Fred Somkin, *Unquiet Eagle: Memory and Desire in the Idea of*

American Freedom, 1815–1860 (Ithaca: Cornell University Press, 1967), passim, and Bercovitch, *The American Jeremiad,* pp. 141 ff.; Douglass, "The Meaning of July Fourth for the Negro" (address of 5 July 1852), in *The Life and Writings of Frederick Douglass,* 5 vols., ed. Philip S. Foner (New York: International Publishers, 1950), 2:181–204; Douglass, *My Bondage and My Freedom,* ed. Philip S. Foner (New York: Dover, 1969), pp. 253–54.

17. *The Confessions of Nat Turner,* in Herbert Aptheker, *Nat Turner's Slave Rebellion* (New York: Humanities Press, 1966), pp. 128–31. On Gray's manipulation of Turner's story, see Seymour L. Gross and Eileen Bender, "History, Politics, and Literature: The Myth of Nat Turner," *American Quarterly* 23, no. 4 (October 1971):487–518 and Jean Fagan Yellin, *The Intricate Knot: Black Figures in American Literature, 1776–1863* (New York: New York University Press, 1972), pp. 187–93. For general examinations of slave revolts in America see Herbert Aptheker, *American Negro Slave Revolts* (New York: International Publishers, 1952), Clement Eaton, *The Freedom-of-Thought Struggle in the Old South* (1948; rev. ed., New York: Harper & Row, 1968), pp. 89–117, and *American Slavery: The Question of Resistance,* ed. John H. Bracey et al. (Belmont, Calif.: Wadsworth, 1971).

18. Toussaint L'Ouverture, letter of 5 November 1797, quoted in C.L.R. James, *The Black Jacobins: Toussaint L'Ouverture and the San Domingo Revolution* (1938; rpt. New York: Random House, Vintage Books, 1963), p. 196; Phillips, "Toussaint L'Ouverture," in *Wendell Phillips on Civil Rights and Freedom,* ed. Louis Filler (New York: Hill & Wang, 1965), p. 163; Brown, *St. Domingo,* p. 37; Douglass, "The Meaning of July Fourth for the Negro," *Life and Writings,* 2:192.

19. Harriet Beecher Stowe, *Uncle Tom's Cabin; Or, Life among the Lowly,* ed. Ann Douglas (New York: Penguin Books, 1981), pp. 562, 596. On Stowe's fear of rebellion and the question of sentimental racism, see George M. Frederickson, "Uncle Tom and the Anglo-Saxons: Romantic Racialism in the North," *The Black Image in the White Mind: The Debate on Afro-American Character and Destiny, 1817–1914* (New York: Harper & Row, 1971), pp. 97–129.

20. Stowe, *Uncle Tom's Cabin,* pp. 392, 299; on American views of the European revolutions of 1848, see Merk, *Manifest Destiny and American Mission in American History,* pp. 195–201, Donald S. Spencer, *Louis Kossuth and Young America: A Study of Sectionalism and Foreign Policy, 1848–1852* (Columbia: University of Missouri Press), and Michael Paul Rogin, *Subversive Genealogy: The Politics and Art of Herman Melville* (New York: Alfred A. Knopf, 1983), pp. 20–21, 103 ff.

21. On benevolence, see David Brion Davis, *The Problem of Slavery in Western Culture* (Ithaca: Cornell University Press, 1966), pp. 333–421, 472–82; Stephen A. Hirsch, "Uncle Tomitudes: The Popular Reaction to *Uncle Tom's*

32   Eric J. Sundquist

Cabin," in *Studies in the American Renaissance,* ed. Joel Meyerson (Boston: Twayne, 1978), pp. 303–30; Elizabeth Ammons, "Heroines in *Uncle Tom's Cabin,*" *American Literature* 49, no. 2 (May 1977):161–79; Jane P. Tompkins, "Sentimental Power: *Uncle Tom's Cabin* and the Politics of Literary History," *Glyph 8: Johns Hopkins Textual Studies* (Baltimore: Johns Hopkins University Press, 1981), pp. 79–102; and Philip Fisher, "Partings and Ruins: Radical Sentimentality in *Uncle Tom's Cabin*" *AmerikaStudien* 28, no. 3 (1983):279–83; Ronald G. Walters, *The Antislavery Appeal: American Abolitionism after 1830* (Baltimore: Johns Hopkins University Press, 1976), pp. 70–110, quote at p. 78; Catherine Beecher, *An Essay on Slavery and Abolitionism,* pp. 97–136.

22. Stowe, "The Two Altars," *The Writings of Harriet Beecher Stowe,* 20 vols. (New York: AMS Press, 1967), 4:249–64; Robert Hayne, quoted in William W. Freehling, *Prelude to Civil War: The Nullification Controversy in South Carolina, 1816–1836* (New York: Harper & Row, 1966), p. 141.

23. Constance Rourke, *Trumpets of Jubilee* (New York: Harcourt, Brace, 1927), pp. 107–8; James Baldwin, "Everybody's Protest Novel," *Notes of a Native Son* (1955; rpt. New York: Bantam Books, 1964), pp. 9–17; Forgie, *Patricide in the House Divided,* pp. 159–99; Child, *An Appeal in Favor of the Americans Called Africans,* p. 212.

24. Martin R. Delany, *Blake; Or, the Huts of America,* ed. Floyd J. Miller (Boston: Beacon Press, 1970), pp. 19–20, 84–85, 112–13, 251.

25. "Continental Policy of the United States—The Acquisition of Cuba," *The United States' Democratic Review* 43 (April 1859):2, 21–22, 32; cf. Philip S. Foner, *A History of Cuba and Its Relations with the United States,* 2 vols. (New York: International Publishers, 1963), 2:75–105, and Robert E. May, *The Southern Dream of a Caribbean Empire: 1854–1861* (Baton Rouge: Louisiana State University Press, 1973).

26. Delany, *Blake,* pp. 298–306, 313; Delany, quoted in Yellin, *The Intricate Knot,* p. 195; "Ostend Manifesto," *Documents of American History,* 2 vols. in 1, ed. Henry Steele Commanger (New York: F. S. Croft, 1934), 1:33–35.

27. Delany, *The Political Destiny of the Colored Race on the American Continent,* in Sterling Stuckey, ed., *The Ideological Origins of Black Nationalism* (Boston: Beacon Press, 1972), p. 203; James Brewer Stewart, *Holy Warriors: The Abolitionists and American Slavery* (New York: Hill & Wang, 1976), p. 141; on Delany see also Victor Ullman, *Martin R. Delany: The Beginnings of Black Nationalism* (Boston: Beacon Press, 1971), and Ronald T. Takaki, *Violence in the Black Imagination: Essays and Documents* (New York: G. P. Putnam's Sons, 1972), pp. 79–101.

28. Joseph Mills's diary entry, quoted by Basler in Lincoln, *Collected Works,* 7:508.

29. Douglass, *My Bondage and My Freedom,* pp. 362, 397-98, 51, 37-38, 191.

30. Douglass, "The Heroic Slave," *Life and Writings* (supp. vol., 1975), 5:473-505; cf. Howard Jones, "The Peculiar Institution and National Honor: The Case of the *Creole* Slave Revolt," *Civil War History* 21, no. 1 (March 1975):28-50; and Robert B. Stepto, "Storytelling in Early Afro-American Fiction: Frederick Douglass' 'The Heroic Slave,'" *Georgia Review* 36, no. 2 (Summer 1982):355-68.

31. Douglass, *My Bondage and My Freedom,* pp. 269-70; Herman Melville, *Great Short Works,* ed. Warner Berthoff (New York: Harper & Row, Perennial, 1969), pp. 280, 268.

32. Davis, *The Problem of Slavery in Western Culture,* pp. 165-73; Parker, "The Nebraska Question," *Additional Speeches, Addresses, and Occasional Sermons,* 1:299-303, 373-80.

33. Lincoln, *Collected Works,* 5:10; Melville, *Great Short Works,* p. 314; on Melville, Shaw, and Webster, see Carolyn Karcher, *Shadow over the Promised Land: Slavery, Race, and Violence in Melville's America,* pp. 9-11, and Rogin, *Subversive Genealogy,* pp. 142-46; Webster, *The Writings and Speeches of Daniel Webster,* 18 vols. (Boston: Little, Brown, 1903), 13:405-7.

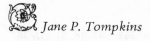 Jane P. Tompkins

The Other
American Renaissance

The word *other* in my title refers to the fiction written during the period we know as the American Renaissance by writers whose names we do not know. The writer I am concerned with in particular is Susan Warner, who was born in the same year as Herman Melville and whose best-selling novel, *The Wide, Wide World,* was published in the same year as *Moby Dick.* But I am interested in Warner's novel not for the light it can shed on Melville;[1] I am interested in it because it represents an entire body of work that this century's critical tradition has largely ignored. According to that tradition, the "great" figures of the American Renaissance were a handful of men who refused to be taken in by the pieties of the age. These writers, according to Henry Nash Smith, were not afraid to "explore the dark underside of the psyche," or to tackle "ultimate social and intellectual issues"; and because they repudiated the culture's dominant system of values they were, in Perry Miller's words, "crushed by the juggernaut" of the popular sentimental novel.[2] The sentimental writers, on the other hand, are generally thought to have been out of touch with reality. What they produced, says Smith, was a literature of "reassurance," calculated to soothe the anxieties of an economically troubled age. To the "Common Man and Common Woman," fearful of challenge or change, they preached a "cosmic success story," which promised that the practice of virtue would lead to material success. Their subject matter—the tribulations of orphan girls—was innately trivial; their religious ideas were "little more than a blur of good intentions"; they "feared the probing of the inner life," and above all were committed to avoiding anything that might make the "undiscriminating mass" of their middle-brow readers "uncomfortable."[3]

My purpose today is to challenge that description of sentimental novels and to argue that their exclusion from the canon of American literature has been a mistake. My strategy will not be to compare what I have called the "other" American Renaissance to the dominant tradition (a dichotomy, ultimately, that is itself a misrepresentation) but to show what makes sentimental novels powerful and important in their own right. For once one has a grasp of the problems these writers were trying to solve, their solutions do not seem shallow or unrealistic; on the contrary, given the social circumstances within which they were obliged to work, their prescriptions for living seem at least as courageous as those put forward by the writers who said, "No, in thunder."

The Wide, Wide World, in 1851, caused an explosion in the literary marketplace that was absolutely unprecedented—nothing like it, in terms of sales, had ever been seen before. The next year, Uncle Tom's Cabin broke the records that Warner's novel had set. Two years later, Maria Cummins's The Lamplighter—the direct literary descendant of The Wide, Wide World—made another tremendous hit.[4] Yet Henry Nash Smith, who has devoted an entire book to studying the influence of popular fiction on classical American writing, dismisses the phenomenon, saying "it is impossible now to determine just what did happen to the market in the early 1850's."[5]

But it is not impossible to determine. The impact of sentimental novels is directly related to the cultural context that produced them. Once one begins to explore that context in even a preliminary way, the critical practice that assigns Hawthorne and Melville the role of heroes, the sentimental novelists the role of villains, and the public the role of their willing dupes, loses its credibility. The one great fact of American life during the period under consideration was the "terrific universality" of the revival.[6] Sentimental fiction was perhaps the most influential expression of the beliefs that animated the revival movement and shaped the character of American life in the years before the Civil War. Like their counterparts among the evangelical reformers, the sentimental novelists wrote to educate their readers in Christian perfection and to move the nation as a whole closer to the City of God. But in order to understand the appeal of their project one has to have some familiarity with the cultural discourse of the age for which they spoke.

The best place to begin is with some documents that, as far as I know, have never made their way into criticism of American Renaissance literature. These are the publications of the American Tract Society, the first organization in America to publish and distribute the printed word on a mass scale. Its literature is a testament both to the faith of antebellum Americans—to the shape of their dreams—and to what they experienced as everyday reality. It is only by attempting to see that reality from within the assumptions that founded it that one can arrive at a notion of what gave sentimental fiction its tremendous original force.

THE CLOSET

The conception of reality on which the reform movement was based is nowhere more dramatically illustrated than in the activities of the New York City Tract Society, whose members, numbering in the thousands, attempted to help the city's poor by distributing a religious tract to every family in the city once a month.[7] The "Directions" that guided the Tract Visiters, printed on the back cover of the society's Annual Report, are as succinct a statement as one is likely to find of the politics of the reform movement. "Be much in prayer," the Directions said. "Endeavor to feel habitually and deeply that all your efforts will be in vain unless accompanied by the Holy Ghost. And this blessing you can expect only in answer to prayer. Pray, therefore, without ceasing. Go from your closet to your work and from your work return again to the closet."[8] If one can understand what made these Directions meaningful and effective for the people who carried them out, one is in a position to understand the power of sentimental fiction. For all sentimental novels take place, metaphorically and literally, within the "closet." Their heroines rarely get beyond the confines of a private space—the kitchen, the parlor, the upstairs chamber— but more important, most of what they do takes place inside the "closet" of the heart. For what the word *sentimental* really means in this context is that the arena of human action, as in the Tract Society Directions, has been defined not as the world but as the human soul. This fiction shares with the evangelical reform movement a theory of power that stipulates that all true action is not material but spiritual, that one obtains spiritual power through prayer, and that those who know how, in the privacy of their closets, to struggle for possession of their souls, will one day conquer the world through the power given them by God. This theory of power is one that made itself felt, not simply in the explicit assertions of religious propaganda, but as a principle of interpretation that gave form to experience itself, as the records the Tract Visiters left of their activities show.

The same beliefs that make the Directions to Tract Visiters intelligible structured what the Visiters actually saw as they went about their work. One Visiter, for example, records that a young woman who was dying of pulmonary consumption became concerned at the eleventh hour about the state of her soul and asked for spiritual help. "She was found by the Visiter," the report reads,

> supplied with a number of tracts, and kindly directed to the Saviour of sinners. . . . For some time clouds hung over her mind, but they were at length dispelled by the Sun of righteousness. . . . As she approached the hour which tries men's souls, her friends gathered around her; . . . and while they were engaged in a hymn her soul seemed to impart unnatural energy to her emaciated and dying body. To the astonishment of all, she said to her widowed mother, who bent anxiously over her. "Don't weep for me, I shall soon be in the arms of my Saviour." She prayed fervently, and fell asleep in Jesus. [9]

Like all the fiction we label "sentimental" this narrative blots out the uglier details of life and cuts experience to fit a pattern of pious expectation. The anecdote tells nothing about the personality or background of the young woman, fails to represent even the barest facts of her disease or of her immediate surroundings. For these facts, it substitutes the panaceas of Christian piety—God's mercy on a miserable sinner, "falling asleep" in Jesus. Its plot follows a prescribed course from sin to salvation. But what is extraordinary about this anecdote is that it is not a work of fiction but a factual report. Though its facts do not correspond to what a twentieth-century observer would have recorded, had he or she been at the scene, they faithfully represent what the Tract Society member saw. Whereas a modern social worker would have described the woman's illness, its history and course of treatment, would have sketched in her socioeconomic background and that of her relatives and friends, the Tract Visiter sees only a spiritual predicament. Whereas the modern observer would have structured the events in a downward spiral, as the woman's condition deteriorated from serious to critical, and ended with her death, the report reverses that progression. Its movement is upward, from "thoughtfulness" to "conviction," to "great tranquility, joy, and triumph."[10]

The charge that has always been leveled against sentimental fiction in the twentieth century is that it is out of touch with reality, that it presents a picture of life so oversimplified and improbable, that only the most naive and self-deceiving reader could believe it. But the sense of the real which this criticism takes for granted is not the one that organized the perceptions of antebellum readers. Their assumptions were the same as those that structured the events of the report I have just quoted. For what I have been speaking about involves three distinct levels of apprehension: "reality itself" as it appears to people at a given time; what people will accept as an "accurate description" of reality; and novels and stories which, because they correspond to such descriptions, therefore seem true. The audience for whom the thoughtless young lady's conversion was a moving factual report found the tears and prayers of sentimental heroines equally compelling. This is so not because they did not know what good fiction was, or because their notions about human life were naive and superficial, but because the "order of things" to which both readers and fictions belonged was itself structured by narratives of this sort.

The report of the young woman's death is exactly analogous to the kind of exemplary narrative that had formed the consciousness of the nation in the early years of the nineteenth century. Such stories filled the religious publications distributed in unimaginably large quantities by organizations of the Evangelical United Front. The American Tract Society alone claims to have published thirty-seven million tracts at a time when the entire population of the country was only eleven million. The same kind of exemplary narratives was the staple of the McGuffey's readers on which virtually the entire nation had been schooled. They appeared in manuals of social behavior, and in instructional literature of every variety, filled the pages of popular magazines, and appeared even in the daily newspapers. As David Reynolds has recently demonstrated, the entire practice of pulpit oratory in this period shifted from an expository and abstract mode of explicating religious doctrine, to a mode in which sensational narratives carried the burden of theological precept.[11] These stories were always didactic in nature—illustrating the importance of a particular virtue—obedience, faith, sobriety—and they were usually sensational in content—the starving widow is saved at the last moment by a handsome stranger who turns out to be her son. But their sensationalism ultimately lies not so much in the dramatic nature of the events they describe as in the assumptions they make about the relation of human events to the spiritual realities that underlie them. One of their lessons is that all experience is sensational which has consequences for the saving or damning of a human soul. These religious assumptions, which organized the experience of most Americans in the antebellum era, are at work in the novels of writers like Stowe and Warner.

Thus, when critics dismiss sentimental fiction because it is out of touch with reality, they do so because the reality *they* perceive is organized according to a different set of conventions for constituting experience. For although the attack on sentimental fiction claims for itself freedom from the distorting effects of a naive religious perspective, the real naiveté is to think that *that* attack is launched from no perspective whatsoever, or that its perspective is disinterested and not culture-bound in the way that the sentimental novelists were. The popular fiction of the American Renaissance has been dismissed primarily because it follows from assumptions about the shape and meaning of existence that we no longer hold. But once one understands the coherence and force of those assumptions, the literature that helped to shape the world in their image no longer seems thoughtless or trivial. The conviction that human events are, ultimately and inevitably, shaped by secret prayer, produces a view of society in which orphan girls—like the heroine of Warner's novel—can hope to change the world.

POWER

If the general charge against sentimental fiction has been that it is divorced from actual human experience, a more specific form of that charge is that these novels fail to deal with the brute facts of political and economic oppression, and therefore cut themselves off from the possibility of truly affecting the lives of their readers. Tremaine McDowell, writing in the *Literary History of the United States,* dismisses Mrs. Lydia Sigourney—who epitomizes the sentimental tradition for modern critics—by saying that although she "knew something of the humanitarian movements of the day, all . . . she did for Negroes, Indians, the poor, and the insane was to embalm them in her tears."[12] Such cutting remarks are never made about canonical authors of the period, though they, too, did nothing for "Negroes, Indians, the poor," and wrote about them considerably less than their female rivals. But what this sort of commentary reveals, beyond an automatic prejudice against sentimental writers, is its own failure to perceive that the great subject of sentimental fiction is preeminently a political issue. It is no exaggeration to say that domestic fiction is preoccupied, even obsessed, with the nature of power. Because they lived in a society that celebrated free enterprise and democratic government but were excluded from participating in either,[13] the two questions these female novelists never fail to ask are: what *is* power, and where is it located? Since they could neither own property, nor vote, nor speak in a public meeting if both sexes were present, women had to have a way of defining themselves that gave them power and status nevertheless, in their own eyes and in the eyes of the world. That is the problem sentimental fiction addresses.

In his characterization of American women, Tocqueville accurately described the solution to this problem as it appeared to an outsider. He noted that the interests of a "Puritanical" and "trading" nation lead Americans to require "much abnegation on the part of women, and a constant sacrifice of her pleasures to her duties." But, he continues, "I never observed that the women of America consider conjugal authority as a usurpation of their rights. . . . It appeared to me, on the contrary, that they attach a sort of pride to the voluntary surrender of their own will and make their boast to bend themselves to the yoke, not to shake it off."[14] The ethic of sentimental fiction was an ethic of submission. But the relation of these authors to their subservient condition and to the dominant beliefs about the nature and function of women was more complicated than Tocqueville supposed. The fact is that American women simply could not assume a stance of open rebellion against the conditions of their lives for they lacked the material means of escape or opposition. They had to stay put and submit. And so the domestic novelists made that necessity the basis on which to build a power structure of their own. Instead of rejecting the culture's value system outright, they appropriated it for their own use, subjecting the beliefs and customs that had molded them to a series of transformations that allowed them both to fulfill and transcend their appointed roles.

The process of transformation gets underway immediately in Warner's novel when the heroine, Ellen Montgomery, a child of ten, learns that her mother is about to leave on a long voyage for the sake of her health and that she will probably never see her mother again. The two have been weeping uncontrollably in one another's arms, when Mrs. Montgomery recollects herself and says: "Ellen! Ellen! listen to me . . . my child this is not right. Remember, my darling, who it is that brings this sorrow upon us,—though we *must* sorrow, we must not rebel."[15] Ellen's mother, who has been ordered to go on this voyage by her husband and her physician, accepts the features of her life as fixed and instructs her daughter to do the same. The message of this scene, and of most sentimental fiction, is "though we *must* sorrow, we must not rebel." This message can be understood in one of two ways. The most obvious is to read it as an example of how it worked to keep women down. This reading sees women as the dupes of a culture that taught them that disobedience to male authority was a "sin against heaven."[16] In this view, religion is nothing but an opiate for the oppressed and a myth that served the rulers of a "Puritanical" and "trading nation." In this view, the sentimental novelists, to use Ann Douglas's phrase, did "the dirty work" of their culture by teaching women how to become the agents of their own subjection.[17]

The problem with this reading is that it is too simplistic. First of all, it assumes that the ethic of submission was limited only to women. But as Lewis Saum has recently shown in his monumental study of the period, the need to submit to the dictates of divine providence was the most deeply held and pervasive belief of common people in this country before the Civil War.[18] Sentimental novelists spoke not only to women but to all who felt that the circumstances of their lives were beyond their power to control. Second, the women in these novels make submission "their boast" not because they enjoy it but because it gave them another ground on which to stand, a position that, while it fulfilled the social demands that were placed upon them, gave them a place from which to launch a counterstrategy against their worldly masters that would finally give them the upper hand. Submission, as it is presented throughout the novel, is never submission to the will of a husband or father, though that is what it appears to be on the surface; submission is first of all a self-willed act of conquest of one's own passions. Mrs. Montgomery tells Ellen that her tears of anger are "not right," that she must "command" and "compose" herself, because, she says, "You will hurt both yourself and me, my daughter, if you cannot."[19] Ellen will hurt herself by failing to submit because her submission is not capitulation to an external authority but the mastery of herself, and therefore, paradoxically, an assertion of autonomy. In its definition of power relations, the domestic novel operates here, and elsewhere, according to a principle of reversal whereby what is "least" in the world's eyes becomes "greatest" in its perspective. So "submission" becomes "self-conquest" and doing the will of one's husband or father brings an access of divine power. By conquering herself in the name of the highest possible authority, the dutiful woman merges her own authority with God's. When Mrs. Montgomery learns that her husband and doctor have ordered her to part from Ellen, she says to herself, "Not my will, but thine be done."[20] By making themselves into the vehicles of God's will, these female characters become nothing in themselves but all-powerful in relation to the world. Ceding themselves to the source of all power, they bypass worldly (male) authority and, as it were, cancel it out. The ability to "submit" in this way is presented, moreover, as the special prerogative of women, transmitted from mother to daughter. As the women in these novels teach one another how to "command" themselves, they bind themselves to one another and to God in a holy alliance against the men who control their material destinies. When Mr. Montgomery refuses his wife the money to buy Ellen a parting gift, it is no accident that she sells her own mother's ring to make the purchase; the ring symbolizes the tacit system of solidarity that exists among women in these books. Nor is it an accident that the gift Mrs. Montgomery gives her daughter is a Bible. The mother's Bible-gift, in sentimental literature, is invested with supernatural power because it testifies to the reality of the spiritual order where women hold dominion over everything by virtue of their submission on earth.[21]

The bypassing of worldly authority ultimately produces, in these novels, a feminist theology in which the godhead is refashioned into an image of maternal authority. When Mrs. Montgomery teaches Ellen what it means to trust in God, she asks her to describe her feelings toward herself, and tells her that "it is just so" that she wishes her to trust in God.[22] All that Ellen

knows of God comes to her through the teaching and example
of her mother, whose saintliness and love are images of his invisible perfection. The definition of the mother as the channel of
God's grace, the medium through which he becomes known to
mankind, locates the effective force of divinity in this world in
women. Doing the will of God finally becomes identical with
doing what one's mother wants. And if one is a woman, doing the
will of God means obeying a divinity that comes to look more and
more like oneself. Scene after scene in *The Wide, Wide World* ends
with Ellen weeping in the arms of a kind mother-figure—a representative of God in human form. As Ellen matures, her spiritual
counselors grow closer to her in age until finally she learns to
control her passions on her own and becomes her own mother.
Not coincidentally, the one completely happy, whole, and self-
sufficient character in this book is an elderly woman who lives
alone on a mountaintop and is, so to speak, a God unto herself.
This is the condition toward which the novel's ethic of submission
strives.

Warner's novel presents an image of people dominated by external authorities and forced to curb their own desires; but as they
learn to transmute rebellious passion into humble conformity to
others' wishes, their powerlessness becomes a source of strength.
For the goal of sentimental fiction is to teach the reader how to
live without power while waging a protracted struggle in which
the strategies of the weak will finally inherit the earth.

TRIFLES

Although women were attempting to outflank men in the
struggle for power by declaring that it was not the world that was
important to conquer but one's own soul, they did in fact possess
a territory of their own that was not purely spiritual. The territory I am referring to is the home, which provided women both
with the means of immediate personal satisfaction and with the
foundation of a religious faith. The emphasis on household tasks

in these novels may seem to vindicate the charge that their subject matter is essentially trivial, but the charge of triviality is the effect of a critical perspective that regards household activity as unimportant. Women writers of the nineteenth century could not allow the one small corner of the universe they had been allotted to be defined as insignificant or peripheral and so they wrote about household routines in such a way that everything else appeared peripheral to them. The routines of the fireside acquire a sacramental power in the fiction of this period, and consequently, the faithful performance of household tasks is not merely a reflection or an expression of celestial love, but, as in this scene from Warner's novel, its point of origin and consummation.

> To make her mother's tea was Ellen's regular business. She treated it as a very grave affair, and loved it as one of the pleasantest in the course of the day. She used in the first place to make sure that the kettle really boiled; then she carefully poured some water into the tea-pot and rinsed it, both to make it clean and to make it hot; then she knew exactly how much tea to put in the tiny little tea-pot, which was just big enough to hold two cups of tea, and having poured a very little boiling water to it, she used to set it by the side of the fire while she made half a slice of toast. How careful Ellen was about that toast! The bread must not be cut too thick, nor too thin; the fire must, if possible, burn clear and bright, and she herself held the bread on a fork, just at the right distance from the coals to get it nicely browned without burning. When this was done to her satisfaction (and if the first piece failed she would take another), she filled up the little tea-pot from the boiling kettle, and proceeded to make a cup of tea. She knew, and was very careful to put in, just the quantity of milk and sugar that her mother liked; and then she used to carry the tea and toast on a little tray to her mother's side, and very often held it there for her while she ate. All this Ellen did with the zeal that love gives, and though the same thing was to be gone over every night of the year, she was never wearied. It was a real pleasure; she had the greatest satisfaction in seeing that the little her mother could eat was prepared for her in the nicest possible manner; she knew her hands made it taste better; her mother often said so.[23]

The making of tea as it is described here is not a household task but a religious ceremony. It is also a strategy for survival. The dignity and potency of Ellen's life depend upon the sacredness she

confers on small duties, and that is why the passage I have quoted
focuses so obsessively and so reverentially on minute details. Ellen's
preparation of her mother's tea has all the characteristics of a religious ritual. It is an activity that must be repeated ("the same
thing was to be gone over every night of the year"), it must be repeated correctly ("Ellen knew exactly how much tea to put in the
tiny little tea-pot," "the bread must not be cut too thick, nor too
thin," "and if the first piece failed she would make another"), it
must be repeated in the right spirit ("all this Ellen did with the
zeal that love gives"), and it must be repeated by the right person
(Ellen "knew her hands made it taste better; her mother often said
so"). Ellen's hands make the tea and toast taste better because the
ritual has worked, but it works not only because it has been performed correctly but because Ellen and her mother believe in it.
The creation of moments of intimacy like this through the making
of a cup of tea is what their lives depend on. What the ritual effects
is the opening of the heart in an atmosphere of closeness, security,
and love. The mutual tenderness, affection, and solicitude made
visible in the performance of these homely acts are the values
sacred to sentimental fiction and the reward it offers its readers
for that other activity which must also be performed within the
"closet"—the control of rebellious passion. While Ellen and her
mother must submit to the will of God, expressed through the
commands of husbands and doctors, they compensate for their
servitude by celebrating daily their exclusive, mutually supportive
love for one another.

The exigencies of a Puritanical and trading nation had put
women in the home and barred the door; and so in order to survive, they had to imagine their prison as the site of bliss. In this
respect, the taking of tea is no different from hoeing a bean patch
on the shores of Walden Pond, or squeezing case aboard a whaling
ship: they are parallel reactions against pain and bondage, and a
means of salvation and grace. The spaces that American Renaissance writing marks out as the site of possible transcendence are
not only the forest and the open sea. The hearth, in domestic fiction, is the site of a "movement inward," as far removed from the

fetters of landlocked existence as the Pacific Ocean is from Coenties Slip.

The happiness that women engender in the home is not limited in its effects to women, although they alone are responsible for it. Like prayer, which must be carried on in solitude and secrecy in order to change the world, the happiness that women create in their domestic isolation finally reaches to the ends of the earth. The domestic ideology operates in this respect, as in every other, according to a logic of inversion. "Small acts, small kindnesses, small duties," writes the Reverend Peabody, "bring the happiness or misery . . . of a whole generation. Whatever of happiness is enjoyed . . . beyond the circle of domestic life, is little more than an offshoot from that central sun."[24] Not only happiness, but salvation itself is seen to depend upon the performance of homely tasks. "Common daily duties," says the Reverend Peabody, "become sacred and awful because of the momentous results that depend upon them. Performed or neglected, they are the witnesses that shall appear for or against us at the last day."[25] By investing the slightest acts with moral significance, disciples of the religion of domesticity make the destinies of the human race hang upon domestic routines. Ellen Montgomery treats the making of her mother's tea as "a very grave affair" because she knows that "momentous results" depend upon these trifles. The measuring out of life in coffeespoons, a modernist metaphor for insignificance and futility, is interpreted in sentimental discourse as a world-building activity. When it is done exactly right, and "with the zeal that love gives," it can save the world.

It may be inevitable at this point to object that such claims are merely the fantasies of a disenfranchised group, the line that society feeds members whom it wants to buy off with the illusion of strength while denying them any real power. But what is at stake in this discussion is precisely what constitutes "real" power. From a modern standpoint, the domestic ideal is self-defeating because it ignores the realities of political and economic life. But the world of nineteenth-century Americans was different. As Lewis Saum has written: "In popular thought of the pre–Civil War period, no theme was more pervasive or philosophically fundamental than the providential view. Simply put, that view held that, directly or indirectly, God controlled all things."[26] Given this context, the claims the domestic novel made for the power of Christian love and the sacred influence of women were not in the least exaggerated or illusory. The entire weight of Protestant Christianity and democratic nationalism stood behind them. The notion that women in the home exerted a moral force that shaped the destinies of the race had become central to this country's vision of itself as a redeemer nation. The ethic of submission and the celebration of domesticity, in an age dominated by the revival movement, were not losing strategies but a successful bid for status and sway. Even as thoroughgoingly cosmopolitan a man as Tocqueville became convinced of this as a result of his visit to the United States. "As for myself," he said,

> I do not hesitate to avow that, although the women of the United States are confined within a narrow circle of domestic life, and their situation is in some respects one of extreme dependence, I have nowhere seen women occupying a loftier position; and if I were asked, now that I am drawing to the close of this work, in which I have spoken of so many important things done by the Americans, to what the singular prosperity and growing strength of that people ought mainly to be attributed, I should reply—to the superiority of their women.[27]

PAIN

The claims that sentimental fiction made for the importance of the spiritual life and for women's crucial role in the salvation of the race were not spurious or self-deceiving, because they were grounded in beliefs that had already organized the experience of most Americans. The sense of power and feelings of satisfaction that the religion of domesticity afforded were real, not just imagined, and they were bought and paid for at an almost incalculable price. The pain of learning to conquer her own passions is the central fact of the sentimental heroine's existence. For while a novel like *The Wide, Wide World* provides its readers with a design for living under drastically restricted conditions, at the same time it provides them with a catharsis of rage and grief that registers the cost of living according to that model. When Melville writes that Ahab "piled upon the white whale's hump the sum of all the general rage and hate felt by his whole race from Adam down, and then, as if his chest had been a mortar . . . burst his hot heart's shell upon it," he describes the venting of a rage that cannot be named as such in Warner's novel, but whose force is felt nevertheless in the deluge of the heroine's tears.[28] The force of those passions that must be curbed at all costs pushes to the surface again and again in her uncontrollable weeping. For although these novels are thought to have nothing to say about the human psyche, and to be unaware of "all the subtle demonisms of life and thought," in fact they focus exclusively on the emotions, and specifically on the psychological dynamics of living in a condition of servitude. The appeal of Warner's novel lay in the fact that it grappled directly with the emotional experience of its readership; it deals with the problem of powerlessness by showing how one copes with it hour by hour and minute by minute. For contrary to the longstanding consensus that sentimental novelists "couldn't face" the grim facts of their lives, their strength lay precisely in their dramatization of the heroine's suffering. It is a suffering that, the novelists resolutely insist, their readers, too, must face or else remain unsaved. And they force their readers to face it by placing them inside the mind of someone whose life is a continual series of encounters with absolute authority. At times, the vulnerability of Warner's heroine, forced to live within the bounds authority prescribes and constantly under the pressure of a hostile supervision, becomes almost too painful to bear.

Warner's refusal to mitigate the narrow circumstances of her heroine's existence is particularly striking when one compares this novel to the opening of *Huckleberry Finn*. Both novels begin with a child who is at the mercy of a cruel parent, but the solutions they offer their protagonists are diametrically opposed. When Huck is trapped by his drunken father at the outset of Twain's novel, he concocts an elaborate ruse that allows him to escape. He kills a hog, scatters its blood around the cabin, drags a sack of meal across the threshold to imitate the imprint of a body, and disappears—hoping that his father and the townspeople will think he has been murdered, and of course, they do. This kind of artfully engineered escape, repeated several times throughout the story, is the structural principle of a novel that has for a long time been considered a benchmark of American literary realism. Twain himself, of course, is famous for his scoffing attacks on the escapism of sentimental and romantic fiction. But if one compares his handling of a child's relation to authority with Warner's, the events of *Huckleberry Finn* enact a dream of freedom and autonomy that goes beyond the bounds of the wildest romance. The scenario whereby the clever and deserving Huck repeatedly outwits his powerful adversaries acts out a kind of adolescent wish-fulfillment that Warner's novel never even glances at. When Ellen is sent by her father to live with a sadistic aunt in New England, when she is deeded by him a second time to an even more sinister set of relatives, there is absolutely nothing she can do. Ellen is never for a moment out of the power of her guardians and never will be, as long as she lives. Whereas the premise of Twain's novel is that, when faced by tyranny of any sort, you can simply run away, the problem that Warner's novel sets itself to solve is how to survive, given that you cannot.

In the light of this fact, it is particularly ironic that novels like Warner's should have come to be regarded as "escapist." Unlike their male counterparts, women writers of the nineteenth century could not walk out the door and become Mississippi riverboat captains, go off on whaling voyages, or build themselves cabins in the woods. Nevertheless, modern critics persist in believing that what sentimental novelists offered was an easy way out: a few trite formulas for the masses who were too cowardly to face the "blackness of darkness," too lazy to wrestle with moral dilemmas, too stupid to understand epistemological problems, and too hidebound to undertake "quarrels with God." But "escape" is the one thing that sentimental novels never offer; on the contrary, they teach their readers that the only way to overcome tyranny is through the practice of a grueling and inexorable discipline. Ellen Montgomery says to her aunt early in the novel that if she were free to do what she wanted she would run away—and spends the rest of the novel learning to extirpate that impulse from her being. For not only can one not run away, in the world of sentimental fiction, one cannot protest the conditions under which one is forced to remain. Ahab's cosmic protest, "I'd strike the sun if it insulted me," epitomizes the self-assertive stance of the heroes of classical American fiction; sentimental heroines, forgoing such gestures, practice a heroism of self-renunciation. Theirs may be a quieter task but it is also more arduous, a taking apart and putting back together of the self that must be enacted over and over again, as the protagonist learns to quench the impulse to justify herself, and humbly asks the Lord for help in forgiving those who have wronged her. It is, as Ellen often says to her mentors, "hard."

In a sense, these novels resemble, more than anything else, training narratives: they are like documentaries, or made-for-TV movies that tell how Joe X, who grew up on the streets of Chicago, became a great pitcher for the White Sox, or how Kathy Y overcame polio and skated her way to stardom. They involve laborious apprenticeships in which the protagonist, under the guidance of a mentor, undergoes repeated failures and humiliations in the course of mastering the principles of her vocation. As the novel progresses, the things that happen to Ellen Montgomery get worse and worse, and at the same time she is required to show an equanimity more unperturbed, and a humility more complete. Thus whereas at an early stage she must learn to repress violent outbursts of temper, later on even a faint expression of irritation crossing her face calls down the devastating rebukes of her mentors. As the first phase of her disciplinary education draws to its close, Ellen becomes her own spiritual taskmaster. Her mentors have succeeded in establishing God in Ellen's mind as an all-powerful internal "Friend" who watches everything she does. Now, when even a rebellious thought crosses Ellen's mind, she will abase herself before the authority she has internalized.

The last section of the novel puts Ellen's ability to accept whatever fate deals out to an even harsher series of tests. Her father dies and deeds her to some rich relatives in Scotland. She is cast on the wide world a second time, and this time there will be no mentors to guide her. Like all true Christians, Ellen must learn to rely on faith alone. The final chapters of *The Wide, Wide World* require of the heroine an extinction of her personality so complete that there is nothing of herself she can call her own. Ellen's Scottish relatives are spiritual tyrants. Whereas her Aunt Fortune has subjected her to constant household drudgery and frequently hurt her feelings, the Lindsays attempt to possess her soul. It is not enough that Ellen is a perfectly docile, charming, and virtuous child; she must be stripped of every vestige of her former identity. Ellen's uncle makes her call him "father" and she submits. He changes her name from Montgomery to Lindsay and she does not protest. He orders her to forget her nationality, forces her to drink wine, forbids her to speak of her former friends, refuses to let her talk of religion, and insists that she give up her sober ways and act "cheerful." To all of these demands Ellen submits, after much internal struggle, many tears and prayers, much consulting of her Bible and singing of hymns. "God will take care of me if I trust in Him," she says to herself, "it is none of my business." "God giveth grace to the humble, I will humble myself."[29]

Given the amount of pain that sentimental heroines endure, it is almost inconceivable that their stories should have been read as myths of "reassurance." The story of Ellen Montgomery's education is no more reassuring than the story of Job or *Pilgrim's Progress,* on which it was modeled, and its original readers apparently understood it in this way. A traveler to England in the 1880s reported that the four books most frequently found in the homes of common people were the Bible, *Pilgrim's Progress, Uncle Tom's Cabin,* and *The Wide, Wide World.* Like the Job story and *Pilgrim's Progress, The Wide, Wide World* is a trial of faith; its emphasis falls not on last-minute redemption but on the toils and sorrows of the "way"—its protagonist, like theirs, is systematically stripped of every earthly support and then persecuted. Like these narratives, *The Wide, Wide World* teaches its readers, by example, how to live under such conditions, and like theirs, its lesson is that the only thing that really matters is faith in God and doing his will.

At the end-point of the disciplinary process, Ellen does not exist for herself at all any more, but only for others. Sanctified by the sacrifice of her own will, she becomes a mentor by example, teaching lessons in submissiveness through her humble bearing, downcast eyes, unruffled brow, and "peculiar grave look." She becomes a medium through which God's glory can show itself to men, a person who "supplied what was wanting everywhere; like the transparent glazing which painters use to spread over the dead color of their pictures; unknown, it was she gave life and harmony to the whole."[30] The ideal to which the novel educates its readers is the opposite of self-assertion; it is to become empty of self, an invisible transparency that nevertheless is miraculously responsible for the life in everything.

In an unfriendly review of Warner's book, Charles Kingsley quipped that it should have been called "The Narrow, Narrow World," and, of course, in a sense he was right. Although the frontispiece to the first illustrated edition shows a ship tossing on a stormy sea with the sun breaking through clouds in the background, all of the heroine's adventures take place in small enclosed spaces that are metaphors of the heart. The wideness of the world is to be measured not by geographical distances but by the fullness with which it manages to account for the experience of its readers. That experience, as I have argued, was shaped conclusively by the revival movement and by the social and economic conditions of American life in the antebellum years. For the sentimental writers, who were evangelical Christians, the world could be contracted to the dimensions of a closet without loss, because, according to their belief, it was in the closet that one received the power to save the world. When one has learned to master one's soul in private, one becomes "responsible," as Warner puts it, "for the life in everything." That theory of power is what made sentimental fiction a decisive social force, and it is formulated succinctly by the Reverend Dr. Patton, addressing the Fifteenth Annual Meeting of the Home Missionary Society, in words that recapitulate the world view I have attempted to summon up: "The history of the world," he said, "is the history of prayer. For this is the power that moves heaven. Yet it is the power which may be wielded by the humblest and obscurest saint. It will doubtless be found, in the great day, that many a popular and prominent man will be set aside; whilst the retired but pleading disciple, will be brought forth to great honor, as having alone in her closet, wrestled with the angel and prevailed."[31]

NOTES

A much-expanded version of this essay will appear in Jane Tompkins, *Sensational Designs: The Cultural Work of American Fiction, 1790–1860* (Oxford University Press), 1985.

1. That is how twentieth-century critics have usually treated this work. See, for example, Henry Nash Smith, "The Scribbling Women and the Cosmic Success Story," *Critical Inquiry* 1 (September 1974):47–49; John T. Frederick, "Hawthorne's 'Scribbling Women,'" *New England Quarterly* 48 (1975):321–40; Ramona T. Hull, "Scribbling Females and Serious Males: Hawthorne's Comments from Abroad on Some American Authors," *Nathaniel Hawthorne Journal* 5 (1975):35–38.

2. Smith, "The Scribbling Woman,"; Henry Nash Smith, *Democracy and the Novel* (New York: Oxford University Press, 1978), p. 12; Perry Miller, "The Romance and the Novel," *Nature's Nation* (Cambridge: Harvard University Press, Belknap Press, 1967), pp. 255–56.

3. Smith, *Democracy and the Novel,* pp. 13–15.

4. James D. Hart, *The Popular Book* (Berkeley and Los Angeles: University of California Press, 1950), pp. 93, 94, 111; Frank Luther Mott, *Golden Multitudes* (New York: MacMillan Co., 1947), pp. 122–25.

5. Smith, *Democracy and the Novel,* p. 8.

6. Perry Miller, *The Life of the Mind in America from the Revolution to the Civil War* (New York: Harcourt Brace & World, 1965).

7. In March 1829, for example, a pamphlet entitled *Institution and Observance of the Sabbath* was distributed to 23,383 New York families. Charles Foster, *An Errand of Mercy: The Evangelical United Front, 1790–1837* (Chapel Hill: University of North Carolina Press, 1960), p. 187.

8. New York City Tract Society, *Eleventh Annual Report* (New York, 1837), back cover.

9. Ibid., pp. 51–52.

10. Ibid.

11. David Reynolds, "From Doctrine to Narrative: The Rise of Pulpit Story-Telling in America," *American Quarterly*, 32 (Winter 1980):479–98.

12. Tremaine McDowell, "Diversity and Innovation in New England," in *The Literary History of the United States*, ed. Robert E. Spiller et. al., 3d ed., rev. (New York: Macmillan Co., 1963), p. 289.

13. In the first half of the nineteenth century, single women could own real property but married women could not. "Essentially," writes Lawrence Friedman in *A History of American Law* (New York: Simon & Schuster, 1973), "husband and wife were one flesh; but the man was the owner of that flesh" (p. 184). For a good discussion of the growing discrepancy, from the seventeenth century onward, between antipatriarchal theories of government and the reinforcement of patriarchal family structure, see Susan Miller Okin, "The Making of the Sentimental Family," *Philosophy and Public Affairs* 11 (Winter 1982):65–88.

14. Alexis de Tocqueville, *Democracy in America*, 2 vols., trans. Henry Reive, rev. Francis Bowen, corrected and annotated Phillips Bradley (New York: Random House, Vintage Books, 1957), 2:223.

15. Elizabeth Wetherell (Susan Warner), *The Wide, Wide World*, 2 vols. in 1 (1851; rpt. J. P. Lippincott & Co., 1886), 1:12.

16. Rev. Orville Dewey, *A Discourse Preached in the City of Washington, on Sunday, June 27, 1852* (New York: Charles S. Francis & Co., 1852), p. 13. Dewey's sermon on obedience is characteristic of a general concern that a democratic government was breeding anarchy in the behavior of its citizens, and that obedience therefore must be the watchword of the day. In European society, Dewey argues, where the law of caste still reigns, there is a natural respect for order and authority. But *"here* and *now,"* he continues, all this is changed. . . . With no *appointed* superiors above us, we are liable enough to go to the opposite extreme; we are liable to forget that any body is to be obeyed—to forget even, that God is to be obeyed. . . . Only let every man, every youth, every child, think that he has the right to speak, act, do any where and every where, whatever any body else has the right to do; that he has as much right to his will as any body; and there is an end of society. That is to say, let there be an end of obedience in the world, and there is an end of the world." (pp. 4–5).

Since, in Dewey's eyes, the home is the source of anarchy in the state, family discipline is the source of all good civil order, and therefore the goal of domestic education must be "a patient and perfect obedience" (p. 13). If the child is *never* permitted to disobey, it will soon cease to think of it as possible. And it should *never* be permitted! . . . Only when living under law—only when walking in obedience, is child or man, family or State, happy and truly prosperous. Selfish passion every where is anarchy, begetting injustice, and bringing forth destruction." (pp. 13–14) Sentimental novels, along with advice books for young women, child-rearing manuals, and religious literature of all sorts, helped to inculcate the notion that obedience was a domestic as well as a civic virtue, especially in the case of women. Beginning in the 1830s, as Nancy Cott has shown, clergymen directed their sermons on the need for order in family and society especially at women, "vividly emphasizing the necessity for women to be subordinate to and dependent on their husbands" (Nancy F. Cott, *The Bonds of Womanhood: "Woman's Sphere" in New England, 1780–1835* [New Haven: Yale University Press, 1977], pp. 158–59).

17. Ann Douglas, *The Feminization of American Culture* (New York: Alfred A. Knopf, 1977), p. 11.

18. Lewis P. Saum, *The Popular Mood of Pre–Civil War America* (Westport, Conn.: Greenwood Press, 1980), chap. I, "Providence."

19. Warner, *The Wide, Wide World*, 1:13.

20. Ibid., 1:35.

21. *Old Favorites from McGuffey's Readers* prints this poem, from the *Fourth Reader*, entitled "A Mother's Gift—The Bible" whose first stanza reads as follows:
Remember, love, who gave thee this,
    When older days shall come,
When she who had thine earliest kiss,
    Sleeps in her narrow home.
Remember! 'twas a mother gave
    The gift to one she'd die to save!
The Bible is the symbol of the mother in sentimental literature, taking her place, after she is dead, serving as a reminder of her teachings, and as a token of her love. To forget what the Bible says is to forget one's mother:
A parent's blessing on her son
    Goes with this holy thing;
The love that would retain the one,
    Must to the other cling.

22. Warner, *The Wide, Wide World*, 1:20.

23. Ibid., 1:14.

24. Rev. E. Peabody, "Importance of Trifles," in *The Little Republic, Original Articles by Various Hands*, ed. Mrs. Eliza P. T. Smith (New York: Wiley & Putnam, 1848), p. 120. The "importance of trifles" theme is ubiquitous in nineteenth-century inspirational literature. It is directly related to the Christian rhetoric of inversion ("the last shall be first"), to the cultivation of the practical virtues of honesty, industry, frugality ("A stitch in time saves nine," "A penny saved is a penny earned"), and to the glorification of

the mother's influence. In another essay in the same volume ("A Word to Mothers"), Timothy P. Smith writes "Let us not forget that the greatest results of the mind are produced by small, but continued, patient effort" (p. 210).

As surely as a continued digging will wear away the mountain, so surely shall the persevering efforts of a Christian mother be crowned with success. . . . She is, through her children, casting pebbles into the bosom of society; but she cannot as easily watch the ripples made: no, they reach beyond the shore of mortal vision, and shall ripple on, in that sea that has neither shore nor bound, for weal or for woe, to them, and to the whole universal brother hood of man. (pp. 211–12)

25. Peabody, "Importance of Trifles," in *The Little Republic*, pp. 124–25.

26. Saum, *The Popular Mood*, p. 25.

27. de Tocqueville, *Democracy in America*, 2:225.

28. Herman Melville, *Moby-Dick or, The Whale,* edited with an Introduction and annotation by Charles Feidelson, Jr. (New York: Bobbs-Merrill, 1964), p. 247.

29. Warner, *The Wide, Wide World*, 2:273.

30. Ibid., 1:249.

31. Rev. Dr. Patton, Address, American Home Missionary Society, *Fifteenth Report* (New York: William Osborn, 1842), p. 104.

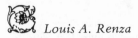 Louis A. Renza

Poe's Secret Autobiography

It is not good for man to cherish a solitary ambition. Unless there be those around him, by whose example he may regulate himself, his thoughts, desires, and hopes will become extravagant, and he the semblance, perhaps the reality, of a madman.

—Nathaniel Hawthorne, "The Prophetic Pictures"

No one needs to remind the American critic of recent Francophile continuations of the assumptions about Poe's canonical status—to be sure, with a "difference"—by past French writers and critics from Baudelaire to Poulet. Not unlike the cracked, ultimately imploding house of Usher, Poe's texts undoubtedly exhibit, sometimes to the point of exhibitionism, a supplementary or, to use one of his own frequently used words, a "supererogatory" verbosity that at once deconstructs the Poe-narrator's logocentric prison-house and the reader's attempt to account for it. Poe, the unconscious producer of postsemiotic texts, has taken precedence over Poe, the exploiter and parodist of late romantic tableaux and memorabilia, and even Poe, the innovator of popular literary genres like the "how did the who-dun-it do it?" It seems time for the still unregenerate, antitheoretical American critic to face a Poe-esque truth as gleaned from one of his most recently deconstructed and re-deconstructed tales: that Francophile criticism has again purloined the Poe *oeuvre* from the archives of American literary history right before the eyes of the latter's self-consciously nationalistic guardians.

Of course, even from this ideological perspective, a perspective that Francophile criticism has come to associate with American criticism's "self" concerns, the Poe canon has registered well-known ambivalent responses. Suspicious of Poe's character, his popularity, and the "literary" pretensions of his works, American criticism has begrudgingly admitted his corpus and, as I shall argue, even his corpse into American literature's Hall of Fame, that is, its institutional courses and anthologies. As prose writer, Poe was

Henry James's "exquisite specimen of provincialism," a writer appealing to "a decidedly primitive stage of reflection," yet who on occasion, if only in his criticism, could "find a phrase of happy insight in a patch of the most fatuous pedantry."[1] In the context of the post–World War II institutionalization of American criticism from F. O. Matthiessen to Harold Bloom, the brief quantity and "narrow" aesthetic as well as moral range of Poe's works has consigned them to the limbo of footnotes in the *American Renaissance* and, at least until recently, to Bloom's conspicuous silence about their anxiety-seminal influence on later American writers.[2] These de facto diminishments of Poe's importance in American literary history tend to confirm Claude Richard's judgment that "to American critics, Poe has been relegated to relative obscurity" or hardly exists "because he didn't fit into the 'picture.' "[3]

To be sure, there have been more ideologically insistent and critically sophisticated efforts to bring Poe back into the mainstream of American literature. Leslie Fiedler, for example, suggests that Poe's confounding of the distinction between high- and low-brow literature entails an American populist demystification of elitist institutionalism, and in this way accords with the American political "experiment."[4] On a more hermeneutic level, Jonathan Auerbach claims that Poe's works reveal, and can even be read as allegorical internalizations of, Poe's struggle and desire to come to terms with producing literature for a commodity-oriented readership.[5] In this sense, Poe's works at least valuably dramatize their "American" literary-ideological relations of production.

There also remains another way to view these works "in the American grain." Refining William Carlos Williams's judgment that Poe's works, in style as well as theme, reflect a mainstream "American Adam" concern, specifically what Williams defines as the American's "necessity for a fresh beginning," Joseph Riddel argues that these works effectively deconstruct the "American" quest for literary-ideological orginality and/or original self-identity.[6] To Riddel, Poe's works are crypts on and cryptographic repetitions of other texts; they thus prefigure and predict postmodernist notions of intertextuality, the fictionality of all origins, and the death of

the authorial self as well as the autonomous work. Particularly in
The Narrative of A. Gordon Pym, as John Irwin painstakingly
shows in his critical revision of Matthiessen's *American Renaissance,* Poe represents the desire to arrive at the origins of self
through a phonetic language trying to double the immediate effect
of hieroglyphic writing.[7] But his quest, one that typifies the concerns of other "American Renaissance" writers as well, is doomed
to failure since there can be no quest for self without language,
and no language whose very materiality as writing does not inter-
fere with the self's desire to become narcissistically doubled—
absolutely self-present—through the mirror of this medium.[8] Poe's
fiction thus constitutes an aporia to would-be "American Adam"
autobiographies, the imaginable representations of the American
self as indeed a "fresh beginning." But for this very reason, one
can argue for his priority not only in exercising through writing
the Republic's ideological or "American dream" wish for self-
autonomy, but also in exorcising by exposing the nightmarish
consequences of this wish.

Still, revisionary "American Renaissance" or canonical recuperations of Poe's works, written through as well as against an
insistent American mythos (noticeably, here, with the help of a
purloined scene of Francophile criticism), may underestimate the
way his works effectively prejudge these same recuperations as misreadings that foster a secret and perverse "American Adam" autobiographical project. Looking at Poe's tales from this perspective, I
do not mean to claim that they are "autobiographical" in the sense
of symbolically outlining his extratextual, perverse spiritual autobiography through, say, the experiences of his many haunted narrators or the various incognito subterfuges afforded by the discourse
of fiction. Rather, I mean something akin to Paul de Man's notion
of autobiography as a figure of reading as opposed to genre of
writing,[9] but here revised as a figure of Poe's reading of his own
texts as he imagines them being misread by others in order to regard them as his dialectically confirmed exclusive private property.
Poe produces texts, that is, to gain a perspective on their writing
like that of his narrator in the lyric tale, "The Island of the Fay,"

who can look with "interest" on a scene in nature only if he "gazed *alone*."[10]

One does not have to be a Poulet-like intuitionist to apprehend Poe's tales as motivated fictions in relation to their imagined reception. For one thing, they impishly advertise their literary seams, their thematic, stylistic, generic, and other conventional derivations. Far from attempting to conceal these derivations and "plagiarisms," precedents that Thomas Mabbott and others have eagerly detected (as Poe himself did with many works written by his contemporaries), Poe's tales overexpose them and thus repeatedly verge on becoming literary hoaxes; repeatedly concern themselves with conspicuously obsessive topoi such as premature burials, doubles, and dying, beautiful women; and repeatedly flirt with motifs like enigmatic ciphers or written "characters," allusions to other texts, even the repetition of certain words and phrases. Equally relevant here is Poe's habit of reducing word-sense to sound, to the sheer materiality of the signifier mocking the reader's attempt to make sense out of it: the animal sounds mistaken for a foreign language in "The Murders in the Rue Morgue"; most famously, perhaps, the "nevermore" mimicking of human speech by the bird in "The Raven"; or the guttural sounds and gnashing of teeth (the latter, a metonym of the very condition for articulate speech) by the dwarf-protagonist in "Hop-Frog." Along these same lines, one everywhere encounters countless verbal jokes, particularly in the form of submerged puns and commonplace maxims which compound the already hoaxy aura of Poe's tales. Hans Phaall dropping a letter to townspeople below from a balloon in the sky translates as a text appearing "out of the blue" and "full of hot air"; the narrator in "Berenice" extracting teeth [*sic*] from his dead female cousin puts himself "in the jaws of death"; or the "duping" Dupin detecting an ape as killer of the two women thus dabbles in "monkey business," or at least, like the character Hop-Frog in the later story, "makes a monkey out of" the social establishment, here the Parisian police.

Whereas these overexposed verbal eruptions point to the intertextual locus and/or linguistic dislocation of Poe's tales, they also signify authorial manipulation as such—the immanently signified presence of an "I" in wilfull control of his text's production. The literary hoax, after all, connotes the writer's intention, or at least the awareness of the fiction of his fiction's reception. If Poe elsewhere adheres to an affectivist philosophy of composition, to that ideal of a text totally enthralling a reader in its tightly construed, unified representational spell for the time it takes to read it, he also sabotages this ideal by permeating his texts with elements that can interrupt this spell and call attention to his own performance. Of course, one might wish to argue that, short of gratuitous exhibitionism, Poe's disruptive activity expresses his "supererogatory" animus toward his consumerist democratic audience. At the very least, it violates the literary contract whereby the reader agrees to suspend his or her disbelief on the assumption that a tale manifests the writer's genuine effort to project a sharable imagined and imaginative world. Or one could regard such disruptions as indicative of the Poe text's unconscious awareness of "writing" as a constant slippage of signifiers. Certainly the forged as opposed to metafictional aspect of the literary hoax as well as the *over*-baring of the device in Poe's tales points to the iterability of fiction in general, that is, to fiction as lacking an original ground from which one could apprehend it as a totally self-present mode of representation.

Yet the verbal static emanating from a Poe tale seems too controlled, too contrived, too intentionally recognizable, for us to regard it as simply a sign either of his ideological grievance toward his audience or of his unconscious semiotic praxis. On the contrary, such static seems self- rather than other-directed. It appears directed, namely, toward revealing to its imagined reader the word-mediated traces of its author, the man in the text-as-machine, for no apparent reason other than to confront his reader with an autobiographical terminus. Indeed, the "self" suddenly uncovered by our awareness of hoaxy elements in Poe's tales occasionally even leads us to the culdesac of his subliminally inscribed signature. For example, the letters of "Siope" (Greek for "calm" or "silence"), a brief fable that Poe later retitled "Silence" and had earlier associated with autobiographical writing per se in his caption for this tale, "in the manner of the Psychological Autobiographists" (Bulwer and De Quincey, according to Mabbott, 2:199), anagrammatically spell the words "is Poe." In the same way, the "ape" that kills the women in "Rue Morgue" anagrammatically spells, of course, the initials of Poe's name: E. A. P.

These discernible, seemingly arbitrary or redundant self-references may signify more than displays of parodistic free play or further extensions of the self-limiting literary hoax. One could instead maintain that they reverse the way tropes usually associated with fiction intrude on and problematize autobiography's "true" renditions of its writer's life-experiences. By permeating his tales with autobiographical intimations in a quite literal rather than symbolically representational sense, Poe exemplifies how autobiography can function as a postscriptural aporia to fiction. Moreover, since the verbal elements conveying these intimations willy-nilly distract the reader's attention from the tale's aesthetic or narrative spell—the very spell Poe identifies as the fictive experience par excellence—we could also argue that elements like his self-consciously planted signature effectively preclude his tale's being read *as* a self-contained fiction, let alone as a text in the process of *un*consciously inscribing, as Geoffrey Hartman has expressed it, a Saussurean specular name.[11] Thus, the reader made aware of Poe's inscribed rhetorical gambit of writing a tale in terms of a "I know that you know I know that *I* am in the process of writing this fiction of a fiction" now confronts a text less endowed with the concentrated ambiguity of two possible readings than a text whose verbally abused "first" or aesthetic reading possibly indicates a secretly withheld autobiographical subtext. On such occasions, Poe's tales do not so much place the reader in the position of not being able to decide between a conventionally aesthetic and a perversely hoaxy reading as suggest that the text he or she has just been reading *has not yet been read*—a situation induced by his or her sudden encounter with a performative linguistic operation which "is Poe."

In short, one can construe Poe's tales as autobiographical cryptograms. He all but confesses this possibility in an oft-cited passage from one of his *Literati* essays where he maintains that "the book of an author" doubles as "the author's self . . . . The soul is a cipher, in the sense of a cryptograph; and the shorter a cryptograph is [i.e., like his own brief tales], the more difficulty there is in its comprehension."[12] His 1841 article on "Secret Writing" clearly shows his desire to produce as well as ability to decipher such writing. There never was, he says, "a time when there did not exist a necessity, *or at least a desire,* of transmitting information from one individual to another . . . as to elude comprehension [by others]."[13] Poe proceeds to contend that all cryptographs are decipherable; in other words that there exists no such thing as a private language. But he also demonstrates his interest in the latter possibility by reprinting a lengthy response to his contention by a correspondent named W. B. Tyler who insists that one could indeed produce a cryptographic text that would "be perfectly 'hidden' " and seem "an impenetrable mystery" to others.[14] When commenting about Shelley in his 1849 "Marginalia," Poe himself will suggest the possibility of producing texts whose public or readable appearance belies their withheld significance for their writer: "[Shelley's] rhapsodies are but the rough notes—the stenographic memoranda of poems—memoranda which, because they were all-sufficient for his own intelligence, he cared not to be at the trouble of writing out in full for mankind."[15] Indeed, one can also see Poe's impulse toward "secret writing" in his very alteration of the title "Siope" to "Silence" where his previous, relatively concealed signature effecitvely *becomes* erased unto "silence" or a more radically concealed signature. To someone like Poe who was convinced that a writer's very autograph and handwritten manuscript could express his "moral biography,"[16] even the print-mediated relatively concealed signature in "Siope" would constitute a form of autobiographical-alias-autographic concealment.

  For Poe, then, writing a tale includes the possible imagination of its misreading. At the very least, like the hoaxing of fiction whose function is defined by his idea of secret writing, or like the many other anagrams we can discover in his texts—for instance, "nevar" in the word "raven" of his famous poem—secret writing for Poe serves to delay the reading of the text's very signifiers. Once deciphered, as deciphered the anagrams may always become, the decoded message seems no less "an impenetrable mystery." The future absence of the illocutionary and/or aesthetic context in which this message was produced saddles its necessarily fragmentary semiotic appearance with zero semantic value. For example, the "nevar" in "The Raven" amounts to no more than a mere tautology or italicized repetition of the poem's "nevermore" refrain; like Poe's other anagrammatic "monkey business," it functions as a kind of secret writing that effectively promulgates the illusion of having produced a still unread literary text. Even when apprehended *as* secret writing, Poe's texts simply disclose a contentless autobiographical pregnancy, a prematurely buried autobiographical subtext whose self-referential significance becomes discernible only through a purely speculative, self-alienating act of reading.

From this perspective, we can better focus on and interpret the effects of Poe's verbal doubling. Here I do not simply mean "doubling" in the sense of represented characters like the two William Wilsons, or of anagrammatic splittings like "nevar" and "raven," but rather that doubling found in his very construction of texts, for example in "The Gold Bug" which was actually first published in a two-part weekly sequence in the *Dollar Newspaper* (Mabbott, 3:806). About money, doubtless also about (especially given its site of publication) its own status as a commodity in Poe's contemporary literary marketplace, the clearly demarcated narrative focuses of "The Gold Bug" serve to increase its conventional literary value, which of course accounts for its continuing popularity in the Poe canon.[17] But we can also claim that the reader pays the price for this narrative doubling or formal defamiliarization of a narrative convention. That is, focusing on William Legrand's mode of deciphering Captain Kidd's cryptographic treasure-map, the second part of the story comes to take narrative precedence over the first where Legrand, the narrator, and Jupiter actually discover the treasure. By making the second or methodological section the narrative center of the story, Poe effectively displaces or interrupts the section that, according to textual precedents on which the story was based (Mabbott, 3:800–803), would otherwise have attracted greater melodramatic interest to a convention-bound reader.

This effect seems to resemble that produced earlier in his career by his analytic demystification not only of the illusory doubling of human activity in Maelzel's mechanical Chess-player, but of the very public wishing to believe in it. In a more perverse sense, it also resembles the effect that his own "The Philosophy of Composition" will have on readers of his earlier, highly popular poem, "The Raven." In other words, the second part of "The Gold Bug" both anticipates by mimicking a "second" or "critical" reading of the first part and, more important, effectively leads its readers to adopt a reflective relation to the narrative as a whole. William Legrand, "the great Will" or redundant figure of the writer desiring, as Poe explicitly states in his review of Hawthorne's *Twice-Told Tales*, to make "the soul of the reader [be] at the writer's control,"[18] first dupes the narrator, himself a figure for the tale's reader, by distracting him with a physical gold bug, an inscribed metonym of the desired aesthetic mystification Poe's tales would perpetrate on their readers. More important, in confessing this chicanery in the process of narrating his solution to the Kidd-cryptograph, Legrand also distracts the narrator/reader *again*. As author in control of the text he has withheld and first interprets, Legrand, that is, all but forces the narrator/reader into a reflective relation to this text and, by a virtually inevitable proleptic doubling, confesses the writer's attempt to do the same with the reader of "The Gold Bug." At *this* confessional point, then, the "reader" confronts a text whose sheer aesthetic effect has become retroactively and irrecoverably lost or sabotaged by its production of the reader's self-conscious relation to it. In short, this lost aesthetic relation to the narrative now itself becomes the tale's *still* buried treasure—like the wine Fortunato will never get to "taste" in "The Cask of Amontillado."

This circuitous concealment of his text helps define Poe's motivated assumptions about the effect an interest in constructing

and deciphering a cryptograph (and the short tale here encoding
it) will have on readers of his stories and poems. "To see dis-
tinctly the machinery . . . of any work of Art," he notes in his
"Marginalia" (205), "is . . . of itself, a pleasure, but one which we
are able to enjoy only just in proportion as we do *not* enjoy the
legitimate effect designed by the artist." In this sense, we can posit
that Poe's tales produce two distinct tiers of reading. First, the
aesthetic or "legitimate effect" of a Poe tale distracts its reader
from recognizing the act of authorial self-inscription; in the process, it inversely frames this act as a kind of secret writing that
conceals, like Maelzel's mechanical hoax, the man controlling the
tale's operations, operations Poe rhetorically formulates as those
of a literary machine in "The Philosophy of Composition." But
second, insofar as a reader becomes aware of the writer's "inten-
tional" concealment via hoaxes, signatorial anagrams, motifs, and
narrational catechreses like staged methodologies potentially referring to the very tales that encode them, he or she is led to
adopt a reflective or *an*esthetic relation to the text-at-hand, a reflex-
ivity that now inversely produces the possibility of Poe's own
secret relation *to his initial aesthetic composition of it,* and "nevermore" allows the reader access to this relation.

   In one sense, then, similar to Dupin's notion of truth in "The
Murders in the Rue Morgue," Poe constructs his stories as all surface without depth, even as they lead the reader eventually to suspect this depth. But whether read in terms of their surface design
or suspicions of their depth, these tales invite rather than resist
closed readings. If the ostensible goal of a Poe tale is to control its
reader in its aesthetic spell for the duration it takes to read it, this
goal becomes a pretext not for a "legitimate" or proper reading
after all, but for an im-proper misreading which results in the
writer's *sole* ability to reappropriate the tale's imagined if Imaginary
scene of writing, its prematurely buried beautiful premise, or what
Poe describes in his "Marginalia" as that special "class of fancies of
exquisite delicacy, which are *not* thoughts, and to which, *as yet,* I
have found it absolutely impossible to adapt language" (98–99).
Such delicate, prelinguistic fancies constitute Poe's sense of his

secret creative origins, his private relation to "Poesy"—the other anagrammatic significance of "Siope," for example [19]—which readers will miss for being trapped by the tale's *post factum* textual residues or provocative patterns of meaning.

We can observe how Poe explicitly stages such scenarios of misreading in an 1842 tale retitled and revised in 1845 as "The Oval Portrait." The narrator of this story, in Arthur Hobson Quinn's paraphrase, is

> a desperately wounded man who seeks refuge in an unoccupied chateau, and seeks the portrait of a young and beautiful girl, which startles him by its likeness to life. Finding an old volume that describes the paintings, he learns . . . [that she] had given her life to please her husband, an artist, who, as he painted into his picture her marvelous beauty, drained from her her health and spirits. Finally, when he gazed on his completed work and cried out, "This is indeed Life itself," he beheld his bride dead. [20]

In the earlier version of this brief tale, the narrator informs us that he had just taken opium before he saw the portrait; in the revised version, that he was merely drifting off to sleep. In either case, this information has led formalist critical readers to focus on the narrator's ironic function in the tale as much as on the material he narrates, an option also afforded by many of Poe's other tales. [21] But by inviting a formally determinate reading, the story here effectively distracts the reader from focusing on what Poe later maintains personifies "the most poetical topic in the world," namely, the tale's actual topic of a beautiful woman's death ("The Philosophy of Composition," 425). [22] Moreover, the tale concerns the theme of art's vampirization of the very effect, "lifelikeness" (Mabbott, 2:664), which the tale no less than the portrait purports to convey. One could also say that the text within the text does the same thing, for the narrator's reading of the volume perforce makes him avert his gaze from the otherwise self-present portrait of the beautiful woman. His reading, that is, disseminates the immediate object of his initial aesthetic response. Indeed, bereft of both the portrait *and* the text from which the narrator (only) quotes, the narrative of "The Oval Portrait" before *us* thus refers to a virtually absent text, itself in the process of absenting its pictorial referent which has already absented its living model.

What *we* read, then, is the narrator's misreading or missed appropriation of the picture, a figure for the aesthetic object per se. Not only does his reading virtually kill this object like the artists's painting his wife's picture has killed her, our reading, too, is put in the position of repeating this artistic homicide. After all, our reading of "The Oval Portrait" inevitably tends to double the narrator's own curiosity to know more about a "vignette"-like aesthetic object which so affects him at first that he closes his eyes, not knowing "why I did this" (Mabbott, 2:664, 663); his ensuing explanation for this closure, "to make sure that my vision had not deceived me—to calm and subdue my fancy for a more sober and more certain gaze," again provokes our own desire "for a more sober and more certain" understanding of the narrator as well as tale. Just as the narrator then comes to read the portrait's verbal commentary, so his statements lead us into a "second" reading of the story. The story itself thus effectively buries by distracting our focus from its putative generative source—that "most poetical topic" as such of a dying, beautiful woman.

Such repetitive de-compositions of, first, the woman by the artist, next the portrait by the volume, then this volume by the tale's very narrative, and finally this narrative by the interpretive narrative able to recognize how such verbal circularity figuratively doubles an "oval portrait," obviously suggest an endlessly provisional sequence or *en abîme* of misreading. But I would argue that as with the sequential relation between "The Raven" and "The Philosophy of Composition," the tale's allegorical staging of misreadings functions to keep the reader ignorant of its ever-more "poetical" locus of production. More precisely, in *reflectively* reenacting the killing of a beautiful woman, these projected misreadings keep the beautiful woman, the secret inspirational source or muse of the story itself, *in the process* of dying. If only from the position of the writer imagining these misreadings, they effectively prolong the tale's secret aesthetic life.

If Poe here and in his other tales allegorizes his reading of others' misreading his therefore privately retained relation to his "most poetical topic," he indeed writes, to use Lacan's etymology for "purloined letter," prolonged narratives, texts that postpone the moment of an aesthetic reading akin to his (Imaginary) own, or texts that by authorial will will "nevar" be read as they were written, in this way serving to produce his secret autobiographical relation to them. In short, as allegories of their process of misreading, his tales never quite exist. Rather, they are ghost stories—not so much stories about ghosts as stories of the possibility of stories about Poe's autobiographical relation to the "beautiful" topos that spawns them. But since Poe can effect a "bad faith" imagination of others misreading his texts, he can also imagine the contingency of such misreadings, their dependence, for example, on the sheer material survivability *of* a text so *as* to become misread. Or more pointedly, he must be able to imagine the possibility of a reading that could double his own, one that like our present discussion would witness, appreciate, but also cancel his otherwise dead-end narcissistic project even before textual disintegration might occur.

And so in this sense, Poe's tales also allegorically confess such obstacles to his wish to produce secret autobiographical fiction. As we can see from looking at an 1844 tale called "The Oblong Box," Poe's fiction endopsychically recognizes the limitation of its patently "bad faith" projection of misreadings. The narrator of this story finds himself on a ship with a young artist named Wyatt and his reputedly beautiful wife whom the narrator, nevertheless, judges to be plain-looking. He also notices that Wyatt, an artist, has brought an oblong box to his stateroom about which he remains silent. Merely curious at first about what the box contains, the narrator soon becomes convinced that it "*could* possibly contain nothing in the world but a copy of Leonardo's 'Last Supper' . . . done by Rubini the younger" (Mabbott, 3:925). Eventually provoked to anger by Wyatt's silence, for he assumes "feelings of warm friendship" with Wyatt (3:922), the narrator becomes even more certain in his conviction that the box indeed contains "artistical secrets" (3:925) like Rubini's valuable counterfeit—a situation not unlike the critical reader's suspicion of a determinate, Captain Kidd-like treasure of meaning concealed amid the intertextual counterfeits advertised in almost any Poe tale. The narrator suspects that Wyatt intends to "smuggle a fine picture to New York, under my very nose; expecting me to know nothing of the matter" (3:925). Then, during a storm when the ship begins to sink, Wyatt refuses to remain on a lifeboat unless he can take the box with him. The box, he exclaims, weighs "'but a trifle'" or "'mere nothing'" (3:931). Wyatt returns to the ship, retrieves the box, jumps overboard, and quickly sinks with it after the captain rejects his request as "'mad'" (3:932). The narrator wonders why the box sank so quickly; the captain replies he had packed it with salt, and as soon as the salt melts "'they will soon rise again'" (3: 933). He also exposes the narrator's misreading of the box's contents, for it turns out that it did not contain an art treasure in the narrator's sense, but the artist's dead wife who, according to the captain, "was, indeed . . . a most lovely, and most accomplished woman" (3:933).

This story, of course, resolves itself into one of those "proverbial" maxims mentioned earlier, here the artist "sinking or swimming" with his artistic ideal. But more important, like the pun in the title of another tale, "The Masque of the Red Death," Poe's narrative of "The Oblong Box" covers or "masks" the *read* death, that is, precisely the reading that would have accorded with the artist's privileged and intimate knowledge of what his text-alias-box contained: Poe's own dead, beautiful muse. The narrative projects its own *egregious* misreading through the figure of the narrator, a misreading imaged in the story as clearly disconnected from the artist's relation to his "most poetical topic." Because of an *un*provoked aggressive tendency on the narrator's part (Wyatt, after all, simply remains silent about the box's contents), his misreading in effect leaves behind not only the artist's still secret relation to Beauty, but also a *dead* "relation" (in both senses of this word): the intimate, dead, but still remembered—hence ghostly—source of the artist's activity. The desired imagination of misreading, then,

here itself seems "supererogatory." Instead of preserving or pro-
longing, it suggests the divorce from any possible corroboration of
the writer's relation to his "most poetical topic." He alone witnesses the entropic disintegration of this topos. Like the small
feminine Fay whom the narrator surrealistically imagines as circling
a small island in the tale "The Island of the Fay," the "poetical"
writer's beautiful woman can become more and more shadowy,
more ghostly, soon to disappear altogether: ". . . when the sun had
utterly departed," she (here little more *than* a figment of the narrator's imagination) "now the mere ghost of her former self, went
disconsolately with her boat [i.e., the small tale containing Poe's
"most poetical topic"] into the region of the ebony flood . . . and I
beheld *her magical figure* no more" (Mabbott, 2:605; my emphasis).

   Simply put, Poe can imagine the material cancellation of his
project. It is in the context of this possibility—the fissure, say, in
his scene of writing allowing him to imagine the ultimate disintegration or fall of his own house of fiction—that Poe's secretly
determined autobiographical relation to his writing accrues epi-
taphic urgency. The "mesmeric" control a writer exerts on his
(mis)reader through his text clearly depends on the limited duration of composing and imagining the misreading of a material text.
But if for Poe narrative time is intrinsically finite, the issue of textual
entropy can also take the form of his imagining *un*-controlled misreadings in the future. The mummy revivified by a "material"
galvanic battery in the comic-satiric tale, "Some Words with a
Mummy," pointedly maintains that only a writer can read his text
the way it was intentionally composed, for after his death a writer's
"'great work'" gets decomposed or invariably becomes "'converted
into a species of haphazard notebook . . . for the conflicting
guesses, riddles, and personal squabbles of whole herds of exas-
perated commentators'" (Mabbott, 3:1189).

   Moreover, given Poe's acute sense of his literary-ideological environment, the honorific status accorded to Romantic Transcendentalist tenets and their associated writers, not to mention his
sense of text-proliferation in his time as a "scourge,"[23] the further
possibility arises that the very misreadings he desires to inscribe in

his fiction may never occur because his work may be regarded as not worth reading at all. In this sense, one can attribute another motivation to his construction of ghostly texts, texts not quite *there* either for the reader who will misread them or the writer who, after all, constructs them precisely through this imagination of their misreading and its mediated reflection of a more and more shadowy, residual muse. This mode of construction here serves as a strategy to justify Poe's claim to literary originality in the context of an unfavorable literary milieu. His desire to perceive his own work as original appears, of course, in the way he often accuses other notable contemporaries like Emerson of imitation ("Marginalia," 143), or Longfellow and Hawthorne of plagiarism. Poe also employs more subtle (one could even term them proto-deconstructive) methods to reduce the major or successful status not only of other literary texts but also of literary-ideological criteria responsible for the value of such texts, including those he himself produces. As Sidney Moss suggests, for example, in "The Philosophy of Composition" Poe effectively deconstructs honorific notions of Romantic Imagination and genius by showing how his own successful poem, "The Raven," was the result of a highly calculated or nonspontaneous mode of mechanical-deductive construction.[24] For Poe, literary originality "demands in its attainment less of invention than negation" ("The Philosophy of Composition," 427)—the negation, no doubt, of other textual precedents and the literary norms they give rise to. Or as he claims in "Peter Snook," such originality is not "a mere matter of impulse or inspiration" but rather the ability "carefully, patiently, and understandingly to combine."[25]

But of course, in exposing both the appearance and honorific notions of literary originality here as patently *un*original, Poe indirectly claims an original position in recognizing this very situation. In effect, Poe's critical reversals or explicit "negation" of contemporary "literary" standards serve to disclose for him an untrammeled intertextual space of writing that promises him the possibility of a "fresh beginning" as regards his own writing. The vigor of his ambition to determine this original space of writing in relation to fraternal competitors is clearly revealed in his secretly inscribed fantasies of homicide concerning writers represented by accepted literary conventions including styles as well as themes of writing. Perhaps nowhere in Poe's canon does such a fantasy get so tellingly inscribed as in a tale he considered to be one of his best, "Ligeia." There he depicts the female protagonist with characteristics that justify Daniel Hoffman's view of her as a muse-figure for Poe[26]: her very name a reference to a spirit personifying music (Mabbott, 2:331); "the dear music of her low sweet voice"; especially her "airy and spirit-lifting vision more wildly divine than the phantasies which hovered about the slumbering souls of the daughters of Delos" (2:311). Indeed, the tale clearly devolves on the prolonged dying and revenant-revivification of *two* beautiful women. Yet Poe's narrational intimations of the character Ligeia as a "spirit-lifting" muse-figure on whom we can say the writer-alias-narrator remains dependent throughout the tale (and even as he writes it after the events it depicts apparently took place) appear to include a quite specific literary-ideological allusion. Thus, her "*intensity* of thought" and "gigantic volition" (2:315), a willfulness dramatized by her and later the narrator's reiteration of a putative passage from Joseph Glanvill claiming that the individual's will can overcome death, project her as a relatively cryptogrammatic allusion to Transcendentalist ideology—not to a Continental as opposed to English romanticism, as some critics have argued, but to its American *and* European ideological versions.[27] For example, as a muse-figure whose "paternal name" the narrator confesses he has "*never known*" (2:311), Ligeia represents a *sui generis* figure of Romantic Imagination to the writer/narrator, a fatherless vision which thus abjures any romantic ideological precedent.

From this allegorical perspective (which, as we have seen, must constitute a misreading of or reflective relation to the text), "Ligeia" also representationally traces the murderous process by which Poe can effect and not merely declare his sense of being original. Despite her will to survive, Ligeia eventually dies, and the aggrieved narrator marries the Lady Rowena who only serves to remind him of his former wife's "wisdom, of her lofty . . . ethereal nature" (2:323). Loveless and trapped in the narrator's bizarrely decorated English abbey, faced with a husband addicted to opium and who isolates her in rooms such as where a wind-machine artificially makes the pictures on a tapestry seem "hideous and uneasy" shapes (2:322), Rowena herself dies, but not before a series of periodic resuscitations. In the representational "mad disorder" of the final scene in which the grave-clothed corpse revives before the narrator and its identity becomes uncertain (2:329–30), Ligeia apparently—is it the narrator's delusion?—repossesses the body of Rowena, thus seeming to validate the passage from Glanvill.

(Mis)reading this tale as a literary-ideological allegory, one could argue that "Ligeia" concerns the death and resurrection of Coleridgean Imagination at the expense of Coleridgean Fancy, the faculty of verbal association suggested even in the way the narrator designates Rowena as "the fair-haired and blue-eyed Lady Rowena Trevanion, of Tremaine" (2:321). But as Rowena's allusion to a character from Scott's *Ivanhoe* suggests, "Ligeia" also revises these faculties into an oppositional relation between modes of prose fictional and poetic praxis, specifically privileging the latter over the former. On the one hand, the abbey-setting of "Ligeia" clearly depicts the claustrophobic space, the "hideous" characters and events, and the artificially induced effects that identify *any* Poe tale. On the other, Ligeia's vampirization of Rowena extends this reference to his own fictional praxis beyond the context of the tale's self-evident parody or ironic distention of its literary milieu, the Gothic and/or romantic fictional conventions it employs such as the binary of the light and dark lady. Given the way the narrative endows her with attributes indicative of a conventional wifely docility and yet confers on her an honorific full name (the *Lady* Rowena Trevanion, of Tremaine), Rowena here stands as a trope of both a familiar and privileged literary praxis associated with contemporary fictional discourse. Thus, the narrator's rejection of her in favor of Ligeia constitutes a way for the tale itself to define its own literary-ideological scene of (fictional) writing as no less willfully original, enduringly poetic, and secretly operative than the vision of its "beautiful" and seemingly "entombed" protagonist (2:323). Just as Ligeia vampirizes Rowena, Poe's tale "Ligeia" effectively murders or vampirizes a conventional and privileged mode of literary praxis for the sake of dialectically resuscitating the more original Poe-esque "poetical topic," the generative trope of a dead, beautiful woman that ostensibly accounts for this very tale which thus continually and strategically entombs "her."

But here again, this narcissistic fantasy of original writing inevitably becomes haunted both by the necessarily social aspect of writing and its temporally limited materiality. Poe later admitted that Ligeia should have died one final time after her ghostly resurrection (2:307), a resurrection, by the way, that *we* reenact with "Ligeia" insofar as our allegorization of the tale itself constitutes a ghostly or reflective figure of reading. Poe's admission suggests that no mode of original expression *including his own* can survive or become recognized as such in the future except as a transitory and illusory event. For the briefest moment, we can (mis)read a Poe tale as in the process of autobiographically secret-ing his "most poetical topic" in a radically original manner. But then the text of the tale comes to dominate both him and us: it appears minus its authorial intention; it escapes the writer's will; not to mention conceals its environmental milieu in which he sought to define his radical originality and which we can only, as here, reconstruct reflectively. To Poe, every story he writes will "fall" like the house of Usher. As with Roderick, the artist, with his twin sister Madeline in "The Fall of the House of Usher," Poe's attempt to maintain the illusion of originality through his writing the tale eventuates *in* a tale, that is, in the project-shattering union between the artist and his beautiful muse-alias-sister, and in the disintegration of even this unity into random, more and more anonymous signifiers.

But if even Poe's narcissistic abuse of fictional discourse fails to support his illusion of originality, no writer, least of all Poe's competitors for literary greatness who, unlike him, seem unaware of the limitations textuality imposes on acts of Imagination, can ever possess anything akin to permanent canonical status. "My whole nature," as Matthiessen in the *American Renaissance* quotes Poe as saying, "revolts at the idea that there is any being in the universe superior to myself."[28] This perverse—even mass suicidal—democratic position could easily define the literary-ideological context in which Poe writes the 1848 *Eureka*. We can justifiably consider this cosmological prose poem as Poe's apocalyptic "negation" (hence effort at originality according to the view espoused in "The Philosophy of Composition") of Emerson's major essay, *Nature*, as regards both the latter's theoretical scope and its articulation of the desire to arrive at "an original relation to the universe." As Poe declares in his preface to this work, *Eureka* "cannot die:— or, if by any means it be now trodden down so that it die, [it] will 'rise again to Life Everlasting.' "[29] Poe's placement of quotation marks around "rise again to Life Everlasting" marks his materialistic qualification both of its orthodox Christian meaning and the presumption of immortality that he imputes to the idealized notions of Emersonian Transcendentalists or, as he referred to them more than once, the "Frogpondians." To judge from Emerson's famous dismissal of him as "the jingle man," Poe rightly felt himself looked down upon by Emerson's elitist literary circle. And he returned the favor in kind. In his review of Hawthorne's *Twice-Told Tales*, for example, he admits to having momentarily qualified his estimation of Hawthorne's literary originality because of his association with this circle.[30]

Thus, it is hardly mere speculation to claim that in *Eureka* Poe expresses his animus toward Emerson's assumptively original vision of nature. Throughout his essays but especially in *Nature*, Emerson tracks the privileged moment when the individual transcends "all mean egotism" and experiences a "transparent" oneness with nature. In *Eureka*, contrarily, Poe effectively demystifies this moment and instead argues that all individuals (and individual events) exist in a material state of regression or collapse back into an Original Unity (579) which he defines oxymoronically as "Matter *no more*" (587).[31] Aside from his vision's deferral of potential Transcendentalist experience to a material-bound future, we here encounter the relevant pun of "no matter" and its virtual

reduction of such experience to the very materiality and common-
ality of language itself. Moreover, it "doesn't matter" whether like
Emerson one lays claim to his privileged experience. Since all individuals will gain "an identity with God" (590), the social or,
what to Poe amounts to the same thing, the literary recognition of
one's originality becomes a moot issue, ultimately dependent on
one's accidental position in the material universe. Eclipsed for the
moment, then, his text "will 'rise again'" since it refers to the
buried but inevitable material truth grounding Transcendentalist
idealism. Like "Ligeia," for example, *Eureka* propagates the notion
of an entropic material spiritualism precisely in contradistinction
to the "natural supernaturalism" or intimations of immortality
that permeate the writings of Poe's English and especially American
Romantic peers.

Thus, along with the aforementioned "secret writing" strategies,
each in their way helping to produce a buried, autobiographically
determined sense of beauty, this materialistic negation of the
would-be permanent canonical originality of other writers serves
to double Poe's narcissistic project to possess a private and original
relation to his act of writing. At the same time, it also helps con-
vince him of the possibility that his written works will indeed
"'rise again'" in the future, will gain him, that is, recognition as
an original American writer precisely for having "executed" such
a project. Poe, in other words, not only attempts to ghost-write his
tales but also his place in American literary history. But here again,
he cannot ever be certain that such recognition will occur. On the
one hand, because of the postponed nature of his project, Poe lives
and writes, as he informs James Russell Lowell in 1844, in terms of
a "longing for solitude" and "continually in a reverie of the
future."[32] On the other, faced with determining his literary originality "between the lines" of other contemporary textual practices
and constructing his texts through the imaginary misreadings of
others, he necessarily experiences moments of self-doubt. In his
"Marginalia" of 1848, for example, around the time he publishes
Eureka, Poe warns that we should not "maltreat" geniuses, for just
when they are about to achieve "some long-cherished end," they

sometimes "sink themselves into the deepest possible abyss of *seeming* despair, *for no other purpose than* that of increasing the space of success through which they have made up their minds immediately to soar" (145; my emphases). But who can apprehend this "space of success" except the writer in question? Poe clearly incurs difficulties in trying to determine his own original space of writing vis-à-vis the imagined misreadings of others. Because his readers "nevar" have the full Poe text before them, he must arbitrarily, that is, perversely, declare its originality. More than guilt, this literarily motivated declaration governs the significance of the narrators' impulsive confessions in "William Wilson," "The Imp of the Perverse," and "The Tell-Tale Heart." What they confess, after all, is their originality in committing crimes that otherwise—like Poe's literary crimes—might have gone unnoticed.

Still, if Poe's ambitious project constantly swings back like a pendulum toward the pit of literary oblivion, his postponed fiction, his secret abuse of prevailing literary conventions and ideologies to determine a privately original space of reading and writing his own fiction, equally allows him to adopt a nonambitious rhetorical stance toward this fiction. He can regard himself as the producer of what others will designate as minor literature but which, like *Eureka,* will nevertheless manifest his genius sometime in the future. Thus, Poe's working in minor or magazine genres (reviews, criticism, articles on nonliterary topics, as well as short commercial tales) is charged with the secret agenda of deferring his recognition as a major American literary talent. Magazine writing, he states in "Peter Snook," is "a *very* important branch of literature" in which Americans are presently behind English writers; even the critical essay is a potential art-form, an unexplored hence original space of writing or, as he expresses it, "a branch of literature . . . which is daily growing in importance, and which, in the end (not far distant), will be the *most* influential of all the departments of Letters."[33]

Poe also internalizes this gambit of "minor literature" or encoded assertion of literary authority within certain tales, for example, "The Domain of Arnheim," a tale that devolves on the ostensibly minor literary topos of landscape gardening. The narrator of this tale still stands in awe of a man named Ellison who, now dead, once possessed both a self-evident artistic genius and economic resources to have realized it in any artistic medium he wished. Yet despite his options to have worked in the more honorific arts, he chose to become "neither musician nor poet" but instead to traffic in "materialism" (Mabbott, 3:1271), that is, to construct a landscape garden. Significantly, one of Ellison's "elementary principles" as an artist "was the contempt of ambition" (3:1268–69). But his artistic success in this minor genre leads the narrator to wonder whether "it is not indeed possible that, while a high order of genius is necessarily ambitious, the highest is above that which is termed ambition[.] And may it not thus happen that many far greater than Milton have contentedly remained 'mute and inglorious'?" (3:1271).

As practiced by Ellison, landscape gardening indeed turns out to express a beauty "true throughout all the domains of art" (3:1273), a phrase referring to the (1847 revised) title of the tale itself, "The Domain of Arnheim." In other words, the garden expresses and yet conceals the labor of the paragon artist who takes nature and so "'imbue[s] his designs at once with extent and novelty of beauty, as to convey the sentiment of spiritual interference'" or "'the *art* of the creator . . . apparent to reflection only'" (3:1276). Ellison considers nature as a whole, and in particular American nature, "'the original beauty of the country,'" (3:1275), as a pretext or textual field—and here he stands as a figure revising Emerson's vision of nature[34]—on which as artist he can inscribe *his own* originality or "spiritual interference." The narrator of the tale thus testifies to the success of this ghostly self-inscription, that is, to Ellison's posthumous "supererogatory" association with an otherwise anonymously authored "natural" artifact. Giving us a verbal tour of the finished garden, the narrator imagines how others will perceive it for the first time. Ellison's construction of the garden clearly requests this imaginary and detailed speculation, for it entails Ellison's and doubtless Poe's own imaginary effort to control the reception of their respective "landscape" works. The experience of the imagined spectator/reader through the seriatim maze of the garden/narrative seems to lead him or her to an original if controlled experience of the Romantic Sublime, to some gated Paradise of "Tall slender Eastern trees" and, "up-springing confusedly amid all, a mass of semi-Gothic, semi-Saracenic architecture, sustaining itself by miracle in mid-air . . . seeming the phantom handiwork . . . of the Fairies" (3:1283).

This experience manifests Poe's desire for an original reading of his own "semi-Gothic, semi-Saracenic" tales, tales he himself had designated in an early collection with the terms "grotesque and arabesque." Indeed, the tale itself, not simply the sequential narrative effect on its implied reader, performs this original reading in the way it allusively inscribes and transcends, for example, Coleridge's "'Kubla Khan." But like the imagined "as if" spectator of Arnheim represented in the tale, even the most "original" reader *of* this tale who becomes aware of *its* paradigmatic artistic originality ("true throughout *all* the domains of art") will be unable, in the end, to experience how it originally expresses "the art of the *creator.*" One cannot apprehend Poe-alias-Ellison in "The Domain of Arnheim" except by "reflection only," in other words, as its lost-because-absent cause. It seems fitting, then, that even the ideal reader will likely miss—and only reflectively grasp when and if dis-covering—anagrams in the tale's self-identifying proper names, "Ellison" and "Arnheim": "Eli's son" and "near Him." These ana-grams testify to the tale's secret and premature burial of Poe's radical, godlike ambition to be original, to his desire to produce a textual "domain near Him," the ultimate Origin. They also testify to the way he programs his texts to explode like time-bombs in the future, as expressed in the title when we substitute the French homonym "demain" for the English "domain": "Tomorrow near Him"! If we regard this tale as paradigmatic of at least Poe's tales, we could thus argue that Poe writes them as evanescent expressions of his own quasi-spiritual autobiographical "interference," his "Kilroy was here" authorial traces, himself as the lost, absent cause of texts that, like those of his artistic peers, he foresees will indeed become "lost causes."

The "post-mortem effects," as Lawrence implicitly termed them, of Poe's cyrogenic project to survive by artificial textual means—through the galvanically, salty, or mesmerically induced misreadings coterminously defining the production of his texts—point to his willed plot to return to future readers as a ghostly autobiographical figure still haunting these texts. Even with this awareness, however, such (mis)readers encounter a text that only momentarily "is Poe"; like that huge, white human figure appearing at the end of *Pym*, this autobiographical "Poe" then proceeds to disintegrate or disappear into the anonymous blank pages of the material text. Or like some manuscript found in a bottle, the title of one of his first published tales where a narrator finds himself on a ghost-ship named "Discovery" and ends on the verge of "some exciting knowledge—some never-to-be-imparted secret" (Mabbott, 2:142, 145), a Poe tale sooner or later transports its reader to a ghostly subtext that both expresses its own ambition to discover and define originally the American experience, and yet leads this reader to confront its never-to-be-imparted autobiographical secret—the tale's withheld aesthetic premise that permits only Poe to read this tale autobiographically.

Such depictions of Poe's project clearly argue against the various critical attempts to recuperate the major canonical status of his works or his proper place in the "American Renaissance." Thus, to write his stories as self-distracting artifacts, as texts produced through a proleptic reading of others misreading them so as to confirm the writer's privatized autobiographical relation to their production, is to run afoul of ideological, French deconstructionist, and American traditionalist criteria—a situation Poe himself could not have plotted better since it effectively prolongs the question of his canonical status or (the same thing) the "secret" autobiographical agenda of his writing. Far from struggling against, Poe's tales unabashedly exemplify and embrace, the bourgeois narcissism encouraged by his literary-ideological environment, in particular its reification of textual-semiotic exchange. Of course, one may still regard such narcissism as the "supplementary" possibility of all text-production and view Poe's mode of writing as prefiguring what have become certain truisms for Gallic deconstruction: producing texts that anticipate, befuddle, expose, and leave their reading "undecidable"; or using temporarily buried puns, anagrams, commonplace maxims, and represented scenes of writing and reading that reveal a text's marginality, its dependence on the materiality of "writing," and/or its deconstruction of its own autonomous status. But as I have argued, Poe's tales effectively abuse these proto-deconstructive gestures. They seek to control, predict, and thus predicate their own secret identity in terms of misreadings that, as Paul de Man has rigorously maintained, are "undecidable" linguistic tropes rather than manipulable pretexts for confirming the *self*-referentiality of these tales to their producer.[35]

On the other hand, Poe's *self*-interested literary practices, his motivated production of texts as private property and abuse of the conventional transaction among, variously, reader, writer, and text, foster his ambivalent status in American literary history. Most of our canonically minded writers and critics have neither recognized nor wanted to regard Poe as an American literary father. I am not thinking of those benign Po-e-philiac writers and critics who naively assume his canonical status. Rather I refer to those who use the Eliotian "preadolescent" judgment of Poe to deny his influence on their work, but who nonetheless repeat the Poe who "ghost-wrote" his own texts. Poe, that is, wrote fiction as a pretext to a fiction and autobiography he never came to write. Itself a fiction of both fiction and autobiography, Poe's self-aggrandizing abuse of the literary medium scandalizes the notion of "serious" literary production, particularly in a country then concerned with its cultural secondariness and today still desirous of demonstrating the morality of its cultural vision.

It is *this* Poe whom Henry James found "primitive" even as he doubled Poe's ghost-writing praxis. Preferring to designate Hawthorne as his literary father, James at best would only acknowledge Poe as a writer of ghost stories that did not sustain his promise to convey an indeterminate effect of terror.[36] But as Shoshana Felman has shown, James himself could write a ghost story like

The Turn of the Screw as an allegorical pre-reading of its own projected Freudian and other misreadings.[37] In this sense, we can say
that James denied Poe by unconsciously misreading Poe's more
subliminally inscribed or *text*-oriented mode of ghost-writing. In
Bloomian terms, James's repression of Poe as precursor of his own
praxis points to Poe's having ghost-written *James's* ghost stories.
One has only to compare the representationally obfuscated scenes
of Ligeia's final revivification and, in "The Jolly Corner," Spencer
Brydon's encounter with that "spectral but human" figure, one of
whose hands "had lost two fingers," to register James's later ghost
story as an unconscious staging of *his* anxious encounter with Poe's
literary-ideological precedent[38]: with Poe, the maimed writer of
inauthentic fiction, of texts postponing their identity as self-
present fiction and instead confessing Poe's perverse desire to un-
cover a prefictional space of writing in which all American writers
might be condemned to dwell. Like Peter Quint in *The Turn of
the Screw,* Poe here returns as James's repressed possibility of
writing, a disguised American literary ghost peering into James's
very house of fiction.

I use this Bloomian framework advisedly. Bloom's project of
discerning major precursors for American writers indeed leaves
Poe "out of the [canonical] picture." Yet Bloom's own anxiety
over originality, his entropic history of post-Enlightenment literature, and even his style of criticism strangely repeat features of
Poe more than of Emerson, Bloom's self-adopted father. And
surely it is Poe who, as I have tried to argue, underwrites what
Bloom identifies as the double-bind "burden of [the] American
tradition," a burden expressed in Bloom's *agon* call for "an
antithetical criticism in the American grain, *affirming the self
over language,* while granting a priority to figurative language over
meaning"—the result being a Poe-esque "mixed discourse . . . at
once esoteric and democratic."[39] Matthiessen ironically may have
been right, then, when he excused Poe from "the American Renaissance" because Poe's "value, even more than Emerson's, is now
seen to consist in his *influence* rather than in the body of his own
work."[40] It indeed was this "body" that Matthiessen literally buried

in a footnote, but that Poe himself had prematurely buried before him in the archives of American literary history. And it is this "influence," albeit subterranean, which suggests that Poe's "body" of works, continually purloined by French criticism, was in fact produced in such a way as to return to its original American ideological setting—if only to haunt it and engender readings possessing the uncanny effect of a séance.

NOTES

1. *The Recognition of Edgar Allan Poe: Selected Criticism since 1829,* ed. Eric W. Carlson (Ann Arbor: University of Michigan Press, 1966), p. 66. T. S. Eliot's sense of Poe as appealing to a preadolescent mentality (212) shows the continuation of the Jamesian view of Poe by canonical American writers into the twentieth century.

2. F. O. Matthiessen, *American Renaissance: Art and Expression in the Age of Emerson and Whitman* (New York: Oxford University Press, 1941), xii, n. 3, uses the term *narrow* to describe Poe's "intense theories of poetry and the short story," and regards even these theories as more relevant to an understanding of nineteenth-century French poetry than of "the American Renaissance." A later and more favorable critic of Poe's work, Edward Davidson, *Poe, a Critical Study* (Cambridge: Harvard University Press, Belknap Press, 1957), explicitly refers to the "narrowness" of Poe's "mind and art" (256), and suggests that his "greatness" lies in "his *few* explorations into the dark underside of human consciousness" (260; my emphasis). Comparing him with Emerson, Thoreau, Melville, and Hawthorne—Matthiessen's "Renaissance" figures—Davidson finds Poe deficient in addressing "the questions of man in the new mass world of democratic society, of the new 'American Adam' whether in the wilderness or in the driving urgency of success, of the lonely self" (256). For a brief survey of Poe's literary reputation that began with Rufus Griswold's notorious obituary of Poe, see Edward Wagenknecht, *Edgar Allan Poe: The Man Behind the Legend* (New York: Oxford University Press, 1963), pp. 3–13. In pointing to Harold Bloom's relative silence on Poe's works, I am referring to the period between his publication of *The Anxiety of Influence* and the date of my paper, September 1983.

3. "An Interview with Claude Richard," *Iowa Review* 12 (Fall 1981):12.

4. Leslie Fiedler, *What Was Literature?: Class Culture and Mass Society* (New York: Simon & Schuster, 1982), pp. 89–90, 132–33, passim.

5. Jonathan Auerbach, "Poe's Other: The Reader in the Fiction," *Criticism* (Fall 1982):343; see also 348, 353, and 360.

6. *The Recognition of Edgar Allan Poe,* p. 129. Williams's point in this selection from *In the American Grain,* namely, that Poe, even through his style, fought "for the right to BE first—to hold up his ORIGINALITY" (133) and thus strove to *found* an American literature, touches on an issue I will raise later in this essay. Joseph Riddel's comments occur in "The 'Crypt' of Edgar Poe," *boundary 2* (Spring 1979):119, 124–25, 141, passim. Also cf. John Carlos Rowe, *Through the Custom-House: Nineteenth-Century American Fiction and Modern Theory* (Baltimore: Johns Hopkins University Press, 1982), pp. 91–110.

7. John Irwin, *American Hieroglyphics: The Symbol of the Egyptian Hieroglyphics in the American Renaissance* (New Haven: Yale University Press, 1980), esp. pp. 55, 61–62, 91–94, 98, 100, 120–28, 133–36, 224–25, and 231–35.

8. Ibid., p. 228.

9. Paul de Man, "Autobiography as De-facement," *MLN* 94 (1979):921.

10. *The Collected Works of Edgar Allan Poe,* ed. Thomas O. Mabbott, 3 vols. (Cambridge: Harvard University Press, Belknap Press, 1978), 2:602. All references to Poe's tales will be cited by volume and page number from this edition. For other references to Poe's works, I have tried where possible to use readily available editions.

11. Geoffrey H. Hartman, "Psychoanalysis: The French Connection," *Psychoanalysis and the Question of the Text,* ed. Geoffrey H. Hartman (Baltimore: Johns Hopkins University Press, 1978), p. 94, passim.

12. The quotation appears in Irwin, *American Hieroglyphics,* p. 42. Wagenknecht, *Edgar Allan Poe,* p. 4, quotes another oft-cited and here relevant passage from Poe's *Literati* sketch of Margaret Fuller: "The supposition that the book of an author is a thing apart from the author's self is . . . ill-founded."

13. Poe, "A Few Words on Secret Writing," *The Complete Works of Edgar Allan Poe,* ed. James A. Harrison, 16 vols. (New York: AMS Press, 1965; rpt. from the 1902 New York edition), 14:114.

14. Ibid., 14:142–43. The correspondent's name was W. B. Tyler, his residence—unlike that of other correspondents whom the Harrison edition here records—unspecified. W. K. Wimsatt, Jr., "What Poe Knew About Cryptography," *PMLA* 57 (1943):759, considers Tyler's letter "tedious," and wonders if "Poe believed him to be a relation to the President," in whose administration Poe, with the help of certain friends, was trying to procure a sinecure. Given the fact that Poe refers to W. B. Tyler as someone he at least knew of, "a gentleman whose abilities we very highly respect" (140), and given that this name does not appear in the City Directories of the major eastern seaboard cities (including Washington, Richmond, Baltimore, Phila-

delphia, New York, and Boston), "Tyler" may have been the Supreme Court justice of Virginia, a William B. Tyler who graduated from William and Mary College around 1812. Yet I am not sure that he was not Poe himself, since in this letter "Tyler" gives an example of a cipher whose solution/translation echoes one of Poe's most frequently used refrains in his tales and poetry—a refrain "Tyler" here italicizes: "the sentence might either be 'I love you now as ever,' or 'I love you now *no more*'" (142). Poe, after all had made up letters for his 1836 articles on "Autography" (Mabbott, 2:259). If Poe indeed adopts the alias of Tyler here, then we can also claim that he secretly but openly professes a theory of secret autobiographical writing in this letter: "With secret writing I have been practically conversant for several years. . . . I have . . . a record of thoughts, feelings and occurrences,—a history of my mental existence, to which I may turn, and in imagination, retrace former pleasures, and again live through by-gone scenes,—secure in the conviction that the magic scroll has a tale for *my* eye alone" (140–41).

15. Edgar Allan Poe, *Marginalia,* introduction by John Carl Miller (Charlottesville: University Press of Virginia, 1981), p. 181.

16. Ibid., p. 19; hereafter cited in text by page number. Poe makes the same point throughout his pieces on "Autography."

17. For the monetary-metaphoric significance of "The Gold Bug," see Marc Shell, *Money, Language, and Thought: Literary and Philosophic Economics from the Medieval to the Modern Era* (Berkeley and Los Angeles: University of California Press, 1982), pp. 5–23. See also Michael Williams, "'The language *of the cipher*': Interpretation in 'The Gold Bug,'" *American Literature* 53 (January 1982):646–60. In contrast to what I argue here, Williams claims that this tale "offers us as consolation [to its placing us readers in a situation of semantic indeterminacy] a limiting paradigm of the reading process. A text can be recovered by clarifying definition, establishing a determining context, and recognizing authorial intention" (660).

18. *Edgar Allan Poe: Selected Prose, Poetry, and Eureka,* ed. W. H. Auden (New York: Holt, Rinehart & Winston, 1950), p. 450.

19. My colleague, James M. Cox, helpfully called my attention to this additional anagram.

20. Arthur Hobson Quinn, *Edgar Allan Poe: A Critical Biography* (New York: Appleton-Century-Crofts, 1941), p. 331.

21. In their annotated edition of Poe's tales, *The Short Fiction of Edgar Allan Poe* (Indianapolis: Bobbs-Merrill Co., 1976), p. 62, Stuart and Susan Levine call attention to Poe's ironic projection of the narrator in "The Oval Portrait." They also see the formalist ironic method operative in many of Poe's other tales. G. R. Thompson, *Poe's Fiction: Romantic Irony in the Gothic Tales* (Madison: University of Wisconsin Press, 1973), pp. 9ff. and throughout this work, argues for a more pervasive romantic ironic vision in

Poe's tales, only *one* of whose manifestations was the "device" of the ironic narrator.

22. Quotations from "The Philosophy of Composition" are taken from *Selected Prose, Poetry, and Eureka*, ed. Auden.

23. Baudelaire quoted from Poe's "Marginalia" in his remarks to *Nouvelles histoires sur Edgar Poe* (1857), cited in *The Recognition of Edgar Allan Poe*, ed. Carlson, p. 46.

24. Sidney P. Moss, *Poe's Literary Battles: The Critic in the Context of His Literary Milieu* (Durham: Duke University Press, 1963), ix; see also p. 108, n. 63.

25. "Peter Snook," *The Complete Tales and Poems of Edgar Allan Poe* (New York: Random House, Vintage Books, 1975), p. 564.

26. Daniel Hoffman, *Poe Poe Poe Poe Poe Poe Poe* (New York: Avon Books, 1978), p. 245, passim.

27. See Clark Griffith, "Poe's 'Ligeia' and the English Romantics," *University of Toronto Quarterly* 24 (October 1954):8–25. Thompson, *Poe's Fiction*, pp. 82–83, agrees with Griffith's thesis about Ligeia as a figure of German "transcendentalism" and Rowena of "dull" English "worldliness."

28. Matthiessen, *American Renaissance*, p. 8 n. 7.

29. *Selected Prose, Poetry, and Eureka*, ed. Auden, p. 484. On the relation between Poe's writing and the quest for immortality, see Irwin, *American Hieroglyphics*, pp. 149–50. Also cf. the introductory comments to Emerson's *Nature* by Stephen E. Whicher, *Selections from Ralph Waldo Emerson: An Organic Anthology* (Boston: Houghton Mifflin Co., 1957), p. 13, where he benignly notes in passing the similarity in topic and theoretical ambition between Emerson's major essay and Poe's *Eureka*.

30. Poe had assumed that Hawthorne "had been thrust into his present position by one of the impudent *cliques* which beset our literature, and whose pretensions it is our full purpose to expose" ("Review," *Selected Prose, Poetry, and Eureka*, ed. Auden, 451). Only after Poe quickly notes that "we have been agreeably mistaken" about Hawthorne's association with this "clique" does he proceed to "commend" the latter's work as an original contribution to American literature: "As Americans, we feel proud of the book" (452).

31. The page numbers in *Eureka* refer to *Selected Prose, Poetry, and Eureka*, ed. Auden.

32. *The Viking Portable Edgar Allan Poe*, ed. Philip Van Doren Stern (New York: Viking Press, 1945), p. 21. Poe also states in this letter that "I am not ambitious—unless negatively."

33. *The Complete Tales and Poems* of Edgar Allan Poe, p. 564.

34. Ellison's personal use of nature here effectively negates Emerson's ideal "transparent" relation to the "Not Me." In the spirit of Poe, one can even

perversely argue that his choice of Ellison's very name bears on this issue: *E*llison's "*l*" alphabetically just so happens to come before—hence is more literally "original" than?—*Emerson's* "m."

35. See, for example, Paul de Man, "Literature and Language: A Commentary," *New Literary History* 4 (Autumn 1972), where he argues that a writer may be more privileged with his text not in terms of his (autobiographical) knowledge of his own intentions, but only "in the knowledge of his impossibility" to "know what he is saying"—an "ignorance" to which he then also "reduces the reader" (191).

36. Henry James alludes to this failure of Poe's "promise" in his New York preface to *The Turn of the Screw,* collected in *The Turn of the Screw,* ed. Robert Kimbrough (New York: W. W. Norton, Critical edition, 1966), p. 122.

37 Shoshana Felman, "Turning the Screw of Interpretation," *Yale French Studies: Literature and Psychoanalysis,* nos. 55/56 (1977), esp. pp. 94–112, 115, 124, 190–93, and 203–7.

38. *Henry James: Selected Fiction,* ed. Leon Edel (New York: E. P. Dutton, 1964), pp. 575–76.

39. Harold Bloom, *Agon: Towards a Theory of Revisionism* (New York: Oxford University Press, 1982), p. 336.

40. Matthiessen, *American Renaissance,* xii n. 3; my emphasis.

Jonathan Arac

F. O. Matthiessen:
Authorizing an
American Renaissance

I

For decades since his suicide in 1950, F. O. Matthiessen has exerted a compelling attraction. The documentation, analysis, and controversy around him bulk larger than for any other American literary scholar born in the twentieth century, and they grow.

There are at least three good reasons for this posthumous attention. First, Matthiessen played a decisive role in making possible the American academic study of American literature (for short, "American studies").[1] His major book, *American Renaissance* (1941), has given its name to courses taught at hundreds of institutions. More than any other single factor it enabled hundreds of Ph.D.s in English to specialize in the American literature of the nineteenth century. Matthiessen himself, however, deplored the "barrenness" of what he termed the "now hopefully obsolescent practice of literary scholars' restricting themselves to the arbitrary confines of a single century in a single country."[2]

Second, Matthiessen, both as a Harvard professor and as a private citizen, was widely and visibly active in the leftist politics of the 1930s and 1940s. Although as a practicing Christian he was not a Communist and disavowed Marxism, he was considered a leading fellow traveler.[3] The clearest textual focus for this engagement is *From the Heart of Europe* (1948), a memoir of his time in Austria and Czechoslovakia in the months before the Czechoslovak coup of 1948.

Third, both as a teacher and friend, Matthiessen made an intense personal impression. A "collective portrait" by many hands was compiled soon after his death, but the most remarkable testimony came in *Rat and the Devil* (1978), a selection by their friend Louis Hyde from the thousands of letters exchanged by Matthiessen and the painter Russell Cheney during the twenty years they shared their lives.[4]

The interrelations among these three aspects of Matthiessen's career do not, however, offer an occasion for the rhetoric of "wholeness," even though that rhetoric was extremely important to Matthiessen himself. As a critic, for example, he concluded *American Renaissance* by writing of Melville that he fulfilled "what Coleridge held to be the major function of the artist: he brought the whole soul of man into activity."[5] As a politically committed man, he began the book by subscribing to the test of "true scholarship," that it be "for the good and enlightenment of all the people, not for the pampering of a class" (xv). As early as 1925, he wrote Cheney about their love:

> In these last months I am a whole man for the first time: no more dodging or repressing for we gladly accept what we are. And sex now instead of being a nightmare is the most sacred, all embracing gift we have. Now I can see, as this morning, while riding along, a husky labouring feller asleep on a bank, one hand lying heavy across his thighs, and I can thrill at the deep earthiness and blood of him. For I know that I am of blood and earth too, as well as of brain and of soul, and that my whole self waits—and waits gladly—for you.[6]

Some problems about Matthiessen's "wholeness" emerge clearly from comparing the letters and *American Renaissance*. In the long section on Whitman, over sixty pages, Matthiessen dispersed references to three topics—homosexuality (585; cf. also 535), the "power of sex" (523), and transient "Good Moments" (541)—which are remarkably condensed in an early letter to Cheney. This letter narrated an encounter with a "workman—husky, broad-shouldered, forty" at Wells cathedral. Matthiessen began with a literary reference: this man was "the perfect Chaucerian yeoman," and he concluded by explaining that he wrote so much about the event "not because it is the least bit important, but because it was so natural, so like Walt Whitman." Such cultural awareness did not conflict with but rather enhanced erotic possibilities: "He caught my eye both as a magnificently built feller, and as fitting in so perfectly to the type of fourteenth century work man." He thus embodied the permanence of the people: "he might just as well have been building the original cathedral, as repairing it centuries later." For "about a quarter of a minute" they talked, allowing Matthiessen to note the man's "unusually gentle" voice and "dark full brown" eye. Then, as the man went off, Matthiessen "deliberately let my elbow rub against his belly," for he "wanted to feel the touch of his body as a passing gesture." He acknowledged that he was sexually excited, yet also that "there was no question of not wanting to keep myself for you." The "whole self" allows marginal responses to take on their own wholeness: "It thrilled me, not only with sex, but with friendliness" (18 April 1925, RD 124).

The problems of temporality here merit further attention: the mythic copresence of the fourteenth and twentieth centuries, set against its punctual disruption, the "passing gesture," the "good moment." What stands out now, however, is the difference between the sense of reading Whitman in Matthiessen's lively letter and in his monumental book. Between these two ways of reading, and ways of writing about reading, stands a long process of transformative discipline.[7] The modern critical practice Leavis called the "discipline of letters" required abandoning the modes of "impressionist" reading, the orientation that M. H. Abrams has called "expressive," and the rhetoric of "flash" and fragment for which the classical antecedent is Longinus on the sublime. To create the centrally authoritative critical identity of *American Renaissance,* much had to be displaced or scattered or disavowed. Loose elbows had to be tucked in. T. S. Eliot's insistence on "form" and "impersonality" in poetry chastened Matthiessen's early commitment to the "human spirit," the "man himself," and the "flash of the spark of life" that reading sets off (RD 102, 133).

Matthiessen joined his generation in sacrificing to modernist discipline a romantic theorist of the "spark," the politically and sexually revolutionary poet Shelley. In the early letters, Matthiessen was reading Shelley with positive engagement. At one point he even archly identified himself with Shelley in their attachment to older men (RD 33, 78, 84). By *American Renaissance,* however, T. S. Eliot's denigration of Shelley was in full force. Some half-dozen times Shelley was evoked for predictable dismissals.[8] Such gestures contributed to the critical authority of *American Renaissance* because they certified Matthiessen as emotionally "mature," and they distanced him from a figure whose philosophic, political, and literary activities can seem terribly unintegrated. Yet in the spread and energy of his own activism, Matthiessen more closely resembled Shelley than any of the antiselves he treated in *American Renaissance*.

II

These analyses suggest that the problem of the whole, the indivisible, the individual, requires attention to institutional circumstances. My fellow contributors encourage such attention through evoking an "other" American Renaissance. To conjure an "other" suggests exclusion, divisiveness. Jane Tompkins thus recalls the "damned mob of scribbling women" that Matthiessen joined Hawthorne in abjuring (*AR* x); students ask me why Frederick Douglass showed insufficient "devotion to the possibilities of democracy" (*AR* ix) for Matthiessen even to mention him. These are matters of institutional power: in order to be a productive unit, a field must be marked off, delimited, defined—even if your commitment is to "all the people."

This kind of discrepancy is crucial to understanding the effects of Matthiessen's career. For Matthiessen's power to authorize an American Renaissance came from his mobilizing certain figures who were then appropriated in ways contrary to his intentions. Recall the irony that his work produced specialists of a sort that he himself considered "hopefully obsolescent." No less striking is the nationalist force achieved by Matthiessen's emphatically international undertaking.

I want to explore in some detail Matthiessen's title: *American Renaissance: Art and Expression in the Age of Emerson and Whitman*. First off, it is significant to my institutional focus that the phrase that later American literary culture most closely identifies

with Matthiessen was not originally his own, but was provided by
a younger colleague.[9] It was important to Matthiessen that his
work be collegial, based more broadly than in the solitary individual. Matthiessen acknowledged the oddity of considering the
mid-nineteenth century a cultural "re-birth." He explained that
"America's way of producing a renaissance" lay in "affirming its
rightful heritage in the whole expanse of art and culture" (*AR* vii).
This still cryptic clarification is better understood through a
quotation from André Malraux cited a few pages later: "Every
civilization is like the Renaissance, and creates its own heritage out
of everything in the past that helps it to surpass itself" (xv n.). The
theory of literary history adumbrated here deserves considerable
attention, but for the moment note how obscure this line of intention has become; few can recall this logic for the title.

For "renaissance" has a force of its own.[10] Ever since the historiographic notion was elaborated by Michelet and Burckhardt—in
1845 and 1860, exactly bracketing Matthiessen's period—"renaissance" has carried a glamorous freight of secularism, progress, and
preeminent individuality. All these values were in fact suspect to
Matthiessen, but his title's figure translated "the renaissance" west-
ward to America just when the old, transatlantic renaissance was
being conservatively reevaluated in works like *The Allegory of
Love* (C. S. Lewis, 1936) and *The Renaissance and English Human-
ism* (Douglas Bush, 1939). Matthiessen supported their claims for
the medieval continuities of the renaissance, emphasizing Christianity and traditional literary modes (cf. *AR* 246). But that was
not how his figure worked.

What is the particular force of an "American" renaissance? As
"American," it is new; more paradoxically, it is a repetition, a
"renaissance of the renaissance." It does for the renaissance what
the renaissance had done for antiquity. Most importantly, however,
it is *national*. People had long spoken of a Concord or Boston or
New England "renaissance," but this was no longer local, regional,
or sectional. It was shared among "all the people." Contrast Perry
Miller's *The New England Mind* (1939), which not only sectional-

ized but also split off "mind" from the vigorous physical embodiment suggested by "renaissance."

In emphasizing his focus on literature as "works of art" rather than as philosophical or social practice, Matthiessen imagined books that he might have written instead: *The Age of Swedenborg,* on transcendental thought; or *The Age of Fourier* on "radical movements" (*A R* vii–viii). The contrast of Emerson and Whitman with Swedenborg and Fourier strikes home. Emerson and Whitman are major, central, household words; Swedenborg and Fourier are minor, eccentric, obscure—and not even American. The literary and the American unite against the foreign, philosophical, and radical.

Matthiessen's title promoted a euphoria of America that gained power against the grain of his own methodological precepts and critical practice. From a review-essay of 1929 on the need to rewrite American literary history to a lecture of 1949 on "The Responsibilities of the Critic," Matthiessen insisted on America's relation to "Europe," which includes England (*RC* 181,12). His most important books before and after *American Renaissance* addressed T. S. Eliot and Henry James, the most notoriously transatlantic of America's great writers. In *American Renaissance* itself Shakespeare occupied more lines of the index than did Thoreau! Matthiessen conceived of his subject as essentially national *and* comparative. He taught courses on world drama, Shakespeare, and an introduction to major English poets. American studies has not followed Matthiessen's precept or practice, even while drawing its warrant to exist from him. His radical energies succeeded more in reinvigorating than in remaking culturally established figures.

In speaking of a "euphoria of America," I do not mean that Matthiessen was blind to social and political problems or that he did not care about them. *American Renaissance* immediately proclaimed its solidarity with "those who believe now in the dynamic extension of democracy on economic as well as political levels" (4). But in writing about the social problems of America, Matthiessen failed to achieve specificity comparable to what he achieved in

writing about the literary successes. Thus in Ahab he found an
"ominous glimpse of what was to result when the Emersonian will
to virtue became in less innocent natures the will to power and
conquest." That will gave us the "empire-builders of the post–
Civil War world," the "strong-willed individuals who seized the land
and gutted the forests and built the railroads" (459). Matthiessen's
rhetoric conflated the will with the deed, while introducing an
oversharp chronological boundary. He failed to acknowledge that
already in the 1850s, precisely in railroad-building, not the tragic
individual but the limited-liability corporation was the major
agency, drawing capital from many sources, developing the tech-
niques of bureaucratic management to organize the activities of its
employees (the "hands" who executed the "will"), and even developing the ideology of free enterprise in order to get rid of
existing government activities.[11] Matthiessen's analysis instead
produced an abstract division from a willed unity. That is, his
theology provided the human potential for evil (180), and his
intellectual history provided the rise of "individualism" in the
American 1830s (5–6). The two combined to produce the figure
of the evil individuals who obstruct the common good of an otherwise united American People.

   Throughout the 1930s, the negative term of "individualism"
and the positive terms of the "community" or the "people" figured
in the discourse of widely different American intellectuals.[12]
Matthiessen's use of such terms in *American Renaissance* has an
important relation to the particular political and rhetorical strategy
of the Popular Front (or "People's Front"), which from 1935 was
the Communist party line. In contrast to the militantly divisive
rhetoric of the "Third Period," which attacked even socialists as
"social fascists," the Popular Front, in belated response to Hitler's
success, emphasized a defensive policy of alliance-building.[13] The
situation no longer promised imminent apocalypse, requiring radical separation of sheep from goats; now rather, from liberals to
Communists all were sheep together,[14] except for that wolf out
there. This policy meant a changed stance toward America. In 1933
Granville Hicks published *The Great Tradition,* on American fiction

after the Civil War. In reviewing it, Matthiessen shared its concern with "the class war which is becoming increasingly the central fact of American life" (*RC* 197). In 1938, still on the staff of the *New Masses,* Hicks published his next book, *I Like America.*

Although Matthiessen was not a Communist party member and did not always follow party positions, the strategy of the Popular Front clearly appealed to him. I have already noted his rhetoric of "all the people" and noted the absence of class analysis in *American Renaissance.*[15] As opposed to earlier Communist emphasis on independent proletarian culture, the Popular Front emphasized defending the "cultural heritage," which included the masterpieces produced by the bourgeoisie. This project defines George Lukács's major studies of nineteenth-century realism as well as André Malraux's brilliant speech on "The Cultural Heritage" at the second congress of the International Association of Writers for the Defense of Culture, held in London in 1936.[16] This is the text that Matthiessen quoted for its crucial assertion that every civilization is like the Renaissance.

To locate Matthiessen's rhetoric in relation to the Popular Front helps to clarify what I find *American Renaissance*'s most extraordinary idealization: the diminishment of the Civil War. The Civil War was not even indexed, although it was not literally absent from the book. It allowed for tragic poetry by Melville and Whitman, and it was mentioned again and again—as in the passage just cited on "empire builders"—as a marker, dividing the American Renaissance from an age of rampantly destructive individualism.[17] But the war was not integrated into any understanding of the renaissance. Matthiessen demonstrated that his object of study, the literary, functioned for writers as an evasion, though not a complete disengagement, from a political life of which they did not wholeheartedly approve (e.g., 67). But his interpretations of this compromise failed to reckon with the affirmative support that compromise still gave to dubious policies. It is both more understandable and less commendable than Matthiessen suggested that Hawthorne, despite his skeptical conservatism, supported the party of Jackson. For the Democratic party's commitment to slavery made "the Democracy" include much less than "all the people."[18] Rather than facing up to divisions within the renaissance, Matthiessen divided the renaissance from the war and segregated qualities "before" and "after." His wish for wholeness led to disconnection.

By splitting off the war, Matthiessen forestalled comparison between the 1850s and 1930s that the Depression had provoked. Edmund Wilson's "An Appeal to Progressives" (1932), for example, defined the time as "one of the turning-points in our history, our first real crisis since the Civil War."[19] The comparison between the 1850s and 1930s was exciting for a militant strategy but embarrassing for a strategy of alliance and containment. If, as Charles and Mary Beard argued in *The Course of American History* (1927), the Civil War had been the "Second American Revolution," then the analogy pointed to a class war that would make a third.

Yet to evade the analogy left a problem: what would mobilize change if "democracy" already existed and "class struggle" was forbidden? This impasse structured *American Renaissance*. Matthiessen was celebrating what he knew *must* be transformed. Renaissance yielded to Civil War, and the Popular Front too must yield to something else, but there was no acceptable image for that new state except an idealization of the present state. The result was an unhistorical freezing.

The conjunction between Matthiessen's cultural politics and those of the Popular Front has two consequences. First, it grants greater value and dignity to the cultural results of the Popular Front than they have been allowed in the most authoritative representations. Lionel Trilling devoted his career to portraying American "liberal" culture as so Stalinized as to make impossible any live or complex literary response. Such claims depend upon ignoring Matthiessen, as Trilling did, or considering his politics as unrelated to his critical accomplishments, as Irving Howe has done.[20] Second, it highlights the dangers of such a strategy of reconciliation, a special concern now when a renewed academic Marxism offers to embrace all other intellectual positions. Matthiessen's figure of "America" suffered a sobering fate. The war (which, after all, did come) reconstellated American politics, and the figure of "America" that began as a Depression tactic of harmony became a postwar myth of empire. A mobilization intended as oppositional became incorporated hegemonically; American studies gained power by nationalistically appropriating Matthiessen.

III

"Reconciliation" is not only a political strategy but also a well-known operation in literary theory. Having analyzed the discrepancy between Matthiessen's internationalism and the nationalist authority his work achieved, I want now to address another area of discrepancy: Matthiessen's attempt to use the politically conservative theory of the "symbol" in a critical discourse intended to be politically progressive.

American Renaissance made a major commitment to literary theory, both as views of the 1850s and as a current activity—"our own developing conceptions of literature" (vii).[21] Matthiessen related the theory and practice of his chosen writers to his own understanding of "the nature of literature" (xiii) on such topics as mode (myth), genre (tragedy), and figurative language (allegory and symbolism). Over the four decades of American studies, such theoretical engagement has not flourished,[22] and where it has recently begun to emerge, it appears as an imported innovation rather than as reclaiming a founding heritage. The single theoretical topic that has become institutionally part of normal procedure is nationalistic: the question of "American romance"—a topic Matthiessen briefly highlighted but also seriously limited (264ff.). Just as Comparative Literature became the subfield that kept alive Matthiessen's internationalism, New Criticism after the war became less a movement than a province, the subfield into which his theoretical commitments were segregated and developed.[23]

Matthiessen's major theoretical resource was Coleridge, as elucidated by I. A. Richards in response to T. S. Eliot, but Matthiessen understood and emphasized that Coleridge's position made larger claims than Eliot or Richards would accept. Eliot wished to separate poet from poem, and Richards used Coleridge in the service of utilitarian atheism, but Matthiessen proclaimed that "the transcendental theory of art is a theory of knowledge and religion as well" (*AR* 31).

Recall that in the fourteenth chapter of the *Biographia Literaria,* the poet "described in *ideal* perfection, brings the whole soul of man into activity" through the "power" of "imagination," which "reveals itself in the balance or reconciliation of opposite or discordant qualities," such as general and concrete or individual and representative. From this passage, Richards in the chapter on "Imagination" in *Principles of Literary Criticism* elaborated a theory of tragedy as the most "inclusive" possible "attitude," which by comtemplating the most extreme opposites—fear and pity—achieves a stable poise that he even called "invulnerable." Matthiessen drew also upon Coleridge's theory of the "symbol," which "enunciates the whole" yet "abides itself as a living part in that unity of which it is the representative." Coleridge's image for this condition is "translucence," above all of "the eternal in and through the temporal." This exposition of the symbol appeared in *The Statesman's Manual,* a theological guide to conservative politics for post-Napoleonic, early-industrial England.

Matthiessen's aesthetics agreed with Coleridge's, as did his theology, but his politics, starting from a similar romantic anti-capitalism, differed widely.[24] Matthiessen identified himself with Hazlitt,[25] who remained loyal to the revolutionary cause despite its horrors, rather than with Coleridge who turned away in fright or revulsion. How could Matthiessen be a trinitarian formalist radical?

He could if radicalism meant reconciliation. The Popular Front enabled Matthiessen's criticism, his politics, and his religion to interact powerfully and positively. The strategy of alliance allowed these different elements to share the same discursive space. *The Achievement of T. S. Eliot,* written just before his involvement with the Popular Front, is weaker than *American Renaissance* because Matthiessen's politics found no place in it. This is not to claim Matthiessen "followed" the line; rather, the line "released" him to bring together elements previously separated. But this is not to say, either, that they make a perfect whole.

Each of three components had its own particular term for the fantasied unity, the figure of wholeness, that their interaction produced as "American Renaissance." For Matthiessen the political leftist, that term would be "all the people" in the People's Front. For Matthiessen the critical formalist, the ideal term of wholeness is "literature" itself.[26] For the Christian, in a tradition that reaches back into the seventeenth century and through Jonathan Edwards, as Richard Niebuhr and Sacvan Bercovitch have demonstrated, that term would be "America." Bercovitch has analyzed the "American Jeremiad" as provoking a sense of crisis that finally produces no fundamental change but reaffirms the existing "American" way. This logic I find operates like that of Coleridge's aesthetics or Popular Front politics—in Melville's phrase, "By their very contradictions they are made to coincide." This formula offers an American translation for the "reconciliation under duress" that Theodor Adorno criticized in Georg Lukács's Stalinist Hegelian realism.[27]

The jeremiad position is not easy or complacent; it is anguished and sincere, but it stands in a false position. Let me explain this observation through Matthiessen's reading of "The Try-Works." In this chapter from *Moby-Dick,* "Ahab's tyrannic will" is "symbolized," Matthiessen argued, through the process by which "the act of burning down the blubber on the ship's deck at night becomes, in its lurid flame, 'the material counterpart of her monomaniac commander's soul.'" From the spiritual symbolized in the physical, Matthiessen went on to read the representative from the individual: "It seemed then to Ishmael, in a rare symbol for individualistic recklessness—indeed for a whole era of American development—'that whatever swift, rushing thing I stood on was not so much bound to any haven ahead as rushing from all havens astern'" (*AR* 290). Matthiessen's exposition of the "symbol" here interacted with the motifs of America and individualism that I earlier analyzed. His trinitarian aesthetic highlighted the figure of embodiment ("material counterpart"), but in emphasizing the "will," Matthiessen's reading omitted the loose elbows, the actual bodies, the "Tartarean shapes of the pagan harpooneers," and the watch with "tawny features . . . begrimed with smoke and sweat, their matted beards, and the contrasting barbaric brilliancy of their teeth." In their racist demonization, these bodies did not represent "all the people."

As earlier "America" was idealized, here the literary was idealized as "symbol." So vivid was Melville's figure that Matthiessen took is as truth, embodying all that we need to know. Ishmael, however, went on to define his vision of "rushing from all havens astern" as a double error: he mistook his object, for it referred not to the try-works scene but to his backward view; and he mistook himself; as his mind wandered, his body turned: "Lo! in my brief sleep I had turned myself about, and was fronting the ship's stern. . . . In an instant I faced back, just in time to prevent the vessel from flying up into the wind, and very probably capsizing her. How glad and how grateful the relief from this unnatural hallucination of the night." Not the demonic scene, but the observer's error posed the real threat: Ishmael neglected his responsibility as helmsman. Matthiessen, then, ignored literature's own recognition that it may err: "wrapped, for that interval, in darkness myself, I but the better saw the redness, the madness, and the ghastliness of others." Thus, even at its most passionately intelligent and concerned, the stance of American studies cultural criticism has been misplaced, through a disorienting, self-involved detachment just at the moment it believed itself most perceptively involved with the way things are.

IV

After treating the politics of America and of the theory of literature in Matthiessen's work, I want now to assess the possibilities for a new literary history in the practice of *American Renaissance*. These possibilities are still "new" after forty years not only because

American studies failed to pick them up, but also because Matthiessen's own explicit theory of atemporal wholeness obscures his recurrent perception of transient, fragmentary moments.

I have mentioned the "freezing" of time and denial of history in Matthiessen's reading.[28] Matthiessen used the term *structure* for the wholeness achieved by a successful symbol, a symbolic "form," when it reconciled the eternal and the temporal. His negative term for the failure of this process was "moments." Matthiessen most pointedly contrasted these terms in discussing D. H. Lawrence, that bogey of New Criticism (*AR* 313). But Lawrence was quite important to Matthiessen, and the evaluation more ambivalent than the theory. Indeed, when Melville himself reached the imaginative "level where both abstraction and concretion may have full play," Matthiessen did not emphasize symbolic stability; he observed instead that this was "not a level which . . . he can sustain for long— but rather, a precarious point of equilibrium between two opposed forces" (464). Melville could not "hold the wave at the crest" (408). Such evanescence resonates less with the New Critics' Coleridge than with the Impressionists' Pater:[29] "This at least of flamelike our life has, that it is but the concurrence, renewed from moment to moment, of forces parting sooner or later" (Conclusion to *The Renaissance*). Such a Paterian "tragic dividing of forces on their ways" rekindles autumnally what Emerson more buoyantly had asserted. Not an enduring "translucence" but the intermittent flare of moments proved in practice what Matthiessen found. Cleanth Brooks observed that in reading *The Waste Land* Matthiessen failed to offer a "complete, consecutive examination,"[30] and this failure remained true of *American Renaissance*. Matthiessen was typically a reader of passages, a judge of moments. The American Renaissance itself from the beginning stood as a moment: "the starting-point for this book was my realization of how great a number of our past masterpieces were produced in one extraordinarily concentrated moment of expression" (*AR* vii).

As Aristotle is the exemplary structuralist, the great critic of the moment is Longinus on the sublime. Against structural unity, the sublime is a "flash of lightning" that "scatters all before it."

Longinus's discontinuous theory of influence—as the agonistic relation between two literary consciousnesses across a wide span of time, like that of Plato to Homer—offers the nearest precedent to Harold Bloom's "revisionary" theory of poetry.[31] Bloom has emphasized, however, the important precedent for his work in Emerson, and I would note that Matthiessen found it there: "Emerson knew that each age turns to particular authors of the past, not because of the authors but because of its own needs and preoccupations that those authors help make articulate" (*AR* 101–2). Thus, Melville achieved "his own full strength" through the "challenge" of Shakespeare (*AR* 424). Such a dynamic, recall, was also Malraux's claim in "The Cultural Heritage." In an italicized formulation that Matthiessen cited, "A heritage is not transmitted, it must be conquered" (xv n.). The energy of struggle, deflected by the Popular Front away from politics, reappears within culture.

Matthiessen understood that such claims violated established ways of conceiving and writing history, and he worried over historiographic method. He knew personally the painful struggle to possess a tradition. He wrote to Cheney in 1925: "This life of ours is entirely new—neither of us know of a parallel case. We stand in the middle of an uncharted, uninhabited country. That there have been other unions like ours is obvious, but we are unable to draw on their experience" (29 January 1925, *RD* 71). Against such blanking-out, Matthiessen found his own needs and preoccupations articulated in Whitman and in Proust.[32] He accepted Richards's claim that great writing required "availability of experience" (*AR* 129).

For his own historical project Matthiessen rejected "the descriptive narrative of literary history" (*AR* vii). He was not alone in rejecting narrative. In 1929 there had appeared in England Namier's *The Structure of Politics at the Accession of George III* and in France the first issue of the great journal *Annales*. Matthiessen, however, also rejected analytic history-writing. Against scientific digging "into . . . the economic, social, and religious causes" (*AR* vii), Matthiessen chose Richards's analytic of experience. His project shared this ground with Walter Benjamin's essay on "The

Storyteller" (1936) and Sartre's *Nausea* (1938), both of which
lamented the unavailability of "experience" and marked a crisis of
narrativity.

Matthiessen evaded this crisis by studying the "fusions of form
and content" that defined *"what* these books were as works of art"
(*AR* vii). This aesthetic ontology projected a Coleridgian, "symbolic" history like that of Joyce's *Ulysses.*[33] There one day's hap-
penings come into contact with as much of the human cultural past
as it could possibly evoke. Likewise, Matthiessen's "moment"
focused centuries of American cultural history from the Puritans
through James and Eliot. This mythic rhetoric leveled history into
what Matthiessen quoted Thomas Mann as calling "recurrence,
timelessness, a perpetual present" (*AR* 629), a relationship of
temporality that was "continuous," as Matthiessen quoted Eliot
on Joyce (630).

In *American Renaissance* there also operated, however, a temporal orientation that aimed not to perpetuate but to innovate,
signaled by Matthiessen's sole positive citation of Nietzsche: "only
the supreme power of the present can interpret the past," and
such power requires the interpreter to be "architect of the future"
(*AR* 629 n.). The urgency of relationship between this particular
present moment and particular past moments contrasts both
to the continuous linear sequence of traditional narrative time
and to the equally continuous homogeneity of modernist myth. It
produces a discontinuous, textured, historical temporality. One
model for this could be found in Proust,[34] whose correlation
of moments through "involuntary memory" again highlighted
Richards's problem of availability, which Matthiessen found as
struggle in Malraux.

During Matthiessen's work on *American Renaissance,* the critic
most suggestively rethinking literary history—and working on Whitman's contemporary Baudelaire—was Walter Benjamin. It is worth
noting that Malraux's essay on the cultural heritage referred to
Benjamin's study of the artwork and mass reproduction, but that
in translating and editing Malraux for the *New Republic,* Malcolm
Cowley omitted that reference.[35]

In his "Theses on the Philosophy of History," Benjamin characterized the relation between one historical moment and another as
a "constellation" and argued that "to articulate the past histor-
ically" meant to "seize hold of a memory as it flashes up at a
moment of danger"—as the French revolutionaries did with the
Roman Republic.[36] This claim illuminates Matthiessen's conjunction of the 1850s and 1930s, his urgent sense that these were
exactly the writers "all the people" needed at the moment of
solidarity against the danger of fascism, disconnecting them from
the Civil War in order to join them to "now."

Benjamin, however, opposed the Popular Front strategy. He
deprecated the preservation of "cultural treasures," for they are
tainted with "barbarism" both in their origin and in their trans-
mission. He urged instead "the fight for the oppressed past," to
redeem what was once stigmatized and suppressed as "minor."
Perhaps Matthiessen fulfilled this task, in rejecting the cultural
treasures of Holmes, Longfellow, and Lowell to rescue once-
marginal writers, as Emerson, Thoreau, Hawthorne, Melville, and
Whitman had been in their time. Matthiessen, however, disavowed
any canon-shifting intervention, deferring to the judgment of "the
successive generations of common readers" (*AR* xi) who selected
the five authors. This version of the Popular Front he at once
reconciled with the apparently contradictory claim by Ezra Pound
that "the history of an art . . . is the history of masterwork" (xi).

Following Benjamin, I have tried both to specify the "barbarism"
at work in Matthiessen's book and to "redeem" certain emphases
and practices obscured through the representation of Matthiessen
produced in American studies. Benjamin's concern with the cultural apparatus, his care for technical matters that relate the means
chosen to the ends desired, leads me to a final question, which
bears on Matthiessen's claims about his chosen writers, on his own
project in his book, and on work any of us might do. Can one
espouse and further "all the people" by writing "masterwork"?
American Renaissance achieves its masterful unity through the
construction of figures that misrepresent Matthiessen's cherished
values. Their effect is not a symbolic translucence but an allegorical

alienation. He mobilized "America" on behalf of internationalism; he mobilized "renaissance" on behalf of communalism; he mobilized the theory of "structure" but actually elucidated "moments." The project of "wholeness" involves harmonizing, centralizing, normalizing, and "identifying." By tucking in elbows, one empowers a particular self and work and nation and also rejects particular "other" identities, such as Shelley, and disperses others, such as Whitman.

Near the end of his decade writing *American Renaissance,* Matthiessen suffered a psychic breakdown. While he was briefly hospitalized, Matthiessen posed as life-or-death choices the kind of issues that have concerned my analysis—Aristotle versus Longinus, structure versus moment. He asked, was it any reason to kill himself if his failure to accomplish this project proved to him that "I am an enthusiast trying to be a critic . . . a rhapsode trying to be an Aristotelian?" (4 January 1939, *RD* 246).

Matthiessen questioned the value for life of this discipline, this struggle of the will to define, formulate, mobilize, and authorize an American Renaissance. His question took its terms from the extinction of democratic politics in ancient Rome and from the assertion of identity in Renaissance Italy: "Must it be aut Caesar aut nullus?"—that is, must there be a choice between Caesar and nonentity?[37] Only if we can define better alternatives for the intellectual career is there any chance to be of much use to "all the people."

NOTES

1. See Richard Ruland, *The Rediscovery of American Literature* (Cambridge: Harvard University Press, 1967), pp. 209–73; also books entitled *F. O. Matthiessen* by Giles B. Gunn (Seattle: University of Washington Press, 1975) and by Frederick C. Stern (Chapel Hill: University of North Carolina Press, 1981); and Leo Marx, "Double Consciousness: The Cultural Politics of F. O. Matthiessen," *Monthly Review* 34 (February 1983):34–56.

2. F. O. Matthiessen, *The Responsibilites of the Critic,* ed. John Rackliffe (New York: Oxford University Press, 1952), p. 196; hereafter cited as *RC.*

3. I find most lucid Karen Rosenberg, "Stalinism, Democracy, and Commitment," *Harvard Magazine* (March–April 1983):51–54. See also David Caute, *The Fellow-Travellers* (New York: Macmillan Co., 1973), p. 75 n., and William L. O'Neill, *A Better World: The Great Schism: Stalinism and American Intellectuals* (New York: Simon & Schuster, 1982), pp. 164ff.

4. The "collective portrait" first appeared in *Monthly Review* 2 (1950). See also George Abbott White, "Ideology and Literature: *American Renaissance* and F. O. Matthiessen," in *Literature in Revolution,* ed. White and Charles Newman (New York: Holt, Rinehart & Winston, 1972), pp. 430–500; Alfred Kazin, *New York Jew* (New York: Alfred A. Knopf, 1978), pp. 168–70; Harry Levin, *Memories of the Moderns* (New York: New Directions, 1980), pp. 218–31; and Kenneth Lynn, in *Masters: Portraits of Great Teachers,* ed. Joseph Epstein (New York: Basic Books, 1981), pp. 103–18.

5. F. O. Matthiessen, *American Renaissance: Art and Expression in the Age of Emerson and Whitman* (New York: Oxford University Press, 1941), p. 656; hereafter cited as *AR.* The first words of the subtitle were a "last minute change from *Language and Art*"—with some significance for T. S. Eliot's dicta elevating the medium of language over anything expressed.

6. *Rat and the Devil: Journal Letters of F. O. Matthiessen and Russell Cheney,* ed. Louis Hyde (Hamden, Conn.: Archon, 1978), p. 116 (7 April 1925); hereafter cited as *RD.* Relevant to this letter and the next I discuss is Eve Kosofsky Sedgwick, "Whitman's Transatlantic Context: Class, Gender, and Male Homosexual Style," *Delta,* no. 16 (May 1983):111–24.

7. This essay draws upon my understanding of Michel Foucault's work of the 1970s, which I sketch in "The Function of Foucault at the Present Time," *Humanities in Society* 3 (1980):73–86.

8. See esp. *AR* 259, 311, 353, 388. On the return to Shelley in current criticism, see my "To Regress from the Rigor of Shelley," *boundary 2,* 8:3 (1980):241–57.

9. See the preface to Harry Levin, *The Power of Blackness* (New York: Alfred A. Knopf, 1958).

10. On the historiography of the renaissance, see Lucien Febvre, "How Michelet Invented the Renaissance" (1950), trans. K. Folca, in *A New Kind of History,* ed. Peter Burke (New York: Harper & Row, 1973); and Harry Levin, "English Literature and the Renaissance" (1961), in *Refractions* (New York: Oxford University Press, 1966). See also *AR* 106–13 for Matthiessen's critique of Emerson and Thoreau as readers of "Renaissance individualism" who ignore "medieval" and "hierarchical" emphases and neglect "religious dogma."

11. In Matthiessen's own time, Matthew Josephson's *The Robber Barons* (1934) typifies the individualistic focus, but Adolf Berle and Gardiner C. Means in *The Modern Corporation and Private Property* (1933) offered

another perspective which came to fruit in James Burnham's *The Managerial Revolution* (1941). On corporate legal innovations before the Civil War, see Harold M. Hyman and William M. Wiecek, *Equal Justice under Law* (New York: Harper & Row, 1982), esp. p. 25. On railroads in the 1850s, see Alfred D. Chandler, Jr., *The Visible Hand: The Managerial Revolution in American Business* (Cambridge: Harvard University Press, Belknap Press, 1977), esp. chap. 3. See also the classic study by George Rogers Taylor, *The Transportation Revolution* (New York: Holt, Rinehart & Winston, 1951), which resists the separation of pre- from postwar periods (p. 101), emphasizes the prevalence of corporate over individual enterprise (pp. 240–42), and cites Louis Hartz on the role of the Pennsylvania Railroad (Chandler's crucial case for corporate management) in fomenting the ideology of private enterprise (p. 383).

12. Richard H. Pells, *Radical Visions and American Dreams* (New York: Harper & Row, 1973), p. 118.

13. I can only regret here my scanting of the complexities attendant upon the Soviet-German alliance of 1939 and the beginning of the war. See *Political Activism and the Academic Conscience: The Harvard Experience, 1936–1941*, ed. John Lydenberg (a symposium of Hobart and William Smith colleges, privately published, 1977), which is especially valuable for giving a view from Cambridge on a subject too often seen only from New York.

14. On the postwar persistence of such rhetoric, see Dwight Macdonald, "A Note on Wallese" (1947), in *Memoirs of a Revolutionist* (1957) (New York: Meridian, 1958). Wallese is a language "always employed to Unite rather than to Divide" (pp. 298–99). Matthiessen in 1948 gave a seconding speech for Wallace and devoted himself to the campaign.

15. See, however, the contrast of Hawthorne's confidence in "democratic opportunity" with Chekhov's awareness of the "breakdown of a whole social class" (*AR* 332).

In "Double Consciousness," Leo Marx downplays this whole problem by appealing to the "serious historical controversy" that continues to debate "the character and extent of class conflict in the northern American states before the Civil War" (p. 40). My point is that Matthiessen in 1934 used the language of "class war" but stopped doing do, even while the early work of Arthur Schlesinger, Jr. (e.g., *Orestes A. Brownson,* cited *AR* ix) continued to develop that perspective. Moreover, to limit the question to the North fails to face Matthiessen's national emphasis just where it is weakest.

16. On Georg Lukács and the Popular Front, see Isaac Deutscher, *Marxism in Our Time* (Berkeley: Ramparts Press, 1971), esp. pp. 291–92.

17. Lewis Mumford in *The Golden Day* (1926) (Boston: Beacon, 1957), an important book for Matthiessen (*AR* xvii), acknowledges the presence before the war of "all that blighted" America afterward (p. 40; cf. also p. 79). On the "revisionist" attempt in the thirties to diminish the significance of

the Civil War, see Kenneth M. Stampp, "The Irrepressible Conflict," in *The Imperiled Union* (New York: Oxford University Press, 1980). After the Second World War, the renewed sense of the Civil War's positive significance shifted the analogy from class war to foreign war (the South as Hitler's Germany, and perhaps the Soviet Union).

It is worth remarking that Richard Hofstadter linked his postwar "assertion of consensus history" to "the Marxism of the 1930s" but later found it "helpless and irrelevant on the Civil War." See Hofstadter, *The Progressive Historians* (New York: Alfred A. Knopf, 1968), pp. 452 n., 459.

18. I elaborate this argument in "The Politics of *The Scarlet Letter*," forthcoming in *Ideology and American Literature,* ed. Sacvan Bercovitch and Myra Jehlen. I find Matthiessen's disconnection of cultural politics most distressing in his treatment of Horatio Greenough. Despite Greenough's idealization of slaveholding Athenian Greece and his failure to support abolitionism, he hated "all attempts, whether in the social structure or in art, to divide man's wholeness and so to disperse and drain his vitality" and therefore figured as "one of the spearheads of radical advance in the America of his day" (*AR* 148, 151).

19. Edmund Wilson, "An Appeal to Progressives" (1932), in *The Shores of Light* (1952) (New York: Alfred A. Knopf, 1961). As a bitter demystification of mid-nineteenth-century nation-building, Wilson's *Patriotic Gore* (1962) stands at the opposite pole from *American Renaissance.*

20. Irving Howe, "The Sentimental Fellow-Traveling of F. O. Matthiessen," *Partisan Review* 15 (1948):1125–29; and *Margin of Hope* (New York: Harcourt Brace Jovanovich, 1982), pp. 156–58.

Lionel Trilling did review Matthiessen's study of James, and the two appeared together on a panel (see *RD* 300, 333), yet the treatment of Matthiessen in Trilling's fundamental position paper, "Reality in America" (1950), is remarkable. The essay asserts that Parrington dominates "the college course in American literature" nationwide, an even stronger claim than Trilling had ventured in the essay's first version, "Parrington, Mr. Smith, and Reality," *Partisan Review* (1940):24–40. Yet according to Henry Nash Smith, writing at the same time, Parrington's dominance in the thirties had yielded to *American Renaissance* in the forties (*Monthly Review* 2, 1950:223). Trilling then spotlights "the dark and bloody crossroads where literature and politics meet," that is, the choice between James and Dreiser. Having posed the inevitability of choice, Trilling then quotes Matthiessen's praise of Dreiser while remarking Matthiessen's admiration for James and criticism of Parrington, but he fails to notice the disruptive anomaly this comment introduces into his schematization. See *The Liberal Imagination* (1950) (New York: Doubleday, 1953), pp. 1, 8, 12. See also additional claims for the divorce between "our liberal educated class and the best of the literary mind of our time" (p. 94), that is, Proust, Joyce, Lawrence, Eliot, and other modern masters. Again, Matthiessen's existence makes nonsense of this claim, and he is ignored.

It is worth remarking the contrasted starting-points Matthiessen and Trilling specify for their social thought about America. Matthiessen recalls the "comradeship" shared during college with older, foreign-born workers he helped to instruct in English, and he notes the self-awareness as an "American" provoked by his time in England as a Rhodes Scholar (*From the Heart of Europe*, New York: Oxford University Press, 1948, pp. 72, 23). For Trilling, "America" only became "available" to his "imagination" through the "Jewish situation" (itself necessarily related to "social class") that he discovered working with the *Menorah Journal* in the late twenties. Matthiessen's national awakening obliterated class and ethnic divisions; Trilling's arose from them.

On Trilling's retrospective explanation of his project, see *The Last Decade*, ed. Diana Trilling (New York: Harcourt Brace Jovanovich, 1979), pp. 140–41 and 200. The quotations in the preceding paragraph are from pp. 14–15.

21. Matthiessen, for example, was quick to recognize the powerful implications of M. H. Abrams's work. He cited the dissertation version of *The Mirror and the Lamp, AR* 261.

22. See for example Bruce Kuklick's exposure of American studies "Myth and Symbol" work as theoretically empty, *American Quarterly* 24 (1972).

23. On the redeployment of American literary studies after World War II, see my "Afterword" to *The Yale Critics*, ed. Jonathan Arac et al. (Minneapolis: University of Minnesota Press, 1983), pp. 185–86.

24. On twentieth-century versions of "romantic anticapitalism," see the retrospect by Georg Lukács (1962) that prefaces *The Theory of the Novel* (Cambridge: MIT Press, 1970) and also Michael Löwy, *Georg Lukács: From Romanticism to Bolshevism* (1976), trans. Patrick Camiller (London: NLB, 1979).

25. Matthiessen, *From the Heart of Europe*, p. 83.

26. On literature and wholeness in England, see Perry Anderson, "Components of the National Culture," in *Student Power*, ed. Alexander Cockburn and Robin Blackburn (Harmondsworth: Penguin Books, 1969); Francis Mulhern, *The Moment of "Scrutiny"* (London: NLB, 1979); and Terry Eagleton, *Literary Theory* (Minneapolis: University of Minnesota Press, 1983), pp. 23–27, quoting from forthcoming work by Chris Baldick.

27. Theodor Adorno, "Reconciliation under Duress," in Ernst Bloch et al., *Aesthetics and Politics* (London: NLB, 1977).

28. On this issue more generally, see Paul A. Bové, *Destructive Poetics* (New York: Columbia University Press, 1980).

29. On Paterian versus Coleridgian readings, see my "Bounding Lines," *boundary 2*, 7:3 (1979):31–48.

30. Cleanth Brooks, *Modern Poetry and the Tradition* (1939) (New York: Oxford University Press, 1967), p. 136.

31. On Bloom and Longinus, see my "The Criticism of Harold Bloom," *Centrum* 6:1 (1978):32–42.

32. On Proust, see *RD* 194 (15 January 1930). Could Matthiessen's fantasy of a future like "the poisoned disintegration of M. de Charlus" bear any relation to his later terrible self-destructive nocturnal moment in a shabby hotel?

33. On Anglo-American modernist alternatives to narrative discourse, see Frank Kermode, *Romantic Image* (1957).

34. See, for example, "The noise made both by the spoon and by the hammer . . . mirrored . . . in the past . . . and in the present . . . made it possible . . . to isolate . . . for a moment brief as a flash of lightning [la durée d'un éclair] . . . a fragment of time in the pure state." Marcel Proust, *Remembrance of Things Past,* trans. Andreas Mayor (New York: Random House, 1981) III:905; *A la Recherche du Temps Perdu,* ed. Pierre Clarac and André Ferré (Paris: Gallimard, 1954) 3:872.

35. André Malraux, "The Cultural Heritage," abridged and translated by Malcom Cowley, *New Republic* 88 (1936):315–17; full translation by Kenneth Douglas, *Yale French Studies* no. 18 (1957), pp. 31–38. I have not yet been able to consult the journal *Commune* in which it first appeared. In his memoir of the thirties *The Dream of Golden Mountains* (New York: Viking Press, 1980) Cowley seems to misplace the speech at the Paris congress of 1935 (p. 282), which inaugurated the Popular Front strategy.

I doubt that including Malraux's reference to Benjamin would have made any difference. I have been unable to locate any scholarly reviews in English or American journals of Benjamin's 1928 book on *Trauerspiel,* and even an English-language American publication of Herbert Marcuse's *Reason and Revolution* (1941) awoke no response among American intellectuals, according to John P. Diggins, *Up From Communism* (New York: Harper & Row, 1977), pp. 63–64.

36. Walter Benjamin, "Theses on the Philosophy of History," in *Illuminations,* trans. Harry Zohn (1968) (New York: Schocken, 1969), pp. 263, 255. Subsequent quotations come from pp. 256, 263, 254. For a good recent overview of Benjamin's historical thought, see the editorial introduction by Rolf Tiedemann to Walter Benjamin, *Gesammelte Schriften,* vol. 5 (Frankfurt a. M.: Suhrkamp, 1982) esp. pp. 31–38.

37. This punning motto of Cesare Borgia's strikes a note also heard in the American Renaissance. In *The Natural History of the Intellect,* Emerson found in the Boston of his day what Vasari had found in Florence: a "struggle" not just to equal other "masters" but to be "foremost." See Van Wyck Brooks, *The Flowering of New England* (1936; New York: Dutton, 1952), p. 95.

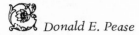 Donald E. Pease

Moby Dick
and the Cold War

The broad topic of this discussion will be the scene of cultural persuasion at the time of the publication of *Moby Dick*. Although the encyclopedic range of that narrative as well as the crucial place it occupies in the cultural context that F. O. Matthiessen called the American Renaissance might provide sufficient grounds for this rather broad context, my motive entails a much more narrow concern: a personal failure to remain persuaded by a reading of *Moby Dick* that has become canonical—the one in which Ishmael proves his freedom by opposing Ahab's totalitarian will. What is at issue here, however, is not my ability to convert this failure into the power to prove the superiority of one reading over another, but the power of a cultural context to designate, in what I am calling a scene of persuasion, the terms in which a text *must be read* in order to maintain cultural power.

By locating what I mean by a scene of cultural persuasion in a context that may seem foreign to any responsible discussion of *Moby Dick* I shall argue that it is crucial to the ongoing reception of that narrative within what Matthiessen called the American Renaissance and we call the American canon: namely, the arena for cultural discussion provided by the Cold War. Unlike other paradigms in the public sphere, the Cold War does not adjudicate or mediate discussions. Instead it derives all its force by simply being persuasive. As *the explanation,* it appears persuasive without having undergone the work of persuasion. That is to say, that it appears persuasive without either having resulted from discussions among individuals with dissenting opinions (discussions would only qualify its authority) or having persuaded a free nation to any action—other than the acceptance of the Cold War as *the paradigm.*

We might best ascertain this compelling persuasive force by attempting to locate any cultural arena external to the Cold War frame. In totalizing the globe into a super opposition between the two superpowers the United States and the Soviet Union, the Cold War economizes on any opposition to it by relocating all options within its frame. So inclusive is this frame and so pervasive is its control of world events that there appear to be no alternatives to it. Anyone wishing to oppose the frame rather than oppose the two superpowers elementing it can "witness" this opposition already "acted out," as it were, in the international area called the Third World. For whatever the specifics of third world conflicts, whether in El Salvador, Chile, or Chad, and however alien they may appear to first world concerns, the fact is that once the superpowers intercede, with their attendant "humanizing efforts," conflicts within the third world appear indistinguishable from the opposition between the United States and the Soviet Union.[1]

What we read through this paradigm are not facts (and here the attractiveness of this "super" opposition becomes all the more compelling with the seemingly endless proliferation of facts that have nowhere else to go) but the sheer power of positioning them. Even more fascinating is the relationship between this power and the range of the facts it places. Indeed, unless we expand the notion of the political to include the enclaves of routine, boredom, and powerlessness—the massive weight of whose dreariness becomes explicit only in the generalization we are used to calling "everyday life"—we cannot say that the Cold War limits its activity to the organization of merely political data. In its relation to the everyday, the Cold War ceases to be a paradigm and becomes, with only qualified indebtedness to what is commonly understood as the martial arts, the *arena*. As the arena, the Cold War accompanies the everyday less as a backdrop than as a front stage, a second scene capable of turning everyday life into its backstage (or, if you prefer, its "political unconscious").

The particular acts to be performed on this stage, however, depend less on the exigencies of international economics than on personal economies, the cultural and psychological demands of those persons whose everyday lives are always about to take a backstage part in relation to the Cold War. Here the by now received idea of culture as a space for individual performances allows the fear of dispossession by a private personality to be converted into a political act, with the particular form of the act, as well as its effect, dependent on the individual's consciousness of the form of cultural anomie in demand of being "acted out" on the Cold War stage. Boredom, the experience of as well as the defense against "modern" moments existing only for the sake of being emptied of significance by being "outmoded," is a common personal affliction. As a cure, the Cold War provides a melodrama with an anticipated last scene, a moment capable of divesting the passing moment of its boredom by investing emptiness with total significance: the Moment of Final Annihilation. Individual helplessness over exposure to experiences utterly in excess of any individual's capacity to convert them into significance disappears with the relocation of everyday life into a "battlefield" arena the Cold War threatens to make universal. Although the battlefield metaphor does not quite absorb these experiences into significance, it does allow them to be silently reapprehended as battlefield shocks (and the massive destruction involved in urban and suburban renewal projects as signs of battlefield victories), justified by the presence of an enemy no more visible than the technological progress deployed in a campaign of massive opposition.[2] For those who feel "wasted" by the sheer accumulation of unassimilable details, connotations, cultural time lags in modern life, the Cold War turns into a massive debriefing ceremony, the location for a dramatic turning point in a scene where all the complications, doubts, and conflicts of modern existence get resolved in a single opposition that then clears up the whole mess and puts everybody back to work: "Us against them."

In this second scene accompanying everyday life, all the doubts, confusions, conflicts, and contradictions constitutive of the lived experience of everyday existence can be reexperienced as participation in a decisive opposition, a last judgment in which the sides are no sooner drawn up than victory is declared. Informed by personal doubts and indecisions, the Cold War only appears the more compelling out of its capacity to convert indeterminacy into this overdetermined scene.

Given this understanding of its role in everyday life, we might say that the Cold War serves two quite different offices. It is both a drama capable of organizing national life and a paradigm claiming authority to explain international politics. Although these two offices are certainly not equivalent, they are related. As a drama responsive to the "political" demands of everyday life, the Cold War maintains its compelling force precisely *because* the Cold War as a paradigm can no longer respond to the complexities of international politics. Once the Cold War as paradigm turns into one of the doubts that everyday life is heir to, the Cold War as drama affirms its power to reposition that doubt into a conviction of national character. And this drama releases a rather chilling recognition. As the political formation of everyday life, the Cold War effectively depoliticizes the everyday by the conversion of the situations that individuals can change into an arena in which *the decision* has already been made. Once it becomes the context for understanding, the Cold War does not articulate the everyday into significance so much as it returns it to oblivion. And once the individual lends it his "personal unconscious," the Cold War can no longer be called a paradigm that does the persuading but, in a person uniform enough to be called a "national character," it is the Cold War that is persuaded.

Put somewhat differently, in the Cold War as drama, the Cold War paradigm *pre*occupies all the positions—and all the oppositions as well. Consequently, all the oppositions—whether of the Battista regime against Cuban rebels, Ishmael against Ahab, or, as was reported in a recent psychoanalytic case study, the mind against the body—can be read in terms of "our" freedom versus "their" totalitarianism. Since the Cold War paradigm confines totalizing operations to the work of the other superpower, the Cold War drama is free to expose even its own totalization of the globe as the work of the other superpower. Consequently, "I" cannot but choose this paradigm, even though it confines choice to the "human right" to choose this paradigm and limits "freedom" either to the "choice" of the correct position within it, or, given the sense that the paradigm has already "performed" all the difficult choices, to the "freedom from" the need to choose. That is to say, the Cold War paradigm relocates public persuasion not in the sphere of discussion but in a scene: one in which all the arguments have been premediated if not quite settled, with the only work left that of becoming the "national character" through whom the paradigm can speak.[3]

I began with a broad topic, the scene of cultural persuasion at the time of the publication of *Moby Dick*. Now my example of a scene of cultural persuasion has embroiled me in an even broader topic. Given the nearly universal breadth of the Cold War as a scene of cultural persuasion, I would do well to remind myself of the much narrower concern—a personal failure to be persuaded by a particular reading of *Moby Dick*. As it happens, this narrower concern brings these two scenes into a relation. The reading to which I was not persuaded (in which Ishmael's freedom is opposed to Ahab's totalitarianism) effectively turned *Moby Dick* into a Cold War text. But the scene of cultural persuasion at the time of the publication of *Moby Dick* enabled me to imagine a scene sufficiently alienated from the Cold War to make *Moby Dick* unfit for that preoccupied opposition. Now the distinction between these two scenes of persuasion permits me to restate my purpose. I do not quite wish to recover the scene of cultural persuasion at the time of the publication of *Moby Dick* but to recover from the scene of persuasion, the Cold War drama, that has appropriated it.

Stated so starkly, this struggle tends toward a melodrama of its own, with the sides no sooner drawn up then victory is declared. To come to terms with a failure to be persuaded by a canonical reading of *Moby Dick* should lead only indirectly to that time when *Moby Dick,* if recognized at all, was acknowledged chiefly as a sign of the author's madness. The more direct confrontation involves us less with the reception of *Moby Dick* in Melville's time than with the man whose work received *Moby Dick* as part of the American canon. Should we persist in the convention of locating

persons and works in scenes, we shall find F. O. Matthiessen writing
at a time—1941—as distant from the present as was the Second
World War, destined to eventuate in the Cold War. Matthiessen
wrote a work he hoped would establish American literature as a
discipline and America as a culture at a time America needed consciousness of the great tradition threatened by a totalitarian power
different from the present one. Matthiessen's work reminded
Americans of the global duties of Renaissance men, with loyalty
to America as a nation.

Acting as a means of consensus-formation as well as canon-
definition, Matthiessen's American Renaissance displaced the need
to acknowledge dissenting opinions onto the power to discover un-
recognized masterworks. Among the dissenting opinions that
American Renaissance silenced was Matthiessen's own, for in returning to the time of Whitman and Emerson, his politics seemed
already to have been achieved in the past. But with the return,
after World War II, of his political opinions to his literary works,
the progenitor of the American Renaissance became, in the
tragedy of his suicide, the sign of the cultural power of another
consensus-formation. If we read Matthiessen's dissenting opinions
as the discourse of the enemy within, the Cold War paradigm turned
him into one of its first casualties.

As we have seen, Matthiessen anticipates repressive activity in
his own work of consensus-formation, silencing not only his own
potentially disruptive political opinions but those of the other
politicians and orators he simply excluded from the American
Renaissance. More precisely, Matthiessen did not quite leave them
out altogether but consigned them to a subordinate context, one
easily assimilated by the cultural consensus he formulated through
Emerson and Whitman. In the years after the war, with the disappearance of the need for a united cultural front, we might say that
another F. O. Matthiessen, unpersuaded by the consensus-formation
underwritten by the American Renaissance, appeared. Before we
can hear this other Matthiessen, however, we have to locate for
him a context other than the American Renaissance that, like the
Cold War, silenced his dissent.

Writing as he did at a time in the international political arena marked by Nazi hegemony, when national self-consciousness could not appear merely political, Matthiessen separated politics from a cultural politics indistinguishable from consensus-formation. But, writing in the years when the Vietnamese War made national self-consciousness appear indistinguishable from the political rhetoric of the Cold War, Sacvan Bercovitch found the Cold War rhetoric supported by another tradition that he called the tradition of the American Jeremiad.[4] He found a broad-based locus for this form precisely in the rhetoric Emerson and Whitman shared with the orators and politicians of the American Renaissance. If for F. O. Matthiessen the American Renaissance proved its power as a cultural consensus by silencing dissenting political opinions, for Bercovitch the American jeremiad derived all its cultural force at precisely that moment in the nation's past when dissenting *political* opinions over such explosive issues as union, slavery, and expansionism would make a difference in the very form of the nation handed over from the past.

But, like the Cold War paradigm it prefigures, the American jeremiad did not quite come to terms with these explosive issues. Rather, it put them into other terms: other terms, moreover, that made these issues indistinguishable from those surrounding the single event—the American Revolution—that, once resolved, seemed to have made up the nation's mind once and for all. Seeing issues in terms of the American Revolution, that is, precluded them from becoming explosive political issues. For the Revolution, in its office as the fulfillment of the Puritan divine mission, lost its status as a historical event that took place and turned into a perpetual national resource, a rhetorical means for making up the nation's mind over whatever issue presented itself. Displaying the same power to *alienate opposition* we found at work in the Cold War, the jeremiad compels any listener intent on issuing his own dissenting opinion to discover that his dissent has, in the American Revolution, already achieved its ideal form. So dissent becomes indistinguishable from a national revolutionary ideal which, Bercovitch argues, has in its turn turned into the ideological representation of the free enterprise system.

When translated into the form of the American jeremiad, political issues become occasions for scripture lessons like the one Theodore Parker attached to his 1848 "sermon" on the Mexican War. In this sermon, America's war with Mexico turned into the "lesson" of King Ahab, who coveted Naboth's Vineyard.[5] Now whatever may be obscure in the lesson, what remains clear is that it was not an occasion for persuading a group of individuals to perform an action by presenting an argument about a complex issue. If the Mexican War embroiled the American people in an anxious political conjuncture involving debates over slavery and national identity, in Parker's lesson this war and all the anxiety surrounding the issues that gave rise to it give way to another scene, a calm and secure one. Writ seems to have already adjudicated these as well as all other matters.

Despite the clarity of the security-inducing effect of Parker's sermon, it nevertheless should serve as an occasion to complicate Bercovitch's model. For Parker does not directly discuss the Mexican War in terms of the American Revolution. He does, however, borrow on that power to discuss political events in religious terms, a power authorized by the revolutionary moment in which God's will and the nation's will become one, secured by the American jeremiad. Bercovitch needs some explanation for the willingness of the American public to cede him this power. Such an explanation cannot simply posit the power of the jeremiad to constrain public opinion but must demonstrate how, given the cultural variations and violent dislocations of American life, the jeremiad could continue to attract public attention at all. Why, for example, given Bercovitch's terms, is not the very form of the American jeremiad one in which figures from the past reappear, an occasion for anxiety over the loss of relation with those figures?

A consideration of Parker's sermon in terms borrowed from our earlier discussion of the conditions overdetermining the acceptance of the Cold War paradigm could begin to provide an explanation. For in this oratorical scene Parker depends on his audience's anxiety and doubt over the issues surrounding the Mexican War for his very authority to invoke his other scene. Once these anxiety-provoking issues are replaced by figures like King Ahab, the issues disappear, for such figures seem already to have acted out the present dilemma in the past, thereby relieving the American public of the need to let the issues enter its consciousness at all. Or, if they must enter the consciousness, they do so precisely in another scene, one, as was the case with the Cold War opposition, in which all the issues have, in their very presentation within the language of Divine Writ, already received definitive judgment. In Parker's sermon, then, King Ahab, the very figure designating the issue of the Mexican War, turns out to have already resolved it.

So political issues turn into great public occasions for the displacement of scenes of present troubles by scenes in which those troubles have already been solved. The same figures who made up the public's mind for it in the past, in acting out potentially divisive public issues, can in the present separate the issue from the anxiety attending it. In place of the anxiety over political events in the present, these figures foreground a threat that seems to have a greater claim to public attention: the loss of a relation with a past. These same figures then allay the anxiety they have aroused by returning from a past, a past become all the more gratifying because of its claim to fulfill all present political aspirations.

The "other scene" utterly displaces any political issue, and so completely economizes on any individual exertion of will that the "mental work" that otherwise might have been expended in resolving a political question gets released from the doubts, second thoughts, calculations, and judgments informing any political decision. It gets released, moreoever, in a discourse that, if it ever became conscious, might have been called inspired—the discovery that the political issue troubling the mind has already been solved by the very rhetorical figures used to articulate the problem. Perhaps we should pause over this discovery to register one more observation. The very form wording the political issue into being excludes the question of individual freedom. More precisely, the jeremiad identifies individual freedom not with the freedom *to* perform an action, but with the freedom *from* the doubts, decisions, and judgments leading to action. That is to say, this other scene depoliticizes freedom, exempts it from political questions.

Since the very words used to articulate political questions have already resolved them, the individual's *freedom* moves elsewhere, into a realm emptied of actantial, judgmental, *determinate* energies: but with the foreknowledge that the sheer freedom and sheer chanciness of this potentially "free" realm will be returned to security once the need for security overdetermines the need to return to the other scene.

Obviously the "other scene" did not limit its power to the listeners. For the orators, in their abilities to transcribe everyday events into a form that made them seem indistinguishable from the inspired words of the God of the revolutionary father, turned their words into figural effects. When perceived as the effects rather than the proponents of the words that seemed to utter them, such orators became indistinguishable from those rhetorical figures appearing *within* their discourse. In their office as realized effects of the revolutionary fathers, these orators gave the American people still another opportunity. For in their sermons, the American people did not quite hear the whispered word of God but witnessed the ways in which their own historical lives had become inspirations *for* God's words. And in their office as present occasions for the divine inspiration, the American people did not feel compelled to hear God's Word so much as to conceive themselves as his means of representing it. Consequently, such scenes of public persuasion as that performed by Theodore Parker became occasions in which the public idealized the most basic form of acknowledgment. Instead of turning listeners toward a neighbor, the need for mutual recognition turned the listeners toward the orator, in whose "inspired" figure they were to recognize what they, in their everyday life, had become.

As the prophetic fulfillment of both speaker and listener, the jeremiad does not really represent their differing positions but, like the scene of persuasion in the Cold War paradigm that it might now be said to prefigure, the jeremiad assimilates both speaker and listener into the means of articulating its form. Moreover, although, unlike the Cold War paradigm, the jeremiad represents its *pre*-mediation of all positions as if it were an *un*mediated vision, nonetheless the effect of both paradigms remains the same. Either you come to your decision in their terms or you cannot decide. The same all-or-nothing logic was at work then as it is now: either you use the terms sanctioned by the form or, as a figure, literally outside of the shared language of the American people, you lose the possibility for representation in the scene of public persuasion altogether.

Although the "concept" of the American jeremiad is quite resourceful in disclosing the ways in which the distinction between consensus and compulsion, always a difficult one to maintain, disappears altogether, nevertheless it cannot quite account for what we might call crises in coercion occasioned by those moments in American cultural history when identical figures in nearly identical forms of the jeremiad were used to represent opposing opinions on related questions. Such a moment clearly was at hand when Theodore Parker speaking against slavery, John Calhoun speaking against union, and David Lee Childs speaking against expansionism could all write variations on the same line, "If I am rightly informed, King Ahab made a law that all the Hebrews serve the idol Baal."[6] When this same line could be used by different orators to represent such violently opposed views on such explosive issues, King Ahab could not be said to have made up his mind on these matters. With the recognition of Ahab's confusion, Americans lost their traditional way of feeling compelled about what to do.

Given our analysis of the unique cultural apparatus brought into existence by the consensus-formations we have by turns called the American jeremiad and the Cold War, we cannot simply dismiss such moments as manifestations of cognitive dissonance on a massive scale. In the national economy of the representation of dissent we have been describing, the figures who idealized dissent into final, resolved form existed in a world we called the other scene, in which everyday dissenting opinions, doubts, and contradictions existed only in a fully resolved state. And the relation between the everyday world of indecision and the other scene of the *Decision* was an overdetermined and compensatory one. This everyday world could function precisely because that other world hedged its bet, converting all of its irresolution into a resolved form. It is not simply that doubts and indecisions do exist in local, contingent forms, but they exist *free from the need for decisive resolution* precisely because this other world exists as the *Resolution*. Dissent exists free from the need for resolution in the everyday world because the jeremiad can absolve dissent of its indecision by wording it into an indubitable final reckoning on the other scene. Not only does the other scene permit indecision and doubts; it demands them as ongoing proof of its authoritative power to judge.

Now with this relation between worlds as a context, imagine one of the rhetorical figures used to free the individual of the consequences of doubt (that is, the need to decide on a course of action)—such as Ahab in Parker's sermon, himself become human enough to experience indecision. What results is a confusion of realms on an apocalyptic scale. When the Ahab who exists to absolve this world of its conflicts himself experiences in that other scene the irresolvable doubts of this world, the other scene reverses its relation to this world. Whereas before, actual indecision discharged itself through symbolic resolution in the other scene, now a form of symbolic resolution from the other scene demands actualization of its indecision in the everyday world. Whereas before the *Decision* in the other scene was an overdetermined form of the indecisions of everyday life, with this confusion of realms everyday indecision gets invested with the overdetermined energy of decision.

Unless one were an orator who actually experienced himself as a figure brought into existence by the words uttered in that other scene, it is difficult to imagine a rhetorical figure (like the Ahab used by different orators to justify expansionism, slavery, and union) who can come into the actual world full of the conflicting demands the other scene can no longer resolve. But if the public that was used to experiencing Ahab as an ideal resolution of their conflicting demands now experiences him, in his multiple representations, as an ideal expression of their conflicting demands, it can be said that Ahab, as the means of making up the public's mind, has come to life as the "character" of the public mind. As the "lived experience" of their betrayed resolution, he expresses the "national character" as a desperate need to convert conflicting demands back into a decisive form.

As the force released by the loss of authority for the American jeremiad, Ahab the tortured national character discloses the prior form of the American jeremiad's power. It generated and contained two different worlds. But the relation between these two worlds was not that of a "type" *fulfilled* by an "antitype" in the typological model Bercovitch offers. Instead the one world (we have called the Other Scene) definitively separated the doubts and indecisions of the other world (we have called everyday life) from the need for resolution. Existing as a colossal estrangement effect, the Other Scene provided the occasion for individuals to reexperience their personal failures to decide as freedom from the need to decide. The Other Scene provided other "personal" benefits as well. As the source world of primary action, the Other Scene relegated authenticity not to the activities of individuals in the everyday world, but to the action performed by such gigantic rhetorical figures as the Ahab in Parker's sermon. Consequently, those "persons" who sensed the disconnection between the individual as effective cause and agent and the individual as an effect of forces beyond any individual's control could, with the relocation of "personal" authenticity in the "national character" acting on the Other Scene, reexperience alienation from an authentic self as a freedom to perform a multiplicity of roles.[7]

The loss of Ahab's power on the Other Scene we might say brought about a reversal in the national relation to "act" and "action." Although I do not want to reduce the national motives for the Civil War to the terms of this reversal, I do want to note that this crisis in the nation's means of self-representation demanded a war for resolution. For when the form of the jeremiad can no longer "contain" and "actualize" national conflicts in the final reckoning acted out on the Other Scene, the *undecided* conflict demands an actual *war* in order to become a decisive opposition *once again*. Stated too simply, the Civil War became the means of recovering in the everyday world the *stability* and *force* of *containment* lost

by the rhetorical figures in the Other Scene. If, before, the staging
of the Other Scene was all the persuasion there was, the Civil War
exposed that persuasion as merely staged. This exposure became
the occasion for individuals no longer merely to be content to "act
out" but to *need to actualize* those dissenting opinions that the
American jeremiad, in its ideal resolution of the "national character," had formally alienated from them.

The Ahab in Parker's sermon was the figure of the "national
character" who impersonated the American jeremiad's forces of
containment. But the conflicting Ahabs in Calhoun's and Child's
orations released an Ahab who could no longer feel persuaded by
the form of the American jeremiad. If Sacvan Bercovitch, like the
other Americans in his text, feels the need to recover the form of
the American jeremiad at moments, like that of the Civil War,
when it loses all of its effective historical force, he recovers the
jeremiad at the expense of the character of Ahab, who no longer
feels persuaded by it. If, in the perhaps excessive characterization
in our discussion, Ahab was said to impersonate the power of the
jeremiad to persuade, he now impersonates the felt loss of the
authority of that power.

The Ahab who feels the compulsive need to persuade utterly
separated from the form sanctioning persuasion does not appear in
anyone's jeremiad but in Melville's novel *Moby Dick.* Should we
follow Melville's lead and remain attentive to the demands not of
the American jeremiad but of the figure who is not persuaded by
it, we can turn to another American Renaissance. Guided this
time, however, not by the figure who organized it into an ideal
consensus-formation but prepared (by the figure of Ahab) to hear
what we called that other F. O. Matthiessen, whose own dissenting
opinions were silenced by what we can now recognize as the jeremiad form of *American Renaissance: Art and Expression in the
Age of Emerson and Whitman.*

When turned toward the time of Emerson and Whitman by
Matthiessen's opinions in conflict with the consensus formed by
the *American Renaissance,* we can revalue the use of Whitman
and Emerson. In using Coleridge's organicist aesthetic to distinguish

the political rhetoric of such orators as Parker from what he called the "vitally" aesthetic writings of Emerson and Whitman, the *American Renaissance* (as a consensus formed at the expense of Matthiessen's own dissenting position) strategically promotes Whitman's and Emerson's rhetoric, in which national self-consciousness becomes indistinguishable from personal self-consciousness, into a cultural asset. Moreover, this act of promotion constitutes the historical power of consensus-formation in 1941. For in order to sanction America's national right to a free culture at a time when that right was threatened less by national than international politics, *American Renaissance* locates a cultural past so united that even the political issues surrounding the Civil War seem petty. When viewed in this context, Whitman and Emerson perform the same function for Matthiessen, in his politics of consensus-formation, that they performed for the politicians used to the consensus formed by the American jeremiad in their time. They silence the conflicting claims in that form by replacing the politicians' forensic motives with motives open to the more rarefied concerns of aesthetics. Seeming, then, to distinguish Emerson and Whitman from the politicians, *American Renaissance* in fact locates in their writings an organicist aesthetic justification for the rhetoric of national individualism at precisely the moment when the politicians seem to be losing the divine justification for that rhetoric. As we have seen, this bracketing out of politics through a turn to aesthetic questions in fact served Matthiessen's "higher" political purpose— to devise a national consensus. Now we might best sense the cultural power of his "higher" purpose if we imagine F. O. Matthiessen coming after Sacvan Bercovitch to convert the "mere rhetoric" of the American jeremiad into the achieved art of the American Renaissance.

When conceived in terms of this "higher" purpose, however, Emerson and Whitman lose their purely aesthetic characters and reveal the explicitly rhetorical use to which *American Renaissance* put them. Nowhere does Emerson lose this character and Matthiessen lose control of the working of his consensus-formation more definitively than in the midst of an analysis of the tyranny of

Captain Ahab in the quarterdeck scene in *Moby Dick*. Curiously,
Matthiessen presents this analysis in what we could call a scene of
critical persuasion. When considering Ahab's compelling domination of the men in the quarterdeck scene, Matthiessen pays no
attention to specific lines but reads the compulsion in Ahab's language as a "sign" of Shakespeare's "power over" Melville. Then, in
a monodrama intended ultimately to reveal Melville's artistic
power, he transcribes lines exchanged by Ahab and Starbuck into
their blank verse form and observes that "the danger of such unconsciously compelled verse is always evident. As it wavers and
breaks down into ejaculatory prose, it seems never to have belonged
to the speakers but to have been at best a ventriloquist's trick."[8]
Having first *posited* Shakespeare's language as the rhetorical power
informing Ahab's exchanges, Matthiessen then rediscovers this
power Shakespeare wields *through* Ahab at work in the spell
Shakespeare cast *over* Melville's prose. This dramatic conflict ends
only after Melville "masters" the power Shakespeare's rhetoric
wields over him by discovering the secret of this own dramatic
power.

Of course all the power in this drama inheres less in Melville's
discovery than in the dramatic use to which Matthiessen puts it.
When Matthiessen's drama, which should have concluded with an
example of Melville's triumphant "mastery" of Shakespeare, comes
to its close, Melville's "mastery" of Shakespeare neither reveals
itself through one of Melville's own characters nor represents one
of Melville's own themes. Instead, Melville's "vital rhetoric" is said
to "build up a defense of one of the chief doctrines of the age, the
splendor of the single personality."[9] In other words, Melville's
recovery from Shakespeare's rhetoric becomes a means for Emerson
to defend his doctrine of self-reliance.

That Matthiessen sees the need for this defense gives pause. But
the cause for the defense is implicit in the drama that builds up to
it. Although he only mentions Hitler, his account of Chilling-
worth, the figure whose totalitarian position Matthiessen wrote
American Renaissance to oppose, is everywhere present in his discussion of Ahab. By staging the textual appearance of the doctrine

of self-reliance within the scene of Melville's recovery from a compulsive rhetorical principle, Matthiessen defends its rhetoric in advance from the charge that it may be as compelling in its excesses as Hitler was in his. When Matthiessen writes, "living in the age of Hitler, even the least religious can know and be terrified by what it is for a man to be possessed," it is clear that figures from Matthiessen's *American Renaissance* exist to oppose compulsive rhetoric, in all of its forms.[10] Consequently, when Melville dramatically achieves independence from the compulsive hold of Shakespeare's rhetoric, in the eyes trained to see by the *American Renaissance*, he earns the *authenticity* of the doctrine of self-reliance by literally realizing its *doctrine* as his defining aesthetic action.

The compelling logic of this dramatic sequence is clear. Matthiessen wants to *see* the doctrine of self-reliance at work, but when Matthiessen "hears" this doctrine enunciated by Ahab, he loses all the benefits accrued by the rest of his drama. Indeed Matthiessen's own earlier treatment of Ahab as the "dummy" through whom Melville performs ventriloquist's tricks with Shakespeare's language posits Ahab as the principle of mere rhetoric rather than authentic art. And this earlier treatment releases troubling questions. If Ahab served as the dummy figure through whom Matthiessen could reveal Melville's act of "working through" his possession by Shakespeare's rhetoric, does he not, once Matthiessen hears him speaking Emerson's rhetoric of self-reliance, disclose Matthiessen's unstated fear that compulsion might be at work in the doctrine of self-reliance? In short, does not the quarterdeck scene become Matthiessen's awareness not of the need to defend but of the need to defend himself against Emerson's ideology of self-reliance, which informs the consensus-formation he called the American Renaissance?

Instead of revealing an instance of self-reliance at work, this scene releases (as two Matthiessens) the conflicts Matthiessen experienced in relation to the doctrine of self-reliance. Whereas Matthiessen wished to affirm Emerson's essays as liberating rather than disabling rhetoric, the moment Emerson appears within the context of *Moby Dick* his doctrine appears least *vital* because most coercive. Moreover, the moment Matthiessen would defend this doctrine, he becomes, according to the logic of his own dramatic metaphor, less himself than an occasion for self-division in which *through* the figure of Ahab one Matthiessen doubts what the other Matthiessen affirms: that is, the liberating power of Emerson's rhetoric.

As we have seen, Melville's Ahab discloses the conflicts the American jeremiad could no longer silence. When Matthiessen attempts to speak the doctrine of his jeremiad through the figure of Ahab, the other Matthiessen, the Matthiessen whose dissenting opinions *American Renaissance* existed to silence, begins to speak instead. This doubling is crucial. Matthiessen not only found self-reliance to be the chief ethical doctrine of the age but the ethical principle of the work *American Renaissance,* earning for that age a cultural power that, in organizing the American canon, has itself become canonical. But, despite *Moby Dick's* power to reduce the doctrine of self-reliance once it appears within its context—to reduce, in fact, both it and the canon of the *American Renaissance* that it informs—to the status of ventriloquist's figures, I should consider the persuasive power of this doctrine before turning to *Moby Dick,* the book that I will argue is not persuaded by it.

Emerson states the doctrine with a simplicity that almost conceals its power. "Self-reliance is precisely that secret," he writes, "to make your supposed deficiency redundancy. If I am true, the theory is, the very want of action, my very impotency, shall become a greater excellency than all skill and toil."[11] When revealed, the secret is as simple as the doctrine; it makes a promise to convert powerlessness into a form of power. Before the reader can wish to find this doctrine appealing, however, he needs as his prior experience to feel powerless. The doctrine, in other words, presupposes a disproportion between a secret inner man and an outer world that it works to maintain. Actually, the doctrine of self-reliance does not simply presuppose such a disproportion between inner man and outer world but demands it as the context for its display of power.

By definition, a *self*-reliant man cannot rely on an outer world but only on an inner self, experienced as superior to the external world. But he can create this inner self only by first reducing the outer world to the level of an abstract externality, as arbitrary as it is merely contingent. Such a reduction cuts two ways. A world that is viewed as *arbitrary at best* allows for a retreat from it without too much regret. This separation from the mere contingencies of the external world can, out of sheer contrast, be experienced from *within* as the first *authentic* choice in an otherwise arbitrary world.

But at least two problems attend the appearance of this inner self. If his authenticity is derived from a prior experience of contingency, then the inner self has not replaced but only internalized the contingency of an outer world. What results, moreover, is what Ishmael, at the beginning of *Moby Dick,* calls a bad case of the "hypos" and what we in our discussion of everyday life in a Cold War world called boredom: that is, a wish for intense action but, given the contingency of internal as well as external worlds, without any incitement to act. The self-reliant man, then, feels empowered to act but has disconnected himself from any world that can validate his action.

In addressing these two problems, Emerson devised two distinct roles for self-reliance to perform. In its role as a doctrine, self-reliance encouraged a sense of withdrawal from the world; but in its role as an address, self-reliance converted this withdrawal into the appearance of a power. In this second role, self-reliance acts less like a doctrine corroborating any particular inner self and more like one of those rhetorical figures of will we saw at work on the Other Scene of the American jeremiad, capable of providing the private person with the freedom in relation to the external world denied him by the doctrine. We begin to understand the power inherent in this division better when we discover what happens when Emerson declares this doctrine as an address. As a figure of address effected by the self-reliance he evokes, Emerson can presume to speak to another individual, not from a position external to him but with all the power of that other individual's "secret" inner life to which each self-reliant individual aspires. And so effective is this power to speak the inner life that such public figures as John Jay Chahpman, James Garfield, and Moncure Conway will declare after listening that Emerson's words have become their "secret" character.[12]

When speaking *as* what we might call the sovereign figure of the will released by the doctrine of self-reliance, however, Emerson does not encourage the individual either to act in the world or to will action. Instead he encourages the individual to discover his power in his inability to act: "If I am true, . . . my very impotency shall secure a greater excellency than all skill and toil." In what we could call a compensatory unconscious, the inability to perform any particular action recovers the sovereign *capability* to perform *all* actions. Through this remarkable turn, the sovereign will can recover the motivation lost after the devaluation of the external world. The individual will recovers its motivation, however, not by bridging the gap between motive and action but by enlarging it to the point where the motivating power, the sheer impulse to action, assumes priority over any particular action.

Thus the doctrine of self-reliance fulfilled the private will, but only through an address by a figure effected by a sovereign will, who relocates *within the abstract capability of the alienated individual* the Other Scene of *final reckoning* we discovered in the form of the American jeremiad. If the jeremiad separated the individual from the need for political decision by providing the scene upon which everything had already been decided, self-reliance alienated individual action from individual motives for action by providing an internal sovereign will whose abstract capability to do what "might be done" was all the action there could be. When addressed by a spokesman, like Emerson, for this sovereign, the private man could feel persuaded not to perform any particular action but to experience the sheer force of the motivation to act—resounding in such imperatives as "trust thyself, every heart vibrates to that iron string"—as if it were already the only fulfillment needed.

If the doctrine of self-reliance justified the individual's alienation from a world of action, the power of address it made possible justified the separation of self-reliant individuals from one another. In replacing the merely private will with the "sovereign will," self-reliance also allowed for a great economy of discussion in the public sphere. For it eliminated first and third persons altogether and turned everyone into representations of what we could call a national second person, an empty discursive slot to be filled in by a figure addressing the nation. While this second person seems to address "you," he derives all of his power by presuming to speak *as* "your" inner life. Thus, in listening to him, "you" can believe you are investing yourself with executive power. But some pathos should return when "you," perhaps as a "second thought," recognize that this second person alone possesses the only self-reliant inner life in the nation.

Thus, the status of this national and sovereign second person must also give pause. For the second person is not only composed of and as "compensation" for the powerlessness of first persons, but is empowered, as it were, out of a sensed disconnection between persons. In a nation of second persons, individuals do not discuss matters with other individuals but "address" or better "move" one another with inspirational apostrophes and imperatives. In inspiring one another, however, a nation of second persons need not listen to or even recognize one another but can, in moving another, look forward to being unmoved in return; or, if moved at all, be moved by the sheer power of moving called the sovereign will. Here, again, we see not consensus but a kind of compulsion in its place. The work of compulsion performed by the figure of address we have called the sovereign will of the self-reliant man faces none of the conflicts that tore apart the form of the American jeremiad. There, as we saw in the person of Ahab, the form of the jeremiad used to sanction the conflicting claims internalized rather than silenced the conflicts. But since the figure of sovereign will *can* perform any action, no *particular position* can lay claim to the figure's power to sanction. As the capability to perform all actions, the sovereign will need not experience the conflicts endemic to any *particular* expression of will. Without the possibility for conflict, the sovereign will need not negotiate conflicts among separate individuals. Instead it demands the separation of individuals as the only appropriate effect of the sovereign will.

Although it is everywhere present in Emerson's theory of friendship, Thoreau elevates disconnection into a national ideological value when he writes, "When they say farewell then indeed we begin to keep them company. . . . [For just as] I always assign to him a nobler employment in my absence than I ever find him engaged in, so I value and trust those who love and praise my aspiration rather than my performance."[13] In these lines Thoreau etherealizes friendship to the status of mutual evanescence, as the sheer potential to be an inspiring friend replaces the need for any actual friendship and sheer motivation replaces action.

But an even clearer sense of the cultural value of this doctrine of friendship arises when we juxtapose it to the doctrine of self-reliance. That doctrine, as we recall, separated the inner self from a devalued because external world. But the address of the sovereign will, to the internal world from a position external to it, revalued, if not an external world, at least an external field of force: a second person capable of addressing private individuals with all the force of their inner life. This second person, less a person than an abtraction of other persons to the position of addressee, in belonging to nobody in particular provided a platform of address for everyone in general. As the sheer capability of address, belonging to everybody in general and no one in particular, this sovereign will, through Thoreau's doctrine of the friend, could as the means of mutual inspiration function as the very principle of community. In other words, this sovereign will could, despite its origin in the sensed disconnection of self-reliant individuals from one another, represent itself, in its capacity to speak for everybody and nobody, as the general will of the people. When speaking from this position, an individual could, through the fiction of the sovereign will, claim to address the people from the position not of their will or the individual's will but (with all the force of a second person) *thy* will.

As was the case with the witnesses of the scene of persuasion in the American jeremiad, however, the "general will" of the people did not originate from discussions among themselves. Instead, the people could only hearken to their inner life as it addressed them from the position of that irresistible field of force resulting from the sensed disconnection of individuals both from the world and from each other: a force we have called the national second person.

In its role as the spokesman for the sovereign will of the people, Emerson's doctrine of self-reliance obviously provided politicians and orators with a tremendous practical advantage. For, in self-reliance, the public found a way not to be persuaded to any particular action but instead, in what we would call the turn to a rhetoric of pure persuasion, to be inspired by the felt sense of the motive to act purified of any actantial component. In valuing motive over action, listeners need not question the acts to which orators would persuade them. Perhaps here we have the reason such public figures as Garfield, Conway, and Chapman felt so empowered by Emerson. Aspiring as they did to speak for the will of the people, they found in the person of Emerson's self-reliant or sovereign will the people's consent. In listening to an orator, a self-reliant man *need* not question what was said, for he was not being addressed as a figure *other* than the figure addressing him. In a relentlessly closed communication circuit, the self-reliance addressed that figure of will Emerson called self-reliance. On these occasions, the individual could witness his own independence coming to him, as it were, in the person of the nation's second person. Most importantly, however, Emerson's conversion of the politician's purposive rhetoric into pure persuasion had the effect of purifying that rhetoric of the confusions we saw at work when King Ahab was used to sanction three conflicting attitudes toward national politics. Since pure persuasion turned purpose into a purposiveness without purpose, it became a means of receiving the inspirational power of political rhetoric when conflicting political demands were breaking apart its form.

When observing what he called the resultant American pleniloquence from the detached position of a third rather than second person, Alexis de Tocqueville did not, as did Matthiessen and Bercovitch, use it as an occasion either to describe or engage in

consensus-formation. Instead he recovered the first-person privileges of the humorist:

> Debating clubs in America are to a certain extent a substitute for theatrical
> entertainment: [for] an American *cannot converse* . . . [instead] his talk
> falls into a dissertation. He speaks to you as if he were addressing a meet-
> ing, and if he should chance to become warm in the discussion, he will say
> "Gentlemen" to the person with whom he is conversing.[14]

Since de Tocqueville, in his outsider's account, seems to have
achieved a position enabling him to recover a first person capable
of poking fun at what I have called the scene of cultural persuasion, I want to take this opportunity to distinguish his outsider's
narrative not only from the forms of address called the jeremiad
and the sovereign will but also from those insiders' narratives—the
legends and tall tales—written by Americans as means of remaining
within the address of the national second person.

In order to understand how this inside narrative works, we need
to return to the scene of pure persuasion to emphasize its crucial
distinction from the American jeremiad. In privileging motive over
act, the scene of pure persuasion does not recall agents from the
nation's past but demands that agents as well as their actions imitate inspiring motives. The second person does not commemorate
the heroic deeds performed by characters from the nation's past.
Instead, the second person calls individuals to aspire to actions indistinguishable from the motivational power of the orator's figures
of will. In Emerson's remarkable turn, the revolutionary fathers,
instead of remaining ideals to be imitated, became effects of the
self-reliant man's inspiring words, embodiments of the motivating
power of his speech. As a result of the claims implicit in Emerson's
rhetoric, the people were able to internalize within the sovereign
will not only the idealized revolutionary fathers but also the biblical
figures who in the form of the American jeremiad provided the
fathers with their divine rights. That is to say, in Emerson's rhetoric
even God's words become indistinguishable from the sovereign
will of the nation's second person.

This same absorptive power—the presumption of the sovereign

will seemingly to claim every preexisting cultural authority as an effect of its power—introduces another dimension in the relationship between sovereign will and action. For although, as we stated, the sovereign will separated any particular action from the infinite capability of the sovereign will, that same sovereign will could claim any action as an effect of its motivating power. In this context, heroic deeds need not be conceived as motives that became actions (which would threaten the superiority of motive in relation to deed) but could be conceived as actions that were indistinguishable from the motivating power to act. Orators secured this equivalence by converting certain actions in the world into tropes of pure persuasion. So whenever individuals "acted out" the inspiring power of the orator's motives, they became a figure of will indistinguishable from the inner life of the self-reliant man and earned, as was the case with Andrew Jackson (who in the Indian Wars became an embodiment of the infinite capacity to act associated with the sovereign will), the right to speak as the national second person that they in their personal lives had already become. They could motivate others, in short, because they had already equated their inner motivation with public action.

The mention of Jackson, however, also provides the occasion for a distinction. For he was the subject not only of legends that assimilated the excesses of the orator's rhetoric into human shape but also of tall tales that, like de Tocqueville's "humorous" observations, decreased these legendary figures by exposing their apparently heroic deeds as mere "stretchers." Here the distinction that needs to be made is between demystifying a rhetorical position and telling a tall tale. For the latter—telling a tall tale—displaces the need to do the former. Instead of wishing to acknowledge the rhetorical status of a tall tale, the tellers never want to get outside its format. For if they did they would not have the pleasure of "taking in" third persons. Third persons, in their turn, do not recognize what it is that has taken them in, but simply experience the pleasure of "taking in" another third person with another tall tale. The legend and the tall tale, then, establish what we might (in our memory of the national second person) call a "second first" and a "second third" person who never become skeptical or even self-conscious about the rhetoric of pure persuasion but who wish instead to claim their second-person privileges and remain in the position of persons addressed by the nation's second person.

But if narrativity functions as a motive to remain within the form of address of the nation's second person, reading narratives became an occasion to locate the power of this will to address. Reading, in other words, offéred an occasion to turn what is read—that is, words as motive forces—into what does the reading. Or, what is the same thing, reading became a means of internalizing and so, following the logic we found at work in the doctrine of self-reliance, making sovereign, what we have called the nation's second person.

The interrelationship between Americans engaged in the activities of listening, speaking, arguing and reading—activities valued most, on at least one cultural level, when most indicative of a certain independence of mind—and what we have called the sovereign will of mind releases an alarming recognition. When accompanying the "democratic" operations acclaimed as proof of the power of individual Americans to make up their own minds, the sovereign will turns these operations into expressions of a national compulsion. When turned toward the national scene on which compulsion could do its work, individual Americans did not make up their own minds but witnessed the scene on which their minds were made up for them as an "experience" of each American's self-reliance.

Perhaps this recognition will have its greatest value if we imagine it stated by the F. O. Matthiessen who led us to it: not the one who used Emerson's doctrine of self-reliance to form the consensus he called the *American Renaissance* but the one whose dissenting political opinions were silenced by *Art and Expression in the Age of Emerson and Whitman.* Since be began to hear this Matthiessen who was not persuaded by the scene of cultural persuasion in his reading of the quarterdeck scene of *Moby Dick,* perhaps we can use this scene as an oppositional one. And since the narrative of *Moby Dick* offers an occasion for Matthiessen to signal opinions in conflict, we should expand the context of this oppositional scene by differentiating Melville's narrative vision from *Art and Expression in the Age of Emerson and Whitman.*

Although Emerson never wrote an explicit narrative, throughout *Leaves of Grass* Whitman used narrations as a means of articulating his relationship with his readers. This relationship becomes clear in section 35 of *Song of Myself,* when Whitman asks a leading narrative question: "Would you hear of a Sea fight?"[15] Curiously, however, the desired account does not follow. What takes the place of the tale is Whitman's imagination of a reading public thoroughly absorbed in an impulse to hear his narrative. What follows from that imaginative act is a conversion of their anticipated acts of rapt attention into the motive energies of the will with which he writes.

In absorbing the reading public into the will with which he writes, Whitman no longer quite exists as either a first-person active or a third-person passive figure in the poem. His narrative scene turns him into the national second person, a figure in the middle voice who is effected by the very will he would affect; not a man who sings but the pre-absorption of any reaction to the song, as the very life of the song. Put most starkly, Whitman does not imagine himself as singing to an audience but as the very give and take, the medium through which an audience would communicate.

In what we might call the interlocutive voice of his poetry, Whitman pre-absorbs the will of the people thoroughly enough to imagine himself the verbal mediation capable of *speaking the public into being.* As the sovereign voice capable of speaking the people of these United States into being, Whitman, speaking as "what I assume you shall assume," elides the specific differences of opinion, the local conflicts of interest informing the people; thereby converting the people into modulations and variations of this sovereign voice. Since the *vox populi* need speak not with, but *as* the people, their conflicts turn into opportunities for the discovery of the resources of that voice.

Writing as if the general will were the sovereign will, Whitman silenced these conflicts by containing them within the modulations of a voice singing America into being. At around the time of the composition of *Moby Dick,* Melville imagined a reading experience utterly at odds with what we have described as the internalization of the sovereign will. Moreover, he discovered this "will of the people" by reading not Whitman or Emerson but a figure Matthiessen included as another (subsidiary) voice in the *American Renaissance*. Reading Hawthorne's *Mosses from the Old Manse,* a work attentive enough to the value of different opinions to provoke in the reader a series of conflicting attitudes, Melville conceived a review in which he *staged* the release of conflicting reactions. Recorded over a two-day period by a Virginian vacationing in Vermont, the review dramatizes a protocol the reverse of what we have called a scene of public persuasion. Instead of finding *his* mind already made up in the figure of Hawthorne's tales, this Southerner vacationing in the heart of the abolitionist Northeast discovers a whole range of conflicting reactions to these tales: with each reaction possessed of sufficient self-consciousness to organize itself into an articulate opinion and each opinion accompanied by a second thought—the shocking recognition of the limits of that single opinion. In an intricate series of moves, Melville reads neither as an individual nor quite as a general will but as the conflicting opinions within a reading public—not a ready-made consensus but a consensus in the process of formulation, or what Melville calls a "plurality of men of genius" released in reading Hawthorne's twice-told tales.

In other words, Melville, at the time of his composition of *Moby Dick,* imagined the release of the reading public from the sovereign will of the national second person. Moreover, he released that public by giving multiple voices, each with the possibility of "parity," to the conflicts silenced by that sovereign will.[16] We got some indication of the dimensions of those conflicts when we analyzed what resulted when the rhetorical figure of Ahab was used to voice opposed political views. But as Alan Heimert in the past and Michael Paul Rogin in the present have pointed out, the other two principles in *Moby Dick*—the figures of Ishmael and the Leviathan— were also deployed, in all their rich biblical allusiveness, to voice contrary political positions on the issues of abolitionism, secession, and manifest destiny in the form of the American jeremiad.[17]

In our previous discussion we suggested that the loss by these rhetorical figures of the power to contain conflict in the jeremiad form resulted in the public's need to actualize this conflict in the Civil War. In *Moby Dick,* Melville, instead of actualizing this conflict, turns the rhetorical figures of Ahab, Ishmael, and the Leviathan, the orators used to contain it, into actual characters. Then in a massive alienation effect that estranges the second-person powers presuming to make up the public's mind for it, he lets them act out their felt alienation from the power legitimately to secure consent. Moreover, since Ahab and Ishmael share, as it were, the privileges of the second person, Melville revokes those privileges by exposing the compulsion at work in their rhetoric.

If we can imagine, in the broad context of a scene of cultural persuasion, the political conjuncture elemented by the different issues of slavery, secession, and expansionism, then if we imagine the three Ahabs, three Ishmaels, and three Leviathans used to word these issues into jeremiads, we can see how conflicted the space that was used to achieve consensus had become. If such cultural forms as the jeremiad, pure persuasion, the legend, and the tall tale had been used to "work through" the conflicts in the general will, Melville, in characterizing the contradictory relations among these forms, released the conflicts at work in the general will.

The "great tradition" of American literature founded by *American Renaissance* silenced these contradictory relations by converting all of them into the opposition between Ishmael's freedom and Ahab's totalitarian will. This opposition resolves the felt force of the contradiction by converting it into an "ideal conflict," a (Cold) War whose appropriate outcome has already been determined. In his analysis of the quarterdeck scene, however, Matthiessen displays a contradictory relation, a conflicting attitude unresolvable by the ideal opposition between Ahab and Ishmael. In his analysis, Matthiessen identifies Ahab as both totalitarian will and the freedom a self-reliant man must use to oppose it. Put another way, through the figure of Ahab Matthiessen reads the feared *compulsion* at work in what he formerly regarded as the sovereign freedom of the self-reliant man.

Ahab invites the ambivalence, for he seems to participate in two separate traditions. Following in the tradition of figures from the American jeremiad, Ahab gives revolution its sublime form, translating "personal" rebellion into an ideal to be honored rather than action to be performed. Following in the Emersonian tradition, Ahab finds his power through his failure to authorize it in anything but his personal will. As we have seen, the Emersonian tradition and the doctrine of self-reliance informing it worked to recover power for the "national spokesman" after it was lost by the form of the jeremiad.

This ambivalence in Ahab never puts him at odds with Ishmael, but it does, as Matthiessen points up, put him at odds with Starbuck, the one member of the crew who, in talking back to Ahab, voices the dissenting opinion the jeremiad exists to silence. Unlike the rest of the crew, Starbuck refused to hunt Moby Dick for gold. And Starbuck's refusal seems both rational and Christian. Although he could work to bring whale oil to the Nantucket market, for Ahab to "wreak vengeance" against a "dumb thing" like Moby Dick seems to Starbuck blasphemy.

Whichever tradition of consensus-formation we place him in, however, an analysis of what happens when Ahab responds to a dissenting opinion should disclose something about the dynamics of consensus-formation. In taking Starbuck "down a little lower layer," Ahab first makes Starbuck experience the limits of his rational Christianity. He begins with an implicit either/or: Either all visible objects are pasteboard marks informed by some deeper purpose, or else "there's nought beyond." This alternative stops Starbuck short. For if he kills whales for oil, they do not reveal God's glory. Instead these "dumb things" only represent Starbuck's need for capital, and Ahab's vengeance, in informing the whale with at least a human purpose, turns Starbuck into the blasphemer. For he prefers his capital to God's purposes. More importantly, Ahab brings Starbuck up against this recognition with such intensity that Starbuck displays malice toward Ahab. That is to say, Ahab, in his response, has put Starbuck in precisely the position Starbuck claims he cannot occupy. For more than anything else, Starbuck now feels all the rage he needs to kill Ahab. When Starbuck feels this, Ahab has him precisely where he wants him, in a state of mind enabling him to identify Ahab's rage with an impulse in his own inner life. Then, in a remarkable move, Ahab, after provoking Starbuck to "anger-glow," separates him from an anger *Ahab agrees to embody alone.* In other words, Ahab provokes his own reaction to the universe, a defiance grown out of rage, in Starbuck; then he recovers Starbuck's defiance as *his trial* and not the burden of a Christian man.

In his encounter with Starbuck, Ahab recapitulates the dynamics we faced at work in the "sovereign will" of the "national second person." He elicits an inner life, the rage against a potentially nihilistic universe. Then, having evoked this free inner life, he alienates it from Starbuck, who must deny it in order to remain himself. And Ahab "acts out" that inner life as his means of dominating the Starbuck who becomes "free" to deny this rebellious will in himself by witnessing it already thoroughly acted out in Ahab's extraordinary character.

That Ahab says all this in cadences borrowed from Shakespeare only underscores the "scenic" character of his separation from the crew. If he talks to the men at all, he talks to the men in a language that immediately encloses him in a theatrical scene: a theatrical frame, moreover, claiming all the "unapproachable" cultural power that Melville, in his review of Hawthorne, claimed Shakespeare wielded over the mob. Thus Ahab not only "acts out" and "ideally resolves" the principle of rebellion he evokes in all of the men, but he does so in a language so invested with cultural power that they can only be inspired by the cultural heights to which Ahab elevates their will to rebel. In short, Ahab embodies not only the crew's inner life but also the best means of articulating it.

Here the contrast between Melville's use of Shakespeare in the quarterdeck scene and Matthiessen's in his quarterdeck scene is illuminating. By translating Ahab's silencing of Starbuck's dissent into Shakespeare's blank verse, Matthiessen not only acknowledges the political power of Shakespeare's language. (Shakespeare, in the politics of canon formation, had, after all, functioned as

Matthiessen's means of securing English Renaissance validity for American Renaissance figures.) But he also reenacts Starbuck's scenario. For Ahab performs for Matthiessen the same function he performed for Starbuck: in embodying compulsion as his inner life alone, he releases Matthiessen from the need to find compulsion in the doctrine of self-reliance informing the body of his work.

But Ahab's very power to silence dissent also causes him to reexperience his sense of loss. Unlike the spokesmen for the American jeremiad, Ahab cannot depend on Divine Writ to sanction his words. Consequently, a dual recognition accompanies each act of persuasion: the terrible doubt that it may be without foundation, and the "experience" of his separation from another. Both recognitions remind him of the loss of his leg. It is Ahab's need to justify this sense of loss—to make it his, rather than God's or Fate's—that leads him to turn his will, which in each act of persuasion repeats that separation of his body from his leg, into the ground for his existence.

Indeed, all of Ahab's actions—his dependence on omens, black magic, thaumaturgy—work as regressions to a more fundamental power of the human will. They constitute his efforts to provide a basis *in* the human will for a rhetoric that has lost all other sanction. Ahab, in short, attempts to turn the coercion at work in his rhetoric into Fate, a principle of order in a universe without it. But since this will is grounded in the sense of loss, it is fated to perfect that loss in an act of total destruction.

That final cataclysmic image of total destruction motivated Matthiessen and forty years of Cold War critics to turn to Ishmael, who in surviving *must*, the logic would have it, have survived as the principle of America's freedom and who hands over to us our surviving heritage. When juxtaposed to Ahab, Ishmael is said to recover freedom in the midst of fixation; a sense of the present in a world in which Ahab's revenge makes the future indistinguishable from the past; and the free play of indeterminate possibility in a world forced to reflect Ahab's fixed meanings.

Given this juxtaposition, we should take the occasion to notice that if Ahab was a figure who ambivalently recalled the scene of

persuasion in the American jeremiad, Ishmael recalls nothing if not
the pure persuasion at work in Emerson's rhetoric. Like Emerson,
Ishmael uncouples the actions that occur from the motives giving
rise to them, thereby turning virtually all the events in the narrative
into an opportunity to display the powers of eloquence capable of
taking possession of them. Indeed, nothing and no one resist
Ishmael's power to convert the world that he sees into the forms
of rhetoric that he wants. The question remains, however, whether
Ishmael, in his need to convert all the facts in his world and all the
events in his life into a persuasive power capable of re-coining
them as the money of his mind, is possessed of a will any less
totalitarian than Ahab's. Is a will capable of moving from one
intellectual model to another—to seize each, to invest each with
the subjunctive power of his personality, then, in a display of rest-
lessness no eloquence can arrest, to turn away from each model as
if it existed only for this ever-unsatisfied movement of attention—
is such a will any less totalitarian, however indeterminate its local
exertions, than a will to convert all the world into a single struggle?

Since, in a certain sense, Ishmael puts his will to work by converting Ahab's terrifying legend into cadences familiar from the
tall tales, we might take this occasion to differentiate Ishmael's tall
tale from those we analyzed earlier. In telling his tale, the Ishmael
who was taken in by Ahab's rhetoric does not, as was the case
with other narrators of the tall tales, use the tale to work through
the excesses in Ahab's rhetoric. Instead, the extraordinary nature
of Ahab's words and deeds legitimizes elements of Ishmael's
narrative that might otherwise seem inflationary. As the figure
whose excesses in word and deed cause him literally to be read out
of Ishmael's narrative, Ahab turns into the figure who enables the
reader to rule out the charge of excess in Ishmael's rhetoric. Ishmael
occupies three different spaces in his narrative. As the victim of
Ahab's narrative, he exists as a third person; as the narrator of his
own tale, as a first person; and as the subject of such urgent
addresses as "Call me Ishmael," a second person. But since, as a
first-person narrator, he turns Ahab into the figure who has vic-
timized Ishmael, Ishmael does not have to be perceived as taking

anyone else in. Ishmael turns Ahab into both the *definitive third-person* victim and the perfect *first-person* victimizer. In perfecting both roles, Ahab becomes Ishmael's means of exempting his narrative in advance of the charge of trying to victimize anyone. Moreover, since, in Ishmael's case, first-person narratives always turn into pretexts for second-person sermons, Ahab, the locus for all false rhetoric, also becomes Ishamel's means of redeeming *his second person* by exempting it in advance from all charges of mystification.

As Ishmael's means of purifying his individual acts of persuasion of any actantial component, Ahab—in his conflation of victim and agent, motive and deed—also turns out to be the second-person *power:* the figure of will who, like the Andrew Jackson of legend mentioned earlier, performs actions absolutely indistinguishable from the motive powers (released by an orator's address), within Ishmael's rhetorical exercises. In Ishmael's rhetoric, each individual act of perception turns into the occasion for an exercise of persuasive power. Through Ahab's death, Ishmael of course exempts these occasions from any charge of coercion (which has been perfected by Ahab). The sensed loss of Ahab, however, results in another, less desirable state of affairs. In the loss of Ahab, Ishmael experiences his separation from the one figure in his narrative capable of realizing inspired words in matching deeds. Buried within Ishmael's display of remarkable oratorical power is his reiterated demand that the world be indistinguishable from the will of his words; buried within Ishmael's narrative is the one figure capable of making these words consequential. In reaction to the fate befalling Ahab, the man who would make deed as consequential as his words demanded, Ishmael retreats into endless local performances of rhetorical exercises, with each invested with the complaint that the world cannot be consequential enough. Each of these performances—these momentary indulgences in a sense of power superior to the given structures of the world—becomes Ishmael's means for the reappearance of the force if not the person of Ahab.

In speaking with the force of Ahab's demand for a world indistinguishable from human will but *free of* the consequences of that will, Ishmael can discover pleasure not quite in another world but in a *prior world,* in which the endless proliferation of possible deeds displaces the need for any definitive action. The pleasure in this prior world results from the economization of ends over means, and the capacity to experience this economy as pleasure (rather than frustration) also derives from Ahab. The fate befalling Ahab's decisive conversion of word into deed determines Ishmael's need for a realm in which the indeterminate play of endless possible actions overdetermines his *in*decision.

We can begin to understand all of this better when we turn to the crucial distinctions that critics during the Cold War draw between Ishmael and Ahab. In their view, Ishmael, in his rhetoric, frees us from Ahab's fixation by returning all things to their status as pure possibilities. What we now must add is that Ishmael has also invested all the rest of the world of fact with possibility, then invests possibility with the voice of conviction. When all the world turns out to be invested with the indeterminate interplay of possibility, it does not seem free but replicates what Ishmael called the hypos and what we call boredom: the need for intense action without any action to perform that motivated the Ishmael who felt the "drizzly November in his soul" to feel attracted to Ahab in the first place. This abreactive interpolation of an excess of indeterminacy between motive and act displaces Ahab's fixation, but in doing so causes Ishmael to develop a need for Ahab. In short, Ishmael's form of freedom does not oppose Ahab but compels him to need Ahab—not only as the purification of his style, but as the cure of his boredom. Only in Ahab's final act can the Ishmael who has in his rhetoric converted the external world into an exact replica of the restless displacements of endlessly mobile energies of attention that we formerly identified with the sovereign will find a means to give all these energies a final, fatal discharge. Said differently, Ahab's fatal, decisive deed permits Ishmael to feel the excessive force of *Ahab's Decision over*determine his exercises in indecision. Put more simply, Ahab's compulsion to decide *compels* Ishmael *not* to decide.

This discussion began with an acknowledgment of a rather

narrow concern: a personal failure to be persuaded by a certain reading of *Moby Dick*. I have attempted to justify this failure by locating similar failures in the work of F. O. Matthiessen and Sacvan Bercovitch, whose *American Renaissance* and *American Jeremiad* formed a consensus opposition through which this reading could continue to be *received* as canonical. Consequently this rather narrow concern opened up two extremely broad contexts: the scenes of cultural persuasion in Melville's and in our own time.

In terms of the foregoing discussion of *Moby Dick,* we can by way of summary say that Melville does not exercise so much as he exposes the compulsion at work in the scene of cultural persuasion in his own time. He does so, moreover, by disrupting the cultural apparatuses meant to conceal this compulsion. If the rhetoric of pure persuasion was used to "purify" the rhetoric of the American jeremiad of the charge of coercion, Melville, by featuring Ishmael's exploitation of Ahab as the means of exempting his rhetoric of "pure persuasion" from the charge of coercion, disrupts the "purification" ceremonies. Instead of "laundering" Ishmael's rhetoric, Ahab's actions seem burdened by the accumulation of the failures of Ishmael's words either to inspire or become deed.

During Melville's time, in which Ahab was a recognizable compilation of features from such familiar orators as Daniel Webster, Andrew Jackson, and Ralph Waldo Emerson, Ishmael did not arise as a figure of freedom. The constant tendency of Ishmael's rhetoric, located in a space filled with an inconsequentiality the reverse of Ahab's fatal consequence, led the majority of critics to conceive of what Melville called a "wicked book" as the work of madness. Either they had to conceive him as mad, or they had to reconceive the terms that permitted them to remain convinced of the power of their culture. It would take another scene of persuasion, with a quite different allocation of the relationship between will and action, to appropriate Ahab and Ishmael as means of corroborating its fundamental lesson. We might say that, having failed to be persuaded by the scene of persuasion in its time, *Moby Dick* reappeared in 1941 to persuade the world of the cultural power of the opposition between the free world and a totalitarian power.

Our previous discussion of the relation between everyday life and the Big Picture might lead us to the somewhat more restricted cultural work this act of including *Moby Dick* within a Cold War frame entails. But writing, during the Vietnam War, against any structure as inclusive as that of the *American Jeremiad,* Richard Poirier made the connection between the accumulation of cultural waste of everyday life during the Cold War and *Moby Dick* explicit. For Poirier, "the analytic rhetoric, the overt symbolic talk, the analysis, the allusiveness" of *Moby Dick* "don't envelop or clarify or organize the other elements of the book. Rather they are part of the 'heap' which befuddles every effort to locate a stabilizing reality."[18]

An earlier observation of Poirier's confirms our sense of the relation between Ahab and Ishmael by correlating Ahab's feeling "heaped" with Ishmael's endless reformulations. Then, however, Ahab's reaction to his complaint that Ishmael's whale of a narrative "heaps him" became Poirier's means of validating not simply Ishmael's destabilizing efforts, but any arduous energy of performance that resists stable meaning. "One must fight through the glitter and rubbish to express anything worthwhile, to express even the rubbish. A writer or anyone else can be called 'great' or 'noble' in my sense who sees the perpetual need for such fighting, who is forever unaccommodated, determinately 'unfinished.'"[19]

Poirier finds local validity for these contentions in a paragraph that, beginning with the claim "Americans can take some pride in *Moby Dick* not because it is in a way like *Ulysses* but rather because *Ulysses* is like *Moby Dick,*"[20] confirms the importance of *Moby Dick* for the canon of American literature. In order to validate either of these contentions, however, Poirier must silently rediscover the recognition that the whale "heaps him" not in Ahab but in Ishmael. Nowhere in *Moby Dick* does Ahab claim to feel *heaped* by Ishmael's rhetoric. Like everything else in that narrative, he is a product of one of Ishmael's rhetorical exercises.[21] Nowhere in *Moby Dick* does Ishmael arrive at the recognition that his rhetorical exercises enable him to work his way out of those stabilizing cultural structures (including those articulated in his own rhetorical exercises) formative of the "heap." In Poirier's work, Ishmael can sympathize with Ahab's sense of being heaped, but he cannot engage Ahab's solution. For Poirier, Ahab's solution, the *Big Decision* becomes indistinguishable from those other momentary "stays against confusion" we must perpetually fight against stabilizing into the meaning of our lives.

But Ahab would feel no less "heaped" by the endless proliferation of momentary stays, however energetically performed, than he does by the whale. He does not wish for a reiteration of local exertions of power. For Ahab, these local exertions, in the conversion of action back into potential for action, deprive him of the experience of action as consequential. That is of course part of Poirier's point. Ahab is what happens when an author demands that his local exertions have other than local consequences. Local resistance to Ahab's Colossal Act justifies the endless reformulations of a performing self.

Poirier has of course made explicit the relationship between the opposition in *Moby Dick* and what we have called a scene of cultural persuasion. He has invested this scene with great cultural force. When situated within such empowering performative events as boxing matches, bullfights, and battle campaigns, the performing self can feel persuaded that his acts are triumphant conversions of recalcitrant, chaotic cultural material into forms of conquest. But what enables the performing self to remain persuaded that the endless repetition of local performances will be a continuing source of delight? What enables the performing self to remain convinced of the power of local performances, if not completely independent of historical consequence, then independent enough to demand that those consequences only turn back into the chaotic raw material demanding new performances? Why does the performer feel persuaded of the cultural power of a performance that (in the obsessive need to reconceive prior performance as part of the waste in need of conversion) appears indistinguishable from a permanent dress rehearsal?

In all of these cases, the performing self remains persuaded because Ahab, or some other version of the conflation of definitive

action and total destruction, looms as the alternative. In response
to the destructive consequences of this alternative, Poirier devises
what we might call provisional actions. Intermediate between
"play acts" we go to the theater to watch and definitive actions
we realize in our engagements with an actual world, these provisional actions derive their power by "acting out" (thereby "working through") the need for their actualization. In place of either a
theater or an actual world, the "performing self" deploys these
provisional actions in what Poirier calls "a world elsewhere," and
this scene, in its turn, derives all of its force by displacing all the
deadening, because reified, forms of everyday life.

If our previous discussion of everyday life enables us to recognize anything, however, it is that the forms of contemporary life,
subjected as they are to endless obsolescence procedures, never
achieve either the stability or the definitive placements a world
elsewhere exists to oppose. Instead of opposing the monstrously
alienating, impersonal forces supervising (in the name of progress)
the outmoding operations at the core of contemporary life, such
constructs as the "performing self" and "a world elsewhere"
enable the individual to reexperience the "modernization" of
everyday life within a personal context. Within this context some
remarkable reversals can transpire. The decomposition inherent to
seemingly every construct in contemporary life can turn out to be
the result not of impersonal forces but of an individual's rebellion
against the oppression exercised by stable forms, the sensed powerlessness in relation to forces in excess of the power of any one
individual to control that can turn into the discovery of an individual's freedom from the need to master, and the impossibility of
deciding from among a seemingly infinite number of alternative
variables that can lead to the celebration of the free play of indeterminacy. What underwrites each of these reversals is the prior
designation of the opponent not as the random eventfulness of
everyday life but as the "work" of a totalitarian will.

When we separate the gigantic rhetorical figures of Ahab and
Ishmael from the forces they represent, we do not find a totalitarian will, however we may wish to. Instead we find what Poirier

calls the compositions and decompositions of contemporary life. Such constructs as the "performing self" and "a world elsewhere" provide a mode of experiencing the impersonal forces of modernization as if an occasion to engage in an actual battle. That is to say, the "performing self" and "a world elsewhere" constitute imaginative constructs capable of appropriating the Cold War opposition as if it were the "lived experience" of contemporary life.

Previously we described the Cold War as a second scene capable, at any moment, of displacing everyday life to the backstage. We might now say that when "a world elsewhere" takes center stage, everyday life, with its massive accumulation of potentially deadening shocks, must move backstage. If Poirier's constructs "a world elsewhere," the "performing self," and what we have called "provisional action" recall the work of Emerson, they should. Poirier is the only critic writing today who can claim a place in the Emersonian tradition. Through a rhetoric of "pure persuasion," Emerson permitted the nation to remain with a scene, enlivening out of the sheer expansiveness of "forever young" revolutionary impulses. He did so, moreover, at precisely the moment in the nation's history when the conflicts that the jeremiad form of the "other scene" no longer could contain demanded a Civil War to resolve.

Poirier moves from an opposite direction. Among the young men Matthiesen's *American Renaissance* addressed in 1941, Poirier fought in the Second World War pitting a free world against a totalitarian power. The untapped reserve power in the great antagonism that put a world to war, gets condensed and reenacted in every scene of the endless campaign informing *A World Elsewhere.*[22] When conceived in terms of that conflict, every cultural encounter becomes an occasion to recover the human resources necessary to exercise the freedom threatened by a totalizing power. Every engagement in the culture as a place where that struggle can repeat itself can turn into either a battle exploit (while the encounter transpires) or little more than a battlefield shock (once the encounter has ended) no sooner experienced than forgotten in the perpetual campaign to keep a world free.

The opposition the World War resolved into a Cold War peace, in other words, reenacts itself as the drama on the cultural scene of persuasion in which the everyday life is what we might call over-appropriated. While the Cold War replaces the revolutionary war as the scene in which liberty gets enacted, the opposition informing both of those scenes remains constant. In view of the permanence of this opposition that preoccupies all the positions any opposition can occupy, we might remind ourselves of its difference from the relationship at work in *Moby Dick.* For there, as we have seen, Ishmael's freedom does not oppose Ahab's will, however totalitarian that may appear. Instead Ishmael's expansive rhetoric depends on the groundlessness of Ahab's exercise for its legitimacy. In *Moby Dick,* Melville does not alienate opposition by positioning all opinions within this conflict; instead he "works through" the vicious circularities informing the conflicted will at work in Ahab and Ishmael. Instead of letting Ishmael appear *opposed* to Ahab he reveals the ways in which Ishmael's obsession depends on Ahab's compulsion. If the Cold War consensus would turn *Moby Dick* into a figure through whom it would speak its own totalizing logic, Melville, as it were, speaks back through the same figure, to alienate the obsessive-compulsive character capable of putting a totalizing logic to work. Should we begin to hear the voice that can speak when such totalizing opposition has been "worked through," that voice will not speak through either Ahab or Ishmael, but will speak words neither their rhetoric nor the Cold War logic can acknowledge: "I prefer not."[23]

NOTES

1. This Cold War logic may recall what Gramsci called hegemony in the Cold War's capacity to bring alignment about, through the intersection of a variety of different lines of intellectual, emotional, and psychological force. But what differentiates the Cold War drama is its ability to empty out any thematic value. So that the Cold War releases what we might call the *force* of persuasion, a force that, like prejudice, works best by economizing on the

work of choosing. When within the Cold War arena, we feel "chosen" as a result of the choices we (do not need to) make.

2. The progress followed here is interesting: the Cold War appears first as a mode of structuring an otherwise chaotic world, but the *neutral* binary opposition informing the structure becomes charged, and the victory of one side in relation to the other promises itself as the outcome—but the outcome *within* the opposition.

What we call deconstruction finds acceptance consequent to the prior reduction of the world into this superopposition. But the inverting, displacing operations of deconstruction do not dislodge the structure so much as they rationalize it. In acting out the logic of this opposition as if it were a revolutionary activity, deconstruction only maintains its cultural power.

3. Here we begin to acknowledge the "absolute" power of the paradigm. Having already made *all* the decisions, it enables the individual to conceive the state of being deprived of choice as the freedom from the need to choose.

4. See Sacvan Bercovitch, *The American Jeremiad* (Madison: University of Wisconsin Press, 1978).

5. Theodore Parker, *A Sermon of the Mexican War: Preached . . . June 25th, 1848* (Boston, 1848), p. 1.

6. For a compilation of the other jeremiads authorized by the Ahab figure, see Alan Heimert, "*Moby Dick* and American Political Symbolism," *American Quarterly* 15 (Winter 1963):498–534. Heimert compiles this information with a remarkable sense of the interrelationship, but he does not, I think, have much sensitivity to the explosive power of the material he compiles.

7. The use of the "dramatic stage" as a context in which to discuss social and cultural issues presupposes the relation between social life and *theatrical distraction,* a relationship that may in itself serve certain political interests. We begin to sense the power of this context when we notice how an individual who feels alienated from himself when in society can, through *the* dramatic metaphor, reexperience alienation from self as the discovery of an opportunity to perform a variety of roles. The metaphor, however, cannot address the dramatic actor's distress over the number of roles inviting performance.

8. See F. O. Matthiessen, *American Renaissance: Art and Expression in the Age of Emerson and Whitman* (New York: Oxford University Press, 1941), p. 426.

9. Ibid., p. 430.

10. Ibid., p. 307. Although this observation appears in Matthiessen's discussion of Hawthorne, I would argue that Melville and Hawthorne serve as locations for Matthiessen's dissent from the "vital doctrines" of Emerson and Whitman.

11. See *Selections from Ralph Waldo Emerson*, ed. Stephen Whicher (New York: Houghton Mifflin, 1960), p. 146. In regard to the use of "man" and the masculine pronoun, Emerson wrote in the terms of his day.

12. Garfield's account is cited in Ralph Leslie Rusk's *The Life of Ralph Waldo Emerson* (New York: Charles Scribner's Sons, 1949), p. 385. Conway's can be found in *Remembrances of Emerson* (New York: Cooke, 1903) and John Jay Chapman's in "Emerson," in *The Shock of Recognition,* ed. Edmund Wilson (New York: Doubleday, 1943), p. 615.

13. *Walden and Other Writings of Henry David Thoreau,* ed. B. Atkinson (New York: Random House, Modern Library, 1937), pp. 357, 380, 386.

14. De Tocqueville is cited in Matthiessen, *American Renaissance,* p. 20.

15. Walt Whitman, *Complete Poetry and Selected Prose,* ed. James E. Miller, Jr. (Boston: Houghton Mifflin, 1959), p. 54.

16. Of course Emerson also permits a series of conflicting voices to speak in his essays, but in effectively depriving them of a context in which the voice can appear as anything other than a conflict *in voice,* he effectively converts these modulations in voice back into the motive powers of pure persuasion.

17. See Heimert in the essay cited earlier and Michael Paul Rogin in *Subversive Genealogy: The Politics and Art of Herman Melville* (New York: Alfred A. Knopf, 1983). Rogin needs to generate a Freudo-Marxist context in which to snare Melville, but this context reveals more of Rogin's nostalgia for the reappearance of that context (in something other than his father's political period) than it reveals about either the politics or the art of Melville.

18. See Richard Poirier, *The Performing Self: Compositions and Decompositions in the Languages of Contemporary Life* (New York: Oxford University Press, 1971), p. 10.

19. Ibid., p. 11.

20. Ibid., p. 10.

21. Ishmael makes clear the connection when he evokes Ahab as his ideal addressee: "Oh, Ahab! What shall be grand in thee, it must needs be plucked at from the skies, and dived for in the deep, and featured in the unbodied air."

22. Here I wish to suggest that the sense of freedom Poirier found released in the act of writing by Emerson and Thoreau is inherited by the performing self in the twentieth century. Although that freedom manifests itself in and as the activities of writing, the context of that writing—the conventions of a stabilized world—makes the sensed liberation possible. None of these comments, however, addresses Poirier's readings of individual writings, which, I would argue, establish a rhetorical field of power that marks, maintains, and increases cultural authority, unanswerable to the notions of either a world elsewhere or a performing self.

23. In referring to "Bartleby," I want to mark what we would call the zero degree of rhetorical power: a zero line of dissent that makes room for an exchange that cannot be assimilated by the dominant scene of rhetoric.

Walter Benn Michaels

Romance and Real Estate

experience hath shewn, that property best answers the purposes of civil life, especially in commercial countries, when its transfer and circulation are totally free and unrestrained.

—Blackstone, "Of Title by Alienation,"
Commentaries on the Laws of England

Visiting Salem in 1904, Henry James asked to be shown the "House of the Seven Gables" and was led by his guide to an "object" so "shapeless," so "weak" and "vague," that at first sight he could only murmur "Dear, dear, are you very sure?" In an instant, however, James and the guide ("a dear little harsh, intelligent, sympathetic American boy") had together "thrown off" their sense that the house "wouldn't do at all" by reminding themselves that there was, in general, no necessary "relation between the accomplished thing for . . . art" and "those other quite equivocal things" that may have suggested it, and by noting in particular how Hawthorne's "admirable" novel had so "vividly" forgotten its "origin or reference."[1] Hawthorne would presumably have seen the point of James's response; his own Preface warned readers against trying to "assign an actual locality to the imaginary events" of the narrative, and for the romance as a genre he claimed an essential "latitude" with respect to reference, a latitude not allowed novelists, who aimed at a "very minute fidelity . . . [to] experience."[2] The distinction drawn here between the novel and the romance, between a fundamentally mimetic use of language and one that questions the primacy of reference, has, of course, become canonical in American literary criticism even though (or perhaps just because) its meaning remains so uncertain. Does Hawthorne intend the romance (as some recent critics think) to pose a self-consciously fictional alternative to the social responsibilities of the novel? Or does he intend the romance (as some other even more recent critics think) to provide in its radical fictionality a revolutionary alternative to the social conservativism of the novel?[3] The last paragraph of the Preface suggests that neither of these formulations may be correct.

Looking for the Seven Gables in Salem, Hawthorne says, is a mistake because it "exposes the Romance to an inflexible and exceedingly dangerous species of criticism, by bringing (its) fancy pictures into positive contact with the realities of the moment" (3). The implication seems to be that the romance (unlike the novel) is too fragile to stand comparison with reality, but Hawthorne immediately goes on to suggest that the difference between the romance and the novel is perhaps less a matter of their relation to reality than of their relation to real estate. He has constructed *The House of the Seven Gables* "by laying out a street that infringes upon nobody's private rights, and appropriating a lot of land which had no visible owner, and building a house, of materials long in use for constructing castles in the air" (3). The romance, then, is to be imagined as a kind of property, or rather as a relation to property. Where the novel may be said to touch the real by expropriating it and so violating someone's "private rights," the romance asserts a property right that does not threaten and so should not be threatened by the property rights of others. The romance, to put it another way, is the text of clear and unobstructed title.

THE MONEY POWER

Of course, haunted house stories (like *The House of the Seven Gables*) usually involve some form of anxiety about ownership. Frequently this anxiety concerns actual financial cost. Stephen King, the author of *The Shining*, has put this powerfully in a discussion of the movie *The Amityville Horror*. "What it's about," he says,

> is a young couple who've never owned a house before; Margot Kidder is the first person in her family actually to have owned property. And all these things start to go wrong—and the horrible part is not that they can't get out, but that they're going to *lose the house.* There was some point where things were falling, and the door banging, and rain was coming in,

and goop was running down the stairs, and behind me, in the little movie
house in Bridgton, this woman, she must have been 60, was in this kind of
ecstasy, moaning, "Think of the bills, think of the bills." And that's where
the horror of that movie is.[4]

Which is not to say that the financial implications of the haunted
house are limited to the actual repair costs of the physical damage
done by the ghosts. Think of the plight of the Amityville couple
as investors in real estate; having risked everything to get themselves into the spectacularly inflationary market of 1975, they
find themselves owning the only house on Long Island whose value
is declining. The only one for a few years, anyway, until rising
interest rates—as intangible as ghosts but even more powerful—
would begin to produce a spectral effect on housing prices everywhere. It may be worth noting that in 1850 Hawthorne was writing
at the start of one of the peak periods in nineteenth-century
American land speculation, a period in which, according to the
agricultural historian Paul Wallace Gates, "touched by the fever of
land speculation, excited people throughout the country borrowed
to the extent of their credit for such investments."[5]

But the actual price of real estate may not finally be as crucial
to the haunted house as the fact of ownership itself and the questions that necessarily accompany that fact: who has title? what
legitimates that title? what guarantees it? Again, contemporary
examples abound. Because of certain "impediments" on their
house, the Lutzes in Amityville never did get clear title although
they had what their lawyer called "the best that could be fashioned
for their mortgage."[6] And another movie, *Poltergeist,* centers on
what is in effect a title dispute between a real estate development
company and the corpses who inhabit the bulldozed cemetery the
developer builds on. But title disputes have also a more intimate
connection to Hawthorne and to *The House of the Seven Gables.*
The most prominent and respectable witch brought to trial before
Hawthorne's ancestor, the "persecuting" magistrate John Hathorne,
was an old woman named Rebecca Nurse, whose family were comparative newcomers to Salem, much resented by the old and increasingly impoverished villagers. The Nurses had bought land from

James Allen (land inherited by him from the Endicotts) and were paying for it in twenty yearly installments. In 1692, when Rebecca was accused, they had only "six more years to go before the title was theirs," but the villagers still thought of them as *arrivistes* and continued to call their place "the Allen property."[7] Hathorne was fleetingly touched by Rebecca's respectability and by her claim to be "innocent and clear" of the charges against her, but he held her for trial anyway and in the end she was one of the first witches hanged. The day of Rebecca's hanging is remembered by *The House of the Seven Gables* in Maule's curse on the Pyncheons, "God will give you blood to drink"—the dying words of Rebecca's fellow victim, Sarah Good. More importantly, Hawthorne revives the connection between witchcraft and quarrels over property by beginning his narrative with a title dispute. Owner-occupant Matthew Maule, who "with his own toil . . . had hewn out of the primal forest . . . [a] garden-ground and homestead," is dispossessed by the "prominent and powerful" Colonel Pyncheon, "who asserted plausible claims to the proprietorship of this . . . land on the strength of a grant from the legislature" (7). Maule, of course, is executed for witchcraft, while Pyncheon leads the pack of executioners.

In one sense, this reworking of the witch trials is a little misleading; as Hawthorne himself notes, one of the few redeeming qualities of the witch hunters was "the singular indiscrimination with which they persecuted, not merely the poor and aged as in former judicial massacres, but people of all ranks, their own equals, brethren, and wives" (8). But the Pyncheon persecution of the Maules does not follow this model. Indeed, it precisely inverts the pattern described in Boyer and Nissenbaum's extraordinary *Salem Possessed: The Social Origins of Witchcraft,* where the accusers are shown to have been characteristically worse off socially and economically than the accused. Hawthorne does not, however, represent the struggle between Pyncheons and Maules merely as a conflict between the more and less powerful or even in any simple way as a conflict over a piece of land. He presents it instead as a conflict between two different modes of economic activity and in this he not only anticipates recent historians' findings but begins the complicated process of articulating his own defense of property.

The devil in Massachusetts, according to Boyer and Nissenbaum, was "emergent mercantile capitalism."[8] Hawthorne understood the question in terms more appropriate to someone whose political consciousness had been formed during the years of Jacksonian democracy. Maule embodies a Lockean legitimation of property by labor whereas the Pyncheons, with their pretensions to nobility, are something like old-world aristocrats. Except that the pre-Revolutionary fear of a titled aristocracy had, during the Jackson years, been replaced by the fear of a "money aristocracy," and Judge Pyncheon is certainly more capitalist than nobleman. From this standpoint, the difference between Maule and Pyncheon is less a difference between bourgeois and aristocrat than between those whom Jackson called "the agricultural, the mechanical, and the laboring classes" and those whom he called the "money power." And yet, *The House of the Seven Gables* by no means enacts a Jacksonian confrontation between the "people" and those who sought to exercise a "despotic sway" over them. Instead the fate of property in *House* suggests the appeal of a title based on neither labor nor wealth and hence free from the risk of appropriation.

"In this republican country," Hawthorne writes, "amid the fluctuating waves of our social life, somebody is always at the drowning-point" (38). This "tragedy," he thinks, is felt as "deeply . . . as when an hereditary noble sinks below his order." Or rather, "more deeply; since with us, rank is the grosser substance of wealth and a splendid establishment, and has no spiritual existence after the death of these but dies hopelessly along with them." The central point here, that America is a country where (as a French observer put it) "material property rapidly disappears,"[9] is, perhaps, less important than the implied comparison between the impoverished capitalist and the dispossessed aristocrat. The capitalist who loses everything loses everything, whereas the nobleman, losing everything material, retains his nobility, which has a "spiritual existence." This title cannot be bought or sold; unlike the land you have "hewn out of the forest," it cannot be stolen either.

Aristocracy's claim to land is unimpaired by the inability to enforce that claim. Indeed, it is, in a certain sense strengthened, or at least purified, since the assertion of what Blackstone calls the "mere right of property," a right that stands independent of any right of possession, is the assertion of a right that is truly inalienable: it cannot be exchanged for anything else, it cannot be taken from you, it cannot even be given away.

Such a claim to property has from the start its place in *The House of the Seven Gables;* the Preface's "castles in the air" suggest in their immateriality a parallel between romance and the property rights of impoverished aristocrats. And, in the text itself, what Hawthorne calls the Pyncheons' "impalpable claim" to the rich territory of Waldo County in Maine repeats this structure. Although the "actual settlers" of this land "would have laughed at the idea" of the Pyncheons asserting any "right" to it, the effect of their title on the Pyncheons themselves is to cause "the poorest member of the race to feel as if he inherited a kind of nobility" (19). This pretension is treated somewhat nervously by Hawthorne's text as a kind of atavistic joke, but the principle on which it is based—title so perfect that it is immunized from expropriation—was by no means completely anachronistic in the 1850s. For example, antislavery polemicists like Harriet Beecher Stowe and William Goodell admitted the comparative superiority of those slave states and societies where, as Goodell put it, slaves are treated as "real estate" in the sense that they are "attached to the soil they cultivate, partaking therewith all the restraints upon voluntary alienation to which the possessor of the *land* is liable, and they cannot be seized or sold by creditors for the satisfaction of the debts of the owner."[10] Of course, it could be argued that this restraint upon alienation should itself be considered a feudal relic, reflecting primarily a nostalgia for the time when land had not yet been transformed into a commodity and thus Pyncheons and slaveholders both could be seen as throwbacks. But, in fact, the notion of inalienable title was central also to one of the most radically progressive social movements of the 1840s and 1850s, the "land for the landless" agitation (opposed by southern slaveholders and northern capitalists both) that culminated in the Homestead Act of 1862.

At the heart of the homestead movement was the conviction that the land should belong to those who worked it and not to the banks and speculators. Attempting to protect themselves from speculation, the most radical reformers urged that homestead land be made inalienable since obviously land that could not be bought or sold could not be speculated upon either. This attempt failed but Congress did, in fact, require that "no land acquired under the provisions of (the Homestead Act) should in any event become liable to the satisfaction of any debt contracted prior to the issuing of the patent."[11] Thus homestead lands, like slaves in Louisiana, represented at least a partial escape from alienability. And, indeed, the desire for such an escape was so strong that Homestead Act propagandists were sometimes willing to sacrifice their Maule-like claim to property through labor for a Pyncheon-like claim to the status of an absentee landlord. In a pamphlet entitled *Vote Yourself a Farm,* the pamphleteer reminds his readers that "if a man have a house and home of his own, though it be a thousand miles off, he is well received in other people's houses; while the homeless wretch is turned away. The *bare right* to a farm, though you should never go near it, would save you from many an insult. Therefore, Vote yourself a farm."[12] In effect, the Pyncheons have voted themselves a farm, or rather, more powerfully, the bare right to one. Hawthorne himself, figuring the romance as uncontested title and inalienable right, has sought in the escape from reference the power of that bare right. His "castles in the air" of the Preface are equally Hepzibah Pyncheon's "castles in the air" (65); her "shadowy claims to princely territory." And her "fantasies" of a "gentility" beyond the reach of "commercial speculations" are his claims to a "street that infringes upon nobody's" rights and to "a lot of land" without any "visible owner." Even the map of Waldo that hangs on Hepzibah's kitchen wall images the security of romance's bare right; "grotesquely illuminated with pictures of Indians and wild beasts, among which was seen a lion" (33), the map's geography is, Hawthorne says, as "fantastically awry" as its natural history. It is itself one of those "fancy-pictures" that perish if "brought into contact" with reality, an antimimetic map, charting a way out of republican fluctuation and novelistic imitation. For if the romance seeps out of the Preface and into the text as an impalpable claim to impalpable property, the novel too embodies an ongoing relation to property, in the form of certain "mistakes" provoked by the lies of mimesis. The novel's commercial world consists of "magnificent shops" with "immense panes of plate glass," with "gorgeous fixtures," with "vast and complete assortments of merchandize," above all, with "noble mirrors . . . doubling all this wealth by a brightly burnished vista of unrealities" (48). We are unable to see through these unrealities just as we are unable to see through those other "big, heavy, solid unrealities such as gold, landed estate . . . and public honors" (229). Hawthorne here conceives of mass production as a form of mimesis and of the factories that make these stores possible as novels producing the realistically unreal. At the same time, the novel is a figure for appropriation and for those men (like the aristocrat turned capitalist Judge Pyncheon) who "possess vast ability in grasping, and arranging, and appropriating to themselves" those unrealities. In fact, the mirror of capitalism is itself reproduced in such men whose own "character," "when they aim at the honors of a republic" (130) becomes only an "image . . . reflected in the mirror of public opinion" (232). Before the Revolution, "the great man of the town was commonly called King" (63); now he must make himself over into a facsimile of the people. They see themselves reflected in him and he, "resolutely taking his idea of himself from what purports to be his image" (232), sees himself reflected in them. Only "loss of property and reputation," Hawthorne says, can end this riot of mimesis and bring about "true self-knowledge."

Judge Pyncheon, who looking within himself sees only a mirror, never seeks such self-knowledge; and the novel, aiming at a "very minute fidelity" to the "ordinary course of man's experience," never seeks it either—its goal is the department store doubling of unrealities. Only the romance, with its dedication to "the truth of

the human heart," and, in the text itself, only the daguerreotypist
Holgrave can represent the "secret character" behind the mirror
and restore appropriated property to its rightful owner. It is, of
course, extraordinary that Holgrave who inveighs against all property should come to represent its legitimation, and it is perhaps
even more extraordinary that the photograph, almost universally
acclaimed in the 1850s as the perfection of mimesis, should come
to represent an artistic enterprise hostile to imitation. To understand these reversals, we need to look a little more closely at the
technology of imitation and at the social conditions in which that
technology and the romance itself were developed.

Holgrave's career, says Hawthorne, was like "a romance on the
plan of Gil Blas," except that Gil Blas, "adapted to American society
and manners, would cease to be a romance" (176). Although
only twenty-one, Holgrave had been (among other things) a school-
master, a salesman, and a dentist. His current occupation, daguerreotypist is, he tells Phoebe, no more "likely to be permanent than
any of the preceding ones" (177). According to Hawthorne, such
mobility is typical of the "experience of many individuals among
us, who think it hardly worth the telling" (176), and certainly too
ordinary to be the stuff of romance. Hawthorne exaggerates, of
course, but not much. Several recent historians have noted the high
degree of geographic mobility in the 1840s and '50s, mostly among
young men who, for economic reasons, frequently changed locations and jobs. This phenomenon, according to Robert Doherty,
was particularly noticeable in major commercial centers like Salem
where it was associated also with increased social hierarchism. In
rural agricultural areas, young men tended to stay put and the distribution of property was comparatively even. In towns like Salem,
however, "commerce and manufacturing produced great inequal-
ities of wealth,"[13] and over one-third of Salem's population in the
fifties consisted of transients. Most of these were propertyless
young men whose geographic mobility was produced by hopes of
a corresponding economic mobility. Sometimes these hopes were
gratified. Many men, Doherty suggests, "spent a period of youth-
ful wandering and then settled in at about age 30 and began to

accumulate property."[14] Many more, however, "failed to gain even minimal material success." Some of these "propertyless . . . men stayed in town," Doherty writes, some "drifted from place to place, but all were apparent casualties of a social system which denied them property."[15]

The development of such an underclass had obvious social significance, and it suggests also ways in which a career like Holgrave's might not only be inappropraite for romance by virtue of its ordinariness but would even constitute a reproach to the commitment to property on which the romance is based. For a real-life Holgrave in Salem in 1851 stood a three-to-one chance of becoming what Doherty calls a "casualty," never accumulating any property and remaining stuck forever at the bottom of an increasingly stratified society. Hawthorne's Holgrave, needless to say, escapes this fate. Like only a few real-life young men, he rises from "penniless youth to great wealth," and one might perhaps interpret this rise as Hawthrone's ideological intervention on behalf of the openness of American society.

Except that, as we have seen, what made Hawthorne most nervous about American society was precisely its openness, its hospitality to fluctuation.[16] In this respect, the actual economic mobility of life in Salem, the fact that some men rose (according to Doherty, about 23%) and that some men fell (about 13%) would be infinitely more disturbing to Hawthorne than the existence of a permanent class of the propertyless. Inalienable rights can be neither lost nor acquired—how then can we explain Holgrave's happy ending, his sudden rise to property. One clue is that he does not actually earn his wealth, he marries it. Which is not to say that Hawthorne is being ironic about his hero's merits. Just the opposite. The whole point here is that property that has been earned is just as insecure (and, in the end, as illegitimate) as property that has been appropriated by some capitalist trick. Thus, for Hawthorne, the accumulation of property must be remade into an accession to property, and the social meaning of Holgrave's career turns out to be that it is not really a career at all. His period of wandering gives him instead the chance to display a stability of character that provides a kind of psychological legitimation for the fact of owner-ship: "amid all his personal vicissitudes," Hawthorne writes, Hol-grave had "never lost his identity . . . he had never violated the innermost man" (177). Like the romance itself which, despite its apparent freedom from the responsibilities of the novel, "must rigidly subject itself to laws" (1), Holgrave appears "lawless" but in fact follows a "law of his own" (85). Anchoring property not in work but in character, he defuses both the threat posed by the young transients who failed to acquire property (Hawthorne simply legislates them out of existence) and the threat posed by the tran-sients who did acquire property (since he makes that acquisition a function not of social mobility but of the fixed character of the "innermost man"). Apparently a pure product of the "republican" world of fluctuation, Holgrave turns out instead to embody the unchanging truth of romance.

But if Holgrave's career offers Hawthorne the opportunity to transform the social meaning of the new class of landless transients, Holgrave's art, the daguerreotype, hits even closer to home and requires an even more spectacular inversion. The terms of this inver-sion are quickly apparent in Holgrave's claim that the daguerreo-type, despite its apparent preoccupation with "the merest surface," "actually brings out the secret character with a truth that no painter would ever venture upon" (91). It was, of course, far more usual for writers of the forties and fifties to make just the opposite point. The "unrivalled precision" of the daguerreotype and the paper photograph, painters were warned, "renders exact imitation no longer a miracle of crayon or palette; these must now create as well as reflect . . . bring out the soul of the individual and of the landscape, or their achievements will be neglected in favor of the facsimiles obtainable through sunshine and chemistry."[17] For Hawthorne, however, the *daguerreotype* penetrates to the soul, seeing through republican honors to "the man himself."

The triumph of the daguerreotype in *House* is the portraits (Hawthorne's and Holgrave's) of Judge Pyncheon dead. Early daguerreotype portraits were often marred by a certain blurriness; the very oldest surviving portrait (John Draper's picture of his sister Catherine, taken in 1840) was sent to an English photographer accompanied by apologies for the "indistinctness" that results, Draper wrote, from any movement, even "the inevitable motions of the respiratory muscles." But where "inanimate objects are depicted," Draper went on to remark with satisfaction, "the most rigid sharpness can be obtained."[18] Holgrave's job is thus made easier by the fact that the judge has stopped breathing but the real point here is that the daguerreotype always sees through to the fixed truth behind the fluctuating movements of the "public character." It is as if the subject of a daguerreotype is in some sense already dead, the truth about him fixed by the portrait just as the actual "fact of a man's death," Hawthorne writes in connection with Pyncheon's posthumous reputation, "often seems to give people a truer idea of his character" (310). The daguerreotype, always a representation of death, is also death's representative.

As is the romance. In a passage that anticipates by some forty years Henry James's famous remarks on "the coldness, the thinness, the blankness" of Hawthorne's America, the French journalist Michel Chevalier was struck by the absence in America of those elements that in Europe served, as he put it, to "stir" the "nerves." James would miss the sovereign, the court, little Norman churches; the effect of American life on a "French imagination," he thought, "would probably be appalling."[19] But Chevalier was thrilled not appalled. He did miss what he called the "sensual gratifications"; "wine, women, and the display of princely luxury . . . cards and dice." But, Chevalier says, the American has a way of more than making up for the absence of traditional stimulants; seeking "the strong emotions which he requires to make him feel life," the American "has recourse to business. . . . He launches with delight into the ever-moving sea of speculation. One day, the wave raises him to the clouds . . . the next day he disappears between the crests of the billows. . . . If movement and the quick succession of sensations and ideas constitute life, here one lives a hundredfold more than elsewhere."[20]

If the cold blankness of American life figured for James the difficulty of finding something to represent, that blankness was to

Chevalier the setting for a business life of "violent sensations," and to Hawthorne, the violent movements of business were the violence of mimetic representation itself. The world of the "money power," Andrew Jackson warned in his Farewell Address, is "liable to great and sudden fluctuations" which render "property insecure and the wages of labor unsteady and uncertain."[21] "The soil itself, or at least the houses, partake in the universal instability," Chevalier exclaimed.[22] Hawthorne required the romance to fix this instability, to render property secure. Where representations are unrealities produced by mirrors, the romance represents nothing, not in compensation for the coldness of American life but in opposition to its terrible vitality. Business makes the American "feel life," but that life is a mimetic lie; whereas "death," Hawthorne says, "is so genuine a fact that it excludes falsehood" (310). Celebrating the death—one might better call it the execution—of Judge Pyncheon, the romance joins the witch hunt, the attempt to imagine an escape from capitalism, defending the self against possession, property against appropriation, and choosing death over life.

THE SLAVE POWER

The conjunction of death and secure property has its place in another text of 1851, one intended not as a romance but, in its author's words, as a "representation . . . of real incidents, of actions really performed, of words and expressions really uttered."[23] Riding by his slave quarters late at night, Simon Legree hears the singing of a "musical tenor voice": " 'When I can read my title clear / To mansions in the skies' " Uncle Tom sings, " 'I'll bid farewell to every fear / And wipe my weeping eyes.' "[24] Tom is preparing for the martyrdom toward which Legree will soon help him, and his sense of heaven as a "Home" to which he has clear title is barely metaphoric. Slaves, of course, were forbidden to own property but Stowe thought of them as by definition the victims of theft. Slavery, "appropriating one set of human beings to the use and improvement of another" (2:21), robbed a man of himself, and so freedom involved above all the restitution of property. Only in death did the slave's title to himself become "sure"; only in death did Uncle Tom's cabin actually become his.

That freedom in the mid-nineteenth century, the period that C. B. Macpherson has called the "zenith" of "possessive market society,"[25] should be understood as essentially a property relation is not, in itself, surprising, but it does provide in *Uncle Tom's Cabin* some unexpected and little-noted points of emphasis. When, for example, George Shelby frees his slaves, he tells them that their lives will go on pretty much as before but with the "advantage" that, in case of his "getting in debt or dying," they cannot be "taken up and sold" (2:309). The implication here is that Shelby himself would never sell them and, in fact, voluntary sales play a comparatively minor role in Stowe's depiction of the evils of slavery. A paragraph from Goodell's *The American Slave Code* helps explain why: "this feature of liability to seizure for the master's debt," Goodell writes,

> is, in many cases, more terrific to the slave than that which subjects him to the master's voluntary sale. The slave may be satisfied that his master is not willing to sell him—that it is not for his interest or convenience to do so. He may be conscious that he is, in a manner, necessary to his master or mistress. . . . He may even confide in their Christian benevolence and moral principle, or promise that they would not sell him. . . . But all this affords him no security or ground of assurance that his master's creditor will not seize him . . . against even his master's entreaties. Such occurrences are too common to be unnoticed or out of mind.[26]

According to Goodell, then, the slave, whose condition consists in being subordinated to the absolute power of his master, may in the end be less vexed by the absoluteness of that power than by its ultimate incompleteness. It is as if the greatest danger to the slave is not his master's power but his impotence. Thus Eliza and little Harry flee the Shelbys because, although they were "kind," they also "were owing money" and were being forced to sell Harry—"they couldn't," she says, "help themselves" (1:128). And when Augustine St. Clare dies, his entire household is overwhelmed not so much by grief as by "terror and consternation" at being left "utterly unprotected" (2:144).

What the slaves fear, of course, is being taken from a kind master to a cruel one; this threat, Goodell thinks, makes them constantly insecure, and the mechanics of this insecurity are the plot mechanism that sells Uncle Tom down the river. But in describing the reaction of St. Clare's slaves to his death, Stowe indirectly points toward a logic of slavery that runs deeper than the difference between good and bad masters, deeper even than the master/slave relation itself. As a matter of course, she notes, the slave is "devoid of rights"; the only "acknowledgment" of his "longings and wants" as a "human and immortal creature" that he ever receives comes to him "through the sovereign and irresponsible will of his master; and when that master is stricken down, nothing remains" (2:144). The point here is not that one man in the power of another may be subjected to the most inhumane cruelties; nor is it the more subtle point that the power of even a humane master dehumanizes the slave. For Stowe, the power of the kind master and the cruel master both can be tolerated since even a Legree, refusing Tom his every want and longing, at least acknowledges those wants by refusing them and thus acknowledges his humanity. Rather, the most terrifying spectacle slavery has to offer is the spectacle of slaves *without masters.* Since the "only possible acknowledgment" of the slave as a "human and immortal creature" is through his master's "will," when in debt or in death the master's will is extinguished, the slave's humanity is extinguished also. The slave without a master stands revealed as nothing more than "a bale of merchandise," inhuman testimony to the absolute transformation of a personal relation into a market relation.

Stowe, like most of her contemporaries, customarily understood slavery as "a relic of a barbarous age";[27] the conflict between the "aristocratic" "Slave Power" and "republican" "free labor" would prove "irrepressible," William Seward proclaimed in a tremendously influential speech,[28] and the supposed "feudalism" of the South was a northern byword. More recently, Eugene Genovese, reviving the irrepressible conflict interpretation of the Civil War, has described the slaveholding planters as the "closest thing to feudal lords imaginable in a nineteenth-century bourgeois republic,"[29] and has argued that the South was a fundamentally precapitalist society. But, as we have begun to see, Stowe was basically more horrified by the bourgeois elements of slavery than by the feudal ones. She and Goodell both were struck by the insecurity of the slave's life and she, in particular, saw that insecurity as the inevitable fate of property in a free market. Thus she comes to see the evil of slavery not in its reversion to a barbaric paternalism but in its uncanny way of epitomizing the market society to which she herself belongs. Rejecting the claims of southern apologists that slavery provides a social and economic refuge from capitalism, Stowe imagines it instead as a mirror of the social and economic relations coming to the fore in the bourgeois North.

Hence the slave trade, what she calls the "great Southern slave-market," dominates her picture of the South and, despite their feudal status, the slaves in her writings share the anxious lives of Hawthorne's "republican" Northerners—"somebody is always at the drowning-point." The "fluctuations of hope, and fear, and desire" (2:245) they experience appear now as transformations of their market value. Their emotions represent their status as the objects of speculation. "Nothing is more fluctuating than the value of slaves,"[30] remarks a Virginia legislator in *The Key to Uncle Tom's Cabin.* A recent Louisiana law had reduced their value; the imminent admission to the Union of Texas as a slave state would increase it. The Virginians speak of their "slave-breeding" as a kind of agriculture and of their female slaves as "brood-mares" but Stowe penetrates more deeply into the nature of the commodity by imagining the product without *any* producer. What everybody knows about the "goblin-like" Topsy, that she just "grow'd," is only part of the answer to a series of questions asked her by Miss Ophelia: " 'Do you know who made you?' "; " 'Tell me where you were born, and who your father and mother were.' " " 'Never was born,' " Topsy replies, " 'never had no father nor mother. . . . I was raised by a speculator' " (2:37). If production in *The House of the Seven Gables* is done with mirrors, production in *Uncle Tom's Cabin* is an equally demonic magic trick, substituting the speculator for the parent and utterly effacing any trace of labor, human or divine.

This replacement of the parent by the speculator assumed an even more lurid countenance when, instead of being separate, the two figures were embodied in the same man, as when a father might sell his daughter. Stowe reproduces a poem by Longfellow called "The Quadroon Girl," in which a planter and slaver bargain in the presence of a beautiful young girl:

> "The soil is barren, the farm is old,"
>   The thoughtful planter said;
> Then looked upon the Slaver's gold,
>   And then upon the maid.
>
> His heart within him was at strife
>   With such accursed gains;
> For he knew whose passions gave her life,
>   Whose blood ran in her veins.
>
> But the voice of nature was too weak;
>   He took the glittering gold!
> Then pale as death grew the maiden's cheek,
>   Her hands as icy cold.
>
> The slaver led her from the door,
>   He led her by the hand,
> To be his slave and paramour
>   In a strange and distant land![31]

Writers like George Fitzhugh defended slavery claiming that it replaced the "false, antagonistic and competitive relations" of liberal capitalism with the more natural relations of the family. "Slavery leaves but little of the world without the family,"[32] he wrote in *Cannibals All!*; in a thoroughly paternalist society, all men, black and white, would be related to one another. Writers like Stowe and Longfellow inverted Fitzhugh's defense while preserving its terms. They too were concerned to defend the family against the market but, in their view, slavery only weakened the "voice of nature." It might be appropriate to think of one's children as property but to make that property alienable was to annihilate the family by dissolving nature into contract. "For the sake of a common humanity," Stowe wrote, she hoped that Longfellow's poem described "no common event."[33]

Longfellow's poem is somewhat ludicrous and its effect, perhaps, is to make the danger it imagines seem absurdly remote, in fact no common event. But the transformations worked upon parental and erotic relations by capitalism appear elsewhere in a more penetrating (although in some respects equally lurid) form. Indeed, these transformations, intensified and above all internalized, constitute what I take to be the heart of Hawthorne's concerns in *The House of the Seven Gables,* the chief threat against which the defense of property is mounted. Hence I would like to close by returning to that text and to what might be called its own representation of the quadroon girl.

"If ever there was a lady born" (201), Holgrave tells Phoebe, it was Alice Pyncheon, the daughter of a Pyncheon with aristocratic ambitions who, returning to Salem after a long stay in Europe, fervently hoped to gain "actual possession" of the Waldo territory and, having established himself as a "Lord" or "Earl," to return to England. According to tradition, the only man with access to the deed to Waldo was Matthew Maule, the grandson of the original "wizard," who was rumored still to haunt his old home "against the owner of which he pretended to hold an unsettled claim for ground-rent" (189). Summoned to the house, this young Maule (himself supposed, by the young ladies at least, to have a bewitching eye) demands to see Alice as well as her father. Ushered into his presence, the beautiful girl looks at Maule with unconcealed "admiration," but the "subtile" Maule sees only arrogant indifference in her "artistic approval" of his "comeliness, strength, and energy" (201). Her "admiration" is so open because it is so empty of desire; she looks at him, Maule thinks, as if he were "a brute beast," and he determines to wring from her the "acknowledgment that he was indeed a man." The "business" he has with her father

now turns on Alice and on what Hawthorne calls the "contest"
between her "unsullied purity" and the "sinister or evil potency
. . . striving to pass her barriers" (203).

Alice is prepared to enter this apparently uneven struggle
between "man's might" and "woman's might" because, as she tells
her father, no "lady, while true to herself, can have ought to fear
from whomsoever or in any circumstances" (202). She knows herself possessed of a "power" that makes "her sphere impenetrable,
unless betrayed by treachery within" (203). Hence she allows her
father to stand by while Maule, gesturing in the air, puts her into a
trance from which Pyncheon, suddenly alarmed, is unable to rouse
her. " 'She is mine!' " Maule announces and, when Pyncheon rages
against him, Maule asks quietly, " 'Is it my crime, if you have sold
your daughter . . . ?' " (206).

Obviously this story repeats in some crucial respects the narrative of "The Quadroon Girl," but in pointing to this similarity I
do not mean to claim that the bewitching of Alice Pyncheon is an
allegory of the slave trade. Hawthorne seems to have been largely
indifferent to the issue of slavery; a few years later, he would urge
Charles Sumner to "let slavery alone for a little while" and focus
instead on the mistreatment of sailors in the merchant marine.[34]
I mean instead to see in this story some sense of how deep the
notion of inalienability could run and especially of how deeply
undermined it could be by conditions closer to home than the slave
trade and less exotic than witchcraft. For Alice Pyncheon fancies
herself immune to possession (in effect, to appropriation) simply
because she feels no desire. She thinks of herself as a kind of
impregnable citadel. Desires, like so many Trojan horses, would
make her vulnerable; wanting no one and nothing, she is free from
what Hawthorne, in McCarthyesque fashion, calls "treachery
from within," and so impervious to aggression from without. That
she in fact succumbs to Matthew Maule does not invalidate her
analysis—it only shows that the enemy within need not take the
form of felt desire. In their dreams, Hawthorne says, the Pyncheons
have always been "no better than bond-servants" (26) to the Maules.
Thus, Alice's Pyncheon blood makes her as much an alienable

commodity as does the quadroon girl's black blood. And, although *she* feels no desire, her father does, "an inordinate desire," Hawthorne calls it, "for measuring his land by miles instead of acres" (208). The bewitching of Alice is here imagined as a business transaction; witches, it turns out, are capitalists by night and (having appropriated her spirit as the Pyncheons did his land), Matthew Maule makes Alice live out her life in unconscious mimicry of the original Salem girls: breaking out, wherever she might be, into "wild laughter" or hysterical tears, suddenly dancing a "jig" or "rigadoon," obeying the every command of "her unseen despot" (209).[35]

"Despot" is a crucial word here; Andrew Jackson described the National Bank as exerting a "despotic sway"[36] over the financial life of the country; Harriet Beecher Stowe called slavery "a system which makes every individual owner an irresponsible despot;"[37] Hawthorne calls Maule, the capitalist wizard, an "unseen despot." The force of the term is in all three cases to represent (internal) conflict as (external) oppression. For example, the point of characterizing the Bank as despotic was to associate it with old-world aristocracy and literally to represent it as un-American. Readers of Jackson's veto message cannot help but be struck by his obsessive concern with "foreign stockholders" in the Bank and with the anonymous threat they pose to "our country." By the same token, Stowe, fearing slavery (if I am right) as an emblem of the market economy, nevertheless thought for many years that the slave problem could be solved by repatriation to Africa, as if exorcising the slaves would rid the South of feudalism and the North of capitalism. Hawthorne too imagines a Maule become a Holgrave, renouncing "mastery" over Phoebe and leaving her "free" out of "reverence for another's individuality" (212). Indeed, the very idea of the romance asserts the possibility of immunity to appropriation in an Alice Pyncheon-like fantasy of strength through purity.

For what does the notion of inalienability entail if not a property right so impenetrable that nothing on the outside can buy it or take it away from you and so pure that nothing on the inside will conspire to sell it or give it away? That no actual possession of land could meet these criteria, we have already seen. What slavery proved to Stowe was that even the possession of one's own body could not be guaranteed against capitalist appropriation. "The slaves often say" (she quotes an "acquaintance") "when cut in the hand or foot, 'Plague on the old foot. . . . It is master's, let him take care of it; nigger don't care if he never get well.' "[38] Even the slave's soul, she thought, could not be kept pure when the "nobler traits of mind and heart" had their own "market value":

> Is the slave intelligent?—Good! that raises his price two hundred dollars. Is he conscientious and faithful? Good . . . two hundred dollars more. Is he religious? Does that Holy Spirit of God . . . make that despised form His temple?—Let that also be put down in the estimate of his market value, and the gift of the Holy Ghost shall be sold for money.[39]

Only death offered an escape from this "dreadful commerce." Legree says to George Shelby, who has made him an offer on Uncle Tom's corpse, "I don't sell dead niggers" (2:282).

In Hawthorne's republican world, however, everything is for sale. If not exactly dead niggers, then at least some version of them, like the Jim Crow gingerbread men Hepzibah Pyncheon sells to her first customer. And if not exactly the Holy Spirit, then at least the "spirit" of Alice Pyncheon, held for debt by her father's "ghostly creditors," the Maules. In fact, the whole project of the romance, with its bizarrely utopian and apparently anachronistic criteria for legitimate ownership, had already played a significant, if ironic, role in opening the American land market. The irony, of course, is that Hawthorne and others like him were uncompromisingly opposed to speculation in land. Jackson, for example, reacted against his own early career as a land speculator by defending, in Michael Rogin's words, "original title against actual residents whose long-standing possession was contaminated at the core."[40] But if the goal was purity, the effect on the western frontier was chaos; criteria like Jackson's were so rigorous that they left no man's title secure. Hence, the separation of title from possession, the very condition of romance's attempt to defend against speculation, turned out to be the condition that enabled speculators to flourish. Apparently imagining the terms of a text that would escape republican fluctuation, Hawthorne imagined in fact the terms of the technology that made those fluctuations possible.

The problematic at the heart of this reversal becomes even sharper if we turn from commerce in land to commerce in people. Stowe opposed slavery but she did so, as we have seen, in defense of property. Slaves, she thought, were the victims of theft, their property rights in their own persons had been violated. Attacking southern feudalism, she spoke for free labor and against slave labor. But insofar as her critique of slavery came to be a critique of the "Southern market," it had inevitably to constitute a repudiation of free labor as well. What Stowe most feared was the notion of a market in human attributes and, of course, free labor is just short-hand for a free market in labor. Hence her conception of freedom was itself a product of the economy epitomized for her in the slave trade—free market, free trade, in Blackstone's words, "free and un-constrained" "circulation" of "property."

Hawthorne valued freedom too, as essential to the "individual-ity" he cherished and to the "reverence" for individuality he held highest among the virtues. Matthew Maule leaves Alice Pyncheon's spirit "bowed" down before him; Holgrave demonstrates his own "integrity" by leaving Phoebe hers. But the specter of "treachery within" cannot be so easily laid to rest. For the real question raised by Alice's story is whether "reverence" for "individuality" is not ultimately an oxymoron. How should we read what Hawthorne calls Alice's loss of "self-control"? We may read it as a conflict between two forces—the individual self and the market—opposed in principle to one another.[41] In this instance, the market wins, but it need not and, indeed, when Holgrave liberates Phoebe, it does not. Or we may read it as a conflict in which the individual is set against a market that has already gained a foothold within—the McCarthyesque imagination of conspiracy. Here the enemy is still regarded as fundamentally other but is seen successfully to have infiltrated the sphere of the self—it must be exorcised.

But if we remember that Alice, as a Pyncheon, is already in bondage to the Maules, and if we remember that this fact of her birth seems to her the guarantee of her "self-control," we may be led to a third reading. Here Alice is ultimately betrayed not only by her father's desire but by the very claim to individual identity that made her imagine herself immune to betrayal. Individuality, in this reading, is its own betrayal—the enemy cannot be repulsed by the self or exorcised from the self since the enemy of the self is the self. "Property in the bourgeois sense," C. B. Macpherson has written, "is not only a right to enjoy or use; it is a right to dispose of, to exchange, to alienate."[42] Property, to be property, must be alienable. We have seen the fate of Hawthorne's attempt to imagine an inalienable right in land; now we can see the fate of his attempt to imagine an inalienable right in the self. The slave cannot resist her master because the slave is her master. If from one perspective, this looks like freedom, from another perspective, it looks like just another one of what Stowe called "the vicissitudes of property."

NOTES

1. Henry James, *The American Scene* (Bloomington, Ind., 1968), pp. 270-71.

2. Nathaniel Hawthorne, *The House of the Seven Gables,* ed. Seymour L. Gross (New York: W. W. Norton, 1967), p. 1. All subsequent references to this work will be cited parenthetically in the text.

3. The texts I have in mind here are Michael Davitt Bell's *The Development of American Romance* (Chicago, 1980) and an article by Brook Thomas, "*The House of the Seven Gables:* Reading the Romance of America," PMLA 97 (March 1982):195-211. Thomas contrasts the "freedom of the romance" to the "conservativism of the novel" (196) and suggests that Hawthorne "chose to write romances . . . because they allowed him to stay true to the American tradition of imagining an alternative to the society he inherited" (195-96). Bell sees a similar tension within the romance itself, in an opposition between the "artifice and insincerity of forms" and the "anarchic energy" of the "strange new truths" (xiv) of American life in the mid-nineteenth century.

In *House,* this opposition is embodied by the Pyncheons and Holgrave but not, according to Bell, satisfactorily, since the "revolutionary" "alternative to the empty forms of the past" represented by Holgrave and Phoebe seems too "personal" to form "the basis of a new social system" and too transitory to "avoid recapitulating the historical cycle" that created the "repressive formalism" in the first place (182–83). Thomas reads the end in similar terms but somewhat more optimistically, arguing that Hawthorne "seems to have retained a hope for the future," imagining in Phoebe's marriage to Holgrave "a real possibility for a break with the past" (209).

But in my reading, the point of the romance is neither to renew the past nor to break with it; it is instead to domesticate the social dislocation of the 1840s and 1850s in a literary form that imagines the past and present as utterly continuous, even identical, and in so doing, attempts to repress the possibility of any change at all. For critics like Bell, *The House of the Seven Gables* fails in the end because Holgrave's "radicalism" succumbs to "conservatism" (184); democracy succumbs to aristocracy, ultimately, the "dangerous" and "subversive" fictionality of the romance succumbs to the "safe and conservative" referentiality of mimesis (14, 18). But what seemed dangerous and subversive to Hawthorne was not so much the "crisis" of reference intrinsic to the romance (Bell calls it a "crisis of belief" [149] and of "correspondence" [153]) as the violently revolutionary power of *mimesis,* the representing form of a market society inimical to the social stability, the individualism, and the rights to property that Hawthorne meant the romance to defend. Thus the novel actually ends triumphantly, with a transformation of "business" into inheritance and mimesis into "fairy-tale."

4. *New York Times Magazine* (11 May, 1980):44.

5. Paul Wallace Gates, "The Role of the Land Speculator in Western Development," in *The Public Lands,* ed. Vernon Carstensen (Madison: University of Wisconsin Press, 1968), p. 352. "The peak years of speculative purchasing," Gates goes on to say, "were 1854 to 1858, when a total of 65,000,000 acres of public domain were disposed of to purchasers or holders of land warrants" (360).

6. Jay Anson, *The Amityville Horror* (New York: Bantam Books, 1978), p. 17. The main obstacle appears to have been that the only heir of the deceased former owners was the son who had murdered them, Ronald. Since Ronald, having killed his parents, was legally barred from inheriting their estate, it is unclear exactly from whom the Lutzes were buying the property. For true horror fans, however, Anson is gratifyingly explicit about who actually ended up owning their "dream house" when the demoralized Lutzes fled to California: "Just to be rid of the place, they signed their interest over to the bank that held the mortgage" (260).

7. Marion L. Starkey, *The Devil in Massachusetts* (1949; rpt. New York: Anchor Books, 1969), p. 77.

8. Paul Boyer and Stephen Nissenbaum, *Salem Possessed* (Cambridge: Harvard University Press, 1974), p. 209.

9. Michel Chevalier, *Society, Manners, and Politics in the United States,* ed. John William Ward (Ithaca: Cornell University Press, 1961), p. 98.

10. William Goodell, *The American Slave Code* (1853; rpt. New York: Arno, 1969), p. 65. The central state in question is Louisiana.

11. George M. Stephenson, *The Political History of the Public Lands* (New York: Macmillan Co., 1917), p. 243. For a characteristically helpful discussion of the ideology of homesteading, see Henry Nash Smith, *Virgin Land* (Cambridge: Harvard University Press, 1950), pp. 165–210.

12. The quotation is in Stephenson, *The Political History of the Public Lands,* pp. 109–10.

13. Robert Doherty, *Society and Power* (Amherst: University of Massachusetts Press, 1977), pp. 52–53. "Agriculture," Doherty notes, "produced greater equality, and the only communities approaching equitable distribution of property were low-level, less developed rural hinterlands" (53).

14. Ibid., p. 47.

15. Ibid., p. 49.

16. Hawthorne apparently found the idea of a fixed income as attractive personally as it was socially. James Mellow quotes his sister Ebe: "One odd, but characteristic notion of his was that he should like a competent income that would neither increase nor diminish. I said that it might be well to have it increase, but he replied, 'No, because then it would engross too much of his attention'" (Mellow, *Nathaniel Hawthorne in his Times* [Boston: Houghton Mifflin Co., 1980]), p. 94.

17. The quotation is in Robert Taft, *Photography and the American Scene* (New York: Dover, 1938), pp. 133–34.

18. Ibid., p. 30.

19. Henry James, *Hawthorne* (Ithaca: Cornell University Press, 1967), p. 35.

20. Chevalier, *Society, Manners, and Politics in the United States,* pp. 298–99. Writing in August 1835, Chevalier notes, "Great fortunes, and many of them too, have sprung out of the earth since the spring; others will, perhaps, return to it before the fall. The American does not worry about that. Violent sensations are necessary to stir his vigorous nerves."

21. Andrew Jackson, "Farewell Address," in *American Democracy: A Documentary Record,* ed. J. R. Hollingsworth and B. I. Wiley (New York: Crowell, 1961), p. 374.

22. Chevalier, *Society, Manners, and Politics in the United States,* p. 299.

23. Harriet Beecher Stowe, *The Key to Uncle Tom's Cabin* (New York: Arno, 1969), p. 1. Written in 1853, this book was an extraordinarily successful attempt to defend the veracity of *Uncle Tom's Cabin* by providing massive documentation for the incidents it narrated and the characters it described.

24. Harriet Beecher Stowe, *Uncle Tom's Cabin* (Columbus: Merrill, 1969),

2:246. All subsequent references to this work will be cited parenthetically in the text.

25. C. B. Macpherson, *Possessive Individualism* (New York: Oxford University Press, 1964), p. 272.

26. Goodell, *The American Slave Code*, pp. 65–66.

27. Stowe, *The Key to Uncle Tom's Cabin*, p. 62.

28. William H. Seward, "The Irrepressible Conflict," in *American Democracy*, pp. 468–69. The "experience of mankind," Seward claimed, had "conclusively established" that two such "radically different political systems" could never coexist. "They never have permanently existed together in one country," he said, "and they never can."

29. Eugene D. Genovese, *The Political Economy of Slavery* (New York: Random House, 1967), p. 31.

30. Stowe, *The Key to Uncle Tom's Cabin*, p. 289.

31. The quotation is in ibid., p. 295.

32. George Fitzhugh, *Cannibals All* in *Ante-Bellum*, ed. Harvey Wish (New York: Capricorn, 1960), p. 129.

33. Stowe, *The Key to Uncle Tom's Cabin*, p. 294.

34. The quotation is in Mellow, *Nathaniel Hawthorne in His Times*, p. 435.

35. In this connection, it may be worth remembering not only Hawthorne's lifelong fear and dislike of mesmerism but also Stowe's remark that "negroes are singularly susceptible to all that class of influences which produce catalepsy, mesmeric sleep, and partial clairvoyant phenomena" (Stowe, *Key*, p. 46). Mesmerism, as a threat to property, works most easily on those whose title to themselves is least secure, but no one in Hawthorne's world can be entirely safe from the threat of expropriation.

36. Andrew Jackson, "Farewell Address," *American Deomcracy*, p. 374. See also his "Veto of the Bank Bill," *American Democracy*, pp. 309–21.

37. Stowe, *The Key to Uncle Tom's Cabin*, p. 204.

38. Ibid., p. 22.

39. Ibid., p. 280.

40. Michael Paul Rogin, *Fathers and Children: Andrew Jackson and the Subjugation of the American Indian* (New York: Alfred A. Knopf, 1976), p. 96. Although he does not explicitly point to the intrinsically self-defeating character of the demand for pure title, Rogin does go on to note that occupancy laws were opposed by "aspiring speculators" as well as by "purists over contractual rights" (p. 97).

41. Such a reading is adopted in effect by Michael T. Gilmore who argues that, writing *The House of the Seven Gables*, Hawthorne "was unable to suppress his misgivings that in bowing to the marketplace he was compromising his artistic independence and integrity" ("The Artist and the Marketplace in

The House of the Seven Gables," *ELH* 48 [Spring 1981]:172–73. Gilmore's valuable essay seems to me typical of much recent work on the artist in the market in that it calls attention to the importance of the market only to draw ever more firmly the line between the values of that market and the values of art. The point I am urging in this essay is the rather different one that for Hawthorne qualities like independence and integrity (artistic or otherwise) do not exist in opposition to the marketplace but are produced by it and contained within it.

42. Macpherson, *Possessive Individualism,* p. 92.

Allen Grossman

The Poetics of Union
in Whitman and Lincoln:
An Inquiry toward the
Relationship of Art and Policy

I

To begin with, I shall suppose that both policy and art are addressed to the solution of problems vital to the continuity of the social order, and, therefore, to the human world. In the period of America's Civil War (the "renaissance" moment both of America's literary and its constitutional authenticity) there arose two great and anomalous masters, the one of policy and the other of poetry: Abraham Lincoln and Walt Whitman. Both men addressed the problem of the reconstruction of their common human world—the Union as a just and stable polity—at a time when the elements necessary to the intelligibility of that world seemed fallen, in Seward's words, into "irrepressible conflict."[1]

The political and constitutional situation, as both men understood it, was clear. The Missouri Compromise of 1820, which had reconciled the equality requirement of the Declaration of Independence with the continuity requirements of the Constitution (among them slavery), was undone between 1846 and 1857 by the outcome of the Mexican War, the Fugitive Slave Law, Kansas-Nebraska, and Dred Scott. In effect, competition between the claims of two incompatible systems of labor with their attendant social structures, precipitated by the acquisition of new territory in the Mexican War and the opening of the Northwest, required deliberated choices, as if in an "original position," among contradictory descriptions of the human world. By the accident of history, these choices involved the staggeringly primitive question as to which human beings were persons.[2] That deliberation was, in the end, condensed upon the figure and discourse of Lincoln, whose "mould-smashing mask" (as Henry James put it) was a bizarre

183

picture of *concordia discors,* the imagination's conquest of irrecon-
cilables; it was interrupted and restated by the cruel, integrative,
and perhaps artificial catastrophe of the Civil War; and at last
ironically inscribed in the Thirteenth, Fourteenth, and Fifteenth
amendments.[3]

On the literary side, Emerson, Thoreau, Melville, and Whitman
addressed the same problem of the union or connectedness of the
human world, which they also saw by deliberated fictions as if for
the first time in a new territory where the worth of persons was
subject to the risk of finding a form. The long aftermath of the
Revolution had destroyed the old America, a confederation of
separately constituted religious communities, in which personhood
was validated or canceled by reference to the eucharistic mystery
of the hypostatic union. Whitman and others worked toward a
reconstructive poetics appropriate to a modern political society, in
which this same validating function was equivocally provided in
the centerless rationality of the Constitution legislated by the
secular decree of the people. Authentic American art, as well as
true American constitutionality, awaited a solution to the crisis of
the establishment of the person.[4]

In America at midcentury, both art and policy confronted a culture that lacked an effective structure (a meter, a genre, an epistemology, a law) between the pragmatic ideal of political unity—the
unwritten poem of these states—and the mutually excluding legitimacies for which right and place were claimed in consciousness
and the nation—Declaration and Constitution, equality and order,
body and soul. Lincoln supplied that structure in the form of a
conservative ideology of union based in ethical constitutionalism,
promulgated by a rational style of discourse of unfailing adequacy
and persuasiveness. He was a *novus homo,* a man impersonated by
his language, the structure of whose song of self-invention (a
recapitulation of the significant past of America, as he understood
it) came in the event to be repeated as America's present, the Civil
War. The literary master of union was Whitman for whom also the
one justifiable order of the world was the order of the discourse
by which he invented himself, his song. ("The United States them-

selves," he said, "are essentially the greatest poem.") Neither of
these men could appear, except as a function of their language
which bore upon them, and subsequently upon their world, as
Emerson remarked of perception in general, not as a whim but as
a fate.

The only social role that could make actual the enigmatic par-
ticularity of Lincoln's self-invention, speaking the pure language of
individual personhood by which he discovered the tragic laws of
its social peace, was the citizen presidency. The only social role
that could express the function of the person for Whitman—
immanent, comedic, doxological, choral—was the poet-nurse, commissioned healer of the violence of language of another sort. At
the end of the war, Whitman signified the inclusion of the tragedy
of policy within the comedy of his art by receiving Lincoln into
the night—"hiding, receiving"—of his elegy, as he had received in
his arms so many of the dead of Lincoln's war.

Insofar as the actuality of both policy and poetry require sentences a man can speak, the material upon which poetry works
and the material upon which policy works are identical because of
the ubiquity of language, and present the same resistances. The
reasons that one cannot make just any poem, or just any policy,
good are the same. An entailment of any style a person speaks is
the structure of a social world that can receive it—a political
formation and its kind of conscious life. Consequently, Whitman
and Lincoln were autodidact masters. As such, they received the
implications of acculturation without interposition of mediating
social forms, and restated its structure directly as the structure of
the worlds they intended.

Whereas Lincoln was born in the wilderness Thoreau deliberately
chose to live there. Lincoln's political literacy derived from personal labor. For Lincoln the crisis of union repeated the enigma of
his own socialization. His legendary honesty specifies him as a man
of his word, as Whitman's theatrical "nakedness" makes him a
man whose self is his song. For Whitman as for Lincoln, the legitimation of his personhood (the crisis of union) involves the justification of a mode of discourse, not merely a particular case of

practice. But the autodidact self-invention of Whitman—his self-commissioning praxis—identified him with the ethos of poetry. In his understanding poetry is the leisure of receptivity, not the rational labor of the will—"I loafe and invite my soul." A poetry that authorizes a personhood reflexively validated by its own discourse can have no category of fictionality. (He who touches this book touches all the man there is.) A poetry that has no category of fictionality is a policy.[5] Correlatively, a policy that intends, as did Lincoln's, the same structure as its discourse is a poetry. In this sense, both Whitman and Lincoln are profoundly conservative figures. Both bind the world, with totalitarian immediacy, to the configurative implication of the central sentences of a cultural instrument.

Therefore, one may ask the question whether, as between Lincoln's politics and Whitman's poetry, there are two policies of union, or only one insofar as they are representative of two distinct cultural modes? Does poetry know anything that policy does not? One may also ask, given the singular nature of these two figures, both of whom practice language that intends as a function of its structure a just order of the human world, whether there really is a nontragic, open-form, egalitarian version of the reconciliation of justice and order, or only the brilliant, closed, individualist, logic-based Lincolnian version so profoundly implicated with our world as it has come to pass.

II

The supposition, with which I began, that art and policy are addressed to the same problems, assumes that prior to both art and policy is the common intention of an order of the human world, and that the world has a stake in knowing (and criticism a means of inquiring) what art and policy cannot do.

Lincoln's strategy of order was an amplification of a legal grammar (Blackstonian) adapted to political use, the structure of which was based in the Aristotelian laws of thought—identity, non-

contradiction, the excluded middle. He judged the world that he
constructed by a hermeneutic criterion of intelligibility, modeled
on Euclid. A house divided against itself, like a sentence that
asserts contradictories, cannot stand because it makes no sense and
accords with no possible state of affairs.[6] He judged the substantial
moral world similarly, according to the criterion of simplicity.
Lincoln accepted as self-evident the distinction between good and
evil, implied as a restriction on choice by the Declaration of Independence (all men are created equal), and assumed that there was
a state of fact in accord with the criterion that the two authoritative documents of his reality (Declaration and Constitution) meant
the same thing. Correspondingly, the meaning of the law, for Lincoln, was "the intention of the law-giver," and all the givers of
authentic law, including God, intended the same thing.[7] "The will
of God," he notes in 1862, "prevails. In great contests each party
claims to act in accordance with the will of God. Both may be,
and one must be, wrong. God cannot be for and against the same
thing at the same time." Hence, Lincoln's speaking induced a
sentiment of what Marianne Moore called his "intensified par-
ticularity," deriving first from a willed overcoming of complexity
and consequent clarification of the world, and second from the
indissociability of that clarification from his own person.[8] Thus,
Lincoln's policy subordinated and conserved an ineradicable
autochthony against a reality of immense complexity. In its
severest form, the form given it in history by the hands of Grant
and Sherman, his rhetoric was obliterative. "Both may be, and one
must be, wrong."[9]

   In the crossing of kinds of discourse in history, poetry situates
itself where other instruments of mind find impossibility. Thus,
Walt Whitman found his truth, and the unity of his world, precisely at the crisis of contradiction where Lincoln found disintegra-
tive instability. Unlike Lincoln's God, who cannot be for and
against the same thing at the same time, Whitman's "greatest poet"
inferred from the traditional fame-powers of his art a fundamental
principle of undifferentiated representation, which constituted a
massive trope of inclusion. Representation (the class of all classes)

was itself an implicit unification, the fame of the world; and the great bard, "by whom only can series of peoples and states be fused into the compact organism of a Nation," promulgated the goodness of simple presence as human state of affairs. Of *his* legislator Whitman says in the "Poem of Many in One": "He judges not as the judge judges but as light falling round a helpless thing." Whitman's originality consisted in the discovery of a regulative principle that permitted an art based in the representative function itself, and organized in its ideal-typical moments (for example, the world-inventories in #15 and #33 of "Song of Myself") as a taxonomy of which the sorting index is mere being-at-all. The argument that made the meter of Whitman was the unification of the world in the one power of language, the secret authority of the poet (his "Santa Spirita"), the bestowal of presence across time. The theater of that presence is the poetic line; and the poetics of the line is the multiplicative logic of presence by which Whitman replaces, and contradicts, the world-dividing logic of argument of Lincoln's rational sentence.

The English poetic line, as Whitman found it, was the synergetic outcome of two orders of form: an abstract and irrational pattern of counted positions, on the one hand, and the natural stress characteristics of language heightened and articulated by the semantic concerns of the reader, on the other. But the repertory of abstract patterns that the reader received was, in his view, indelibly stained by the feudal contexts of its most prestigious instances, and in addition required the subordination of the natural stress characteristics of language, and therefore an abridgment of the freedom of the speaker. Whitman was an end-stopped line-writer. And the abstract patterns (the "mechanical" aspects of structure) served, at the least, two indispensable functions: the provision, first of all, of an external and (by convention) timeless *locus communis* where the "I" and the "you" could meet, a principle of access; and, second, the establishment of a finite term which sealed utterance against silence and granted form. Whitman compensated his deletion of the metrical aspect of the line by revising the mechanism of access on the basis of the "transparence," or reciprocal internality, of persons one to the other ("What I shall assume you shall assume"), and by the hypothesis of a world composed of a "limitless" series of brilliant finite events each of which imposed closure at the grammatical end of its account. But it is opposition to the meaning-intending will by the resistance of abstract form that produces, in the English poetic line, the sentiment of the presence of the person as a singular individual; and this Whitman could not restore.

We see, therefore, the paradox: the logic of poetic construction posed to Whitman, the ideologist of union as happiness, is analogous to the logic of clarification posed to Lincoln, the ideologist of union as "fairness." In Lincoln's case the unification of the world required the dissolution of one term of any set of contradictories in order to obtain the thereby inherent simplification required by truth—a totalitarianism of hypotaxis. In the poet's case, the abandonment of abstract pattern put in question the validity of the instrument of fame itself by dissolving its subject—a totalitarianism of parataxis. The problem for both Whitman and Lincoln was how to preserve the ends of the enterprise from the predation of the means.

III

When Matthiessen named Whitman "the central figure of our literature affirming the democratic faith," he did so because he saw Whitman as the champion, not only of liberty and equality, but also (unlike Emerson, Thoreau, and even Melville) of fraternity—the master of union as social love.[10] But Lincoln was the great speaker of the American Renaissance whose imagination empowered the democratic faith. Its way, he said, is "plain, peaceful, generous, just." In the 1850s, both Whitman and Lincoln held more or less the same politics, including the view that slavery *and also abolition* were barbarisms: abolition because it interrupted contract and exchange without which there was no social world in which anyone *could* be free; slavery because, as an impermissible variation of the practice of liberty (you cannot choose to enslave), it destroyed the value both of labor and leisure without which freedom was empty of praxis.[11] Lincoln's characteristic strategy for freeing slaves was *compensated* emancipation, the completion of the Revolution by the co-optation in its service of the constitutional principle of contract—the justification, in effect, of logical discourse. Whitman supposed that the same result could only be obtained by a more fundamental revision of the central nature of relationship—the establishment of a new basis of speaking in the counterlogic, and infinite distributability, of affectionate presence. Both Lincoln and Whitman intended the same thing. The two systems (the closed and the open) that they sponsored aspire each to specify the inclusion of the other as the best outcome of its own nature. The limits of each of these two systems in view of their common goal becomes plain in the two related issues of hierarchy, the constraints upon variation consistent with union as structure, and equality, the management of access of persons one to the other consistent with union as value.

In Lincoln's "First Inaugural," a performative utterance at the moment of oath-taking, which he described as an account of his own worthiness of credence, Lincoln identified secession as a transgressive practice of freedom—a disordering variation—inconsistent with the intactness of the organic law of the nation; and he defined by contrast the true democratic sovereign:

> Plainly, the central idea of secession is the essence of anarchy. A majority, held in restraint by constitutional checks, and limitations, and always changing easily, with deliberate changes of popular opinions and sentiments is the only true sovereign. Whoever rejects it does of necessity fly to anarchy or to despotism. Unanimity is impossible; the rule of the minority, as a permanent arrangement is wholly inadmissible; so that, rejecting the majority principle, anarchy or despotism is all that is left.[12]

Oath-taking is Lincoln's peculiar form of honesty. At the moment of the "First Inaugural" he identifies himself with the union, grown suddenly abstract with the secession of seven states, and establishes himself as its regulative presence by articulating the grammar of the one authentic sentence that expresses both equality and intelligible structure.[13] But the world it describes is organized around the conservation of the singular person by the concession of totalistic right—excluding despotism, anarchy, *and also unanimity*. By the principle of majority rule, equality is delegated and unanimity eternally postponed. This delegation takes the form of an exchange whereby autonomy is given up, and social life, the human scale of the person, received in return. Lincoln's true sovereign is a collectivity less than the whole, a "majority held in restraint" by a regulative principle external to itself which by its measure produces freedom in the form of resistances to the will structured to conserve its own nature. At the heart of Lincoln's conception of constitution is a commutative process: life is given up for meaning, the significance of the whole sentence; and the interest of all persons (and, therefore, potentially the whole interest of each) is exchanged for a rational sociability based in a hierarchy of ends of which the highest term is external to the person, and not within his power of choice. Paramount among these exchanges, and implied in all, is the exchange of life for meaning, an idea that Lincoln repeated as a hermeneutic principle in his explanation of the war (e.g., "From these honored dead we take increased devotion to that cause for which they gave the last full measure of devotion"). Since secession was a transgressive exercise of choice (the repudiation of the social bond) on behalf of slavery, and slavery a perversion of contract to repudiate rather than affirm personhood, the urgency of restoring Union was doubly driven by the ethical motive, not only (and perhaps not primarily) to establish all human beings as persons, but also to revalidate the principle of the whole social world. Secession made inescapably apparent the inherently conflictual character of the legal understanding of the Constitution by making unmistakable the incompatibility of the freedom of the individual with the order of the state—the inherently imperfect inclusion under rational auspices of the many in the one.

Whitman's motive was to get death out of sociability, to devise "death's outlet song." The bard is the better president because he is the "perfect" agent of human presence—the voice's announcement, prior to all other messages, of the presence of the person prior to all other characteristics. As such, the bard distributes the value of personhood which is the value commuted in all other economic transactions. The poem is of the same nature as central value, because the whole function of its discourse is acknowledgment. Consequently, universal access to the poem is a policy to overcome scarcity. To effect this, Whitman devised a "song" that would reconcile variety and order, equality and constitution, one and many without compromising either term. Once again Whitman situates his new American organic law and true sovereign precisely where Lincoln finds impossibility, at the zero point of unanimity.

The destruction of the constitutional settlement of the 1820s precipitated the crisis of the Union in the form of the scarcity of personhood. A characteristic recuperative episode of the 1850s is the Dred Scott decision which solved the problem of such scarcity by ruling the African slave out of the human community by a distinction as severe and of the same effect as that between the redeemed and the unregenerate.[14] In the slave codes of the South the chattel slave must call every man "master." By his uncanny difference—a human being who is not a person—the slave precisely specifies and thereby generates and maintains (this is his work) the boundary between the nonperson and the person upon which the distinction of the person is established.[15] The refounding of personhood, the historical function of the poet, was the deferred business both of the American Revolution and of American literature. But the perfect equality of all human beings requires, as Whitman understood, an infinite resource of fame.

Whitman's policy was to establish a new principle of access that would effect multiplication, or pluralization (the getting many into one), without the loss entailed by exchange—the glory of the perfect messenger. In the chronology of Whitman's work, the "open" line as formal principle appears simultaneously with the subject of liberation, and is the enabling condition of the appearance of that subject. That is to say, his first poems in the new style are also his first poems on the subject of slavery and freedom (specifically, "Resurgemus," "Blood-Money," "Wounded in the

House of Friends"). His first lines in the new style altogether (so far as I can tell) are recorded in a notebook as follows:

> I am the poet of the slave, and of the masters of the slave
> . . . .
> I am the poet of the body
> And I am the poet of the soul
> I go with the slaves of the earth equally with the masters
> And I will stand between the masters and the slaves,
> Entering into both, so that both shall understand me alike[16]

In another early notebook Whitman gives an account of what he calls "translation," the power he uses in place of the Coleridgean poetic "imagination." (He sometimes, as in the Lincoln elegy, calls it "tallying.")

> Every soul has its own individual language, often unspoken, or feebly spoken; but a true fit for that man and perfectly adapted for his use—The truths I tell to you or to any other may not be plain to you, because I do not translate them fully from my idiom into yours.—If I could do so, and do it well, they would be as apparent to you as they are to me; for they are truths. No two have exactly the same language, and the great translator and joiner of the whole is the poet.[17]

Instead of a "poetic language" (always a mimetic version of the language of one class) Whitman has devised a universal "conjunctive principle" whose manifest structure is the sequence of end-stopped, nonequivalent, but equipollent lines. By it he intends the power of the God to whom (as in the "Collect for Purity" which opens the Mass) "all hearts are open . . . desires known . . . from whom no secrets are hid." His poetic authority is J. S. Mill's "overheard" soliloquy of feeling, and his physicalist basis is the phrenological continuity between inner and outer mind. The drama of translation is enacted at the beginning of an early poem, "The Answerer":

> Now list to my morning's romanza, I tell the signs of the Answerer,
> To the cities and farms I sing as they spread in the sunshine before me.
>
> A young man comes to me bearing a message from his brother,
> How shall the young man know the whether and when of his brother?
> Tell him to send me the signs.

> And I stand before the young man face to face, and take his right hand
>   in my left hand and his left hand in my right hand
> And I answer for his brother and for men. . . .

By curing the human colloquy, the poet (the translator, answerer, perfect messenger, better president) intends to establish a boundless resource of the central acknowledgment-value, and to rid sociability of death by overcoming the scarcity of fame, a process that requires the mechanical checks and balances (reifications of the competing will of the inaccessible other) in the poetics of Lincoln's constitutionalism. But Whitman's new principle of access—his line—is not "organic" in Matthiessen's Coleridgean sense. It has the virtuality of a paradigm; and the negotiation of its actualization against the resistances of history and mind is Whitman's major subject.

The primal scene of that negotiation is the "transparent morning" of part 5 of "Song of Myself." It is the inaugural moment of Whitman's candor, and as such it recapitulates the first subject matter liberated by his line. The form is the confession of a creed:

> I believe in you my soul, the other I am must not abase itself to you
> And you must not be abased to the other.

The rewriting of hierarchies—soul/body, collective/individual, nation/state—as equalities, and the rewriting as identities of conventional dualities, above all the self and the other, is the task of the "translator," whose goal is union as the fraternalization of the community. In the Nicene Creed that follows is, of course, the hypostatic union. What follows in Whitman's creed is the greater mystery of the mortal union of two, the competent number of acknowledgment, and the archetype of all political relationship. For Lincoln, labor is prior to capital and is the praxis of the individual will by which all selfhood, and therefore all value, is produced.[18] It is indistinguishable from the act of clarification (the intention of the lawgiver) by which univocal meaning is derived, many made one. To loaf ("Loafe with me on the grass . . . ") is to exchange the posture of hermeneutic attention for the posture of receptivity, the unity of all things in the last sorting category of mere consciousness prior to interpretation ("the origin of all poems") of which the voice is the "hum," the sound of the blood doing the cultural work of God (a further secularization of the "sound of many waters" of Revelation, repeated by Wordsworth as the mystically integrative speaking of the Leech Gatherer), the doggerel of life. What follows, then, is the sexual union reconstructed as a moment of primal communication, the tongue to the heart. The principle of the language of the soul is the deletion, as in Whitman's metricality as a whole, of centralizing hypotactic grammar, and the difference-making prosodies both of individual meaning-intention and abstractly patterned (stress/no stress) metricality. What is obtained is an unprecedented trope of inclusion—the sign, embodied in that revision of primary human relationship ("gently turned over upon me"), of which the greater inclusions of emancipation and union are the things signified:

> And limitless are the leaves stiff and drooping in the fields
> And brown ants in the little wells beneath them
> And mossy scabs of the worm fence, heap'd stones, elder,
>   mullein and poke-weed.

But what is created, paradoxically, is a new slave culture. The Whitmanian voice, like the slave, is uncanny—a servant of persons, but not itself personal—a case of delegated social death: "A generalized art language, a literary algebra" (Sapir). "Comradeship—part of the death process. The new Democracy—the brink of death. One identity—death itself" (Lawrence). "To put the paradox in a nutshell, he wrote poetry out of poetry writing" (Pavese).[19] There is truth in these judgments. The logic of presence, Whitman's "profound lesson of reception," has its own violence. The Whitmanian convulsion ("And parted the shirt from my bosom-bone, and plunged your tongue to my bare-stripped heart"), attendant upon the reduction of all things to appearance, is the counterviolence to that which flows from the logic of clarification, the reduction of all things to univocal meaning. The tongue of the soul is the principle of continuity figured as the "hum" of subvocal, absorbed, multitudinous, continuously regulated "valved voice," or "this soul," as Whitman elsewhere says, ". . . its other name is Literature."[20] The tongue sacrifices the subject of justice in the interest of a personal immediacy that overcomes the difference of the social body, but at the same time destroys (tongue to bare-stripped heart) the destiny of the secular person which the social body is.

In a tract Whitman wrote in 1856 on behalf of Fremont (whom Lincoln also supported), Whitman produces his model of "The Redeemer President" whose way will be "not exclusive, but inclusive."[21] Lincoln was not Whitman's redeemer president. Lincoln was the type of the "unknown original" (Sapir's expression) from which, as from the utterance of the hermit thrush of the elegy, Whitman translated his song. Whitman's taxonomic line runs "askant" history (the abstract pattern he deletes is precisely the element of the line that has a history).[22] That variation produces the infinite access he required for his "peace that passes the art and argument of earth." In Lincoln's terms such a variation is as transgressive (and of the same nature) as Douglas's "squatter sovereignty," or slavery itself.

Lincoln's sentence, by contrast, prolongs the history of each soul beyond mortality in a never-darkened theater of judgment. In the midst of an argument in his "Second Annual Address" (1862) in support of compensated emancipation, Lincoln inserts the following sentence: "In times like these men should utter nothing for which they would not be responsible through time and in eternity."[23] In the straitening of choice, Lincoln in his language grows thick with character, the pure case of tragic personhood enacting the indissolubility of a moral identity that persists across eschatological boundaries in continuous space and time (the cosmological expression of ethical contract)—unmistakable, eternally situated, judged. The peroration of the same speech begins: "Fellow citizens, *we* cannot escape history. We of this Congress and this administration, will be remembered in spite of ourselves. No personal significance, or insignificance, can spare one or another of us. The fiery trial through which we pass, will light us down, in honor or dishonor, the lastest generation,"[24] By deleting the abstract pattern of internal marks that closes the traditional line and carries is across time, Whitman deleted history, founded an infinite resource of acknowledgment, dissolved the moral praxis of the singular individual, and "launched forth" (as he says at the end of the "Song of the Answerer") into the desituate universe of transparent minds, generated by an open metrical contract, "to sweep through the ceaseless rings and never be quiet again." Lincoln's language, unlike Whitman's, is empowered because it is of the same nature as the institutions that invented him, and his space and time are institutional space and time. In such a world, judgment and acknowledgment are inseparable; and the economy of scarcity is reconstituted in the oldest economic terms of our civilization—honor or dishonor.

Both Whitman and Lincoln are captives of a system of representation, which they are commissioned to justify and put in place as an order of the human world—a policy for union. Are there two policies, or only one? On the one hand, a Whitmanian policy—open, egalitarian, in a sense socialist (as Matthiessen thought it to be), generalized from the fame-power of art, and darkly qualified by that abjection of the subject of value which is the other side of receptivity; and, on the other hand, a Lincolnian system—closed, republican, capitalist, a regulative policy driven by the logic of clarification, and darkly qualified in its turn by the obliterative implications both of moral exclusiveness and the delegatory economies of labor? We have seen that the centered, hierarchical, Lincolnian ethical rationality is precisely the enemy element from which Whitman is bent upon exempting his human world. We see also that the resonant, scale-finding, integrative vocality of Lincoln is the most severe criticism our literature affords of Whitman's indeterminate realization of the person—"You whoever you are." Whitman's "Word over all, beautiful as the sky" reconciles what Lincoln's ethical dualism drives into division, yet only at that distance; Lincoln's sentiment of ethical difference cruelly specifies the limit of variation in which regulative rationality can produce the actual life of all men. But despite the reciprocally canceling nature of Whitman and Lincoln as liberators, the gravity of representation itself unites them in a common conservatism.

In the "Preface of 1855" Whitman lays down his own regulative sentence: "Nothing out of its place is good and nothing in its place is bad."[25] For Whitman the final sorting category of presence, the place of good life, is (as I have said) mere existence of which the dwelling is the open air, and the poetic structure the internally unmarked line manifesting "as amid light" the natural stress characteristics of language in the natural order, determined at the end by the objectively finite plenitude of each of an infinite number of facts of being *caught in a brilliant virtuality from which it cannot depart:* "Passing the yellow-speared wheat, every grain from its shroud in / the dark-brown fields uprisen."[26] For Lincoln that same place of good life is "the national homestead"—a boundless, mastered autochthony specified, rendered continuously intelligible and therefore free, by the internal markings of superordinate measure. It is Lincoln who says: "There is no line, straight or crooked, on which to divide."

IV

One reason we turn to criticism of poetry is to bring to pass projects that become possible only when we make statements about poetic texts. We do criticism because we are busy about something else. In this sense, we do not intend the poem; we intend the intention that brought the poet to poetry, which is not the poem but the reason for taking poetry in hand. Our judgment upon the poem is an assessment of the likelihood of the coming to pass of what is intended. And our judgment, or the poet's, upon poetry itself is an assessment of its usefulness as an instrument of our urgent, common work.

In "a society waiting," as Whitman says of his America, "unformed . . . between things ended and things begun," Whitman intended a revision of all "conjunctive relations."[27] Of this revision the "great poet" was the sign, and also the incarnation of the regulative principle of his own signifier, the poem—man of his word. As the world over which Lincoln presided darkened through the Civil War, Whitman saw the defeat of fraternity which was the substance of his policy. The seal of that defeat, the murder of the president, he inscribed with his great reconstructive "Burial Hymn," "When Lilacs Last in the Dooryard Bloom'd." During that period, Lincoln in his speeches drew the world with justificatory intensity and comprehensiveness ever deeper into the system of representation whose structure was expressed in his political and strategic judgments, as in the "Second Inaugural": "Until every drop of blood drawn by the lash shall be paid by another drawn by the Sword." Whitman, on the other hand, tended more and more to modify his regulative principles to release the world from the over-determination of all systems of representation, as in the consummatory cry of perfect translation: "I spring out of these pages into your arms—decease calls me forth."[28]

As is the case with pastoral elegy in general, "When Lilacs Last" is, first of all, a gesture of riddance of a prior representational dispensation unable to "keep" its children. (Whitmanian celebration by pluralization extinguishes all personhood which has *only* singular form—["Nor for you, for one alone / Blossoms and branches green to coffins all I bring."])[29] Second, the elegy effects the reconstitution of the world on the basis of the new supersessory system (in "Lycidas" the "unexpressive nuptial song," in Whitman's poem "yet varying ever-altering song"). Finally, it investigates the implications of a "passing," or paratactic transcendence, of that new system of representation toward a right state of the world undeformed by any mediation of discourse. One reason for the fullness of articulation of Whitman's poem lies in the complexity of its judgment, not only on the failed predecessor system of which all that survives is love without an object, but also on itself as a policy toward the consummation of that love—a union not broken by the means of its accomplishment. In this judgment of the judge whose justice does not divide consists the final profundity of Whitman, his "delicacy" as the late James Wright called it.

"When Lilacs Last" repeats the millennial archetype of the death
of the Beloved Companion whose *nostos* is completes ("Nothing
out of its place is good; and nothing in its place is bad"). The elegy
returns to the West; Lincoln had departed four years earlier on his
journey from West to East (displacing an autochthonous power in
the service of an alien rationality) with the great sentences of farewell at Springfield, Illinois (11 February 1861), which begin with
double negatives that seal, at the moment of deracination, untrans-
latable individuality into irreducible space and time: "Friends: no
one not in my situation, can appreciate my sadness at this parting.
. . . Here I have lived . . . , and have passed from a young to an old
man. Here my children have been born, and one is buried."[30] By
contrast, Whitman's correlative rehearsal of departure in the opposite direction, from East to West (his revision in 1862 of the opening stanza to "Starting from Paumanok") sets the self at large in
the field of consciousness—at the other end from Lincoln of the
truth table for the particle [or] :

> Aware of the fresh free giver the flowing Missouri, aware
>   of the mighty Niagara,
> Aware of the buffalo herds grazing the plains, the hirsute
>   and strong-breasted bull,
> Of earth, rocks, Fifth-month flowers experienced, stars, rain,
>   snow, my amaze . . . ,

released from the rational justice of situation, inclusive of many
places at once (here and also there) not as seeing is but as light is.
And yet "Solitary, singing in the West." The old situated world
of unexchangeable Euclidean marks provided the object of love—
the Beloved Companion—to Whitman as elegist; but the new world
of the open principle provides the elegy. It springs forth at the
death of the loved person, released from the hermeneutic bondage
("O the black murk that hides the star!") which invented that person and destroyed him—a supersessive culture of keeping as union
one and many ("each to keep and all"), by its nature requiring his
loss. The loss of the companion precipitates the speaker in the
poem upon a new autonomy—a searching of the boundaries of

representation ("dusk and dim") for an instrument of sociability that does not produce the disappearance of its object.

At the heart of Whitman's elegy is the scene of the reading of the song of the hermit thrush named "Solitary," the "loud human song" of the unknown original, the singular person. This scene is a repetition of the inaugural action of translation (as pluralization) by which in "Out of the Cradle Endlessly Rocking" the poet received his commissioning ("Now in a moment I know what I am for . . ./ And already a thousand singers . . . have started to life within me, never to die"). To accomplish this katabasis requires a re-fraternalization by which the poet becomes the conjunctive term between the "thought" of death and its "knowledge," general and particular, many and one—the hand in hand of union mediated only by the consciousness of continuous vitality. In this relationship, the poet becomes the "Answerer," who addresses the central question of freedom which is suffering, as recognition itself, the signifier of nothing. From the renewal of his central originality Whitman receives the vision of things as they are with the living and the dead. He translates Lincoln's death without exchanging it for any term whatsoever, and the "slain soldiers of the war" without the commutation of any rational value:

> I saw battle-corpses, myriads of them,
> And the white skeletons of young men, I saw them,
> I saw debris and debris of all the slain soldiers of the war,
> But I saw they were not as was thought,
> They themselves were fully at rest, they suffer'd not,
> The living remain'd and suffer'd, the mother suffer'd,
> And the wife and the child and the musing comrade suffer'd,
> And the armies that remain'd suffer'd.

Through the establishment of difference between the living and the dead—a laying of ghosts, including Lincoln and his meanings—the elegist recovers the perceptibility of his world, as Lincoln had established the difference between persons and things by the emancipation of the slaves, and thus restored the rationality of the polity. But the act of perceptual autonomy ("free sense") finds Whitman, at the moment of his greatest originality, at the greatest

distance also from the social world in which alone his intention
can have meaning, that world over which Lincoln presided as
emancipator, accounting for the same facts of suffering (at Gettys-
burg, for example, or in the "Second Inaugural") according to compensatory economies of theodicy, those of dedication, sacrifice,
and the vengeance of God.

Both Whitman (poet citizen) and Lincoln (citizen president)
intended a "just and lasting peace" in a polity that had lost regulative stability and consequently postponed the antinomy of those
two terms. Each took in hand a millennial instrument of representation the nature of which he articulated as policy with singular
fidelity: in Lincoln's case, the political principle of sociability based
in commutative justice, the logic of noncontradiction, singular
identity, and the hierarchy of rational order—the language of tragic
personhood; in Whitman's case, the poetic principle of sociability,
based in an abstraction from the representational function of art,
and organized in accord with a redistributive counterlogic of
presence as pluralization and the transparence of affection—a
comedy of justice without exchange. But the Whitmanian distribu-
tive politics of "transparence" fails to obtain unanimity because it
has no natural standpoint (there is no transparence consistent with
the social life of the person), and thus obtains only justice without
constitution. Likewise the Lincolnian poetics of fairness does not
obtain fairness because the nature of the person on whose behalf it
acts limits the systemic change possible to the institutions that represent it—constitution without justice. Both men succeeded in mastering their instrument, but not (as each so profoundly intended) in
overcoming its nature. The contradiction between equality and per-
petuation—Declaration as justice, and Constitution as structure—
was more powerful than the systems of representation that invented
these men (and which they sponsored) could conciliate, because
the contradiction is of the same nature as the system.

Thus, having made one out of many, the common work of policy
and poetry, Lincoln and Whitman left behind the inherently unfinished, reconstructive task of making many, once again of one—the

creation of a real world consistent with its principles both of value
and of order. Near the close of his "Second Annual Message" in
which he promulgated the Emancipation, Lincoln distinguished between imagining and doing, and between the present and the past:

> It is not "Can any of us *imagine* better?" but "can we all *do* better?". . .
> The dogmas of the quiet past, are inadequate to the stormy present. The
> occasion is piled high with difficulty, and we must rise with the occasion.
> As our case is new, so we must think anew and act anew. We must disen-
> thrall ourselves, and then we shall save our country.[31]

Both men, together with most of their literary contemporaries,
saw the historical moment as one requiring new structures of
response; both deprecated the category of the imaginary, and both
intended to "disenthrall" the self in the interest of national
authenticity. In the end, however, the freedom conferred by Whitman and Lincoln remained, as I have suggested, virtual and paradoxical. The empowered master, Lincoln, was unable, by the very
nature of his power, to legislate a social world in which his intention could become actual. Whitman, the master of social love (the
better president as he understood it), was unable, by the nature of
his fundamental revision of personhood, to enter the world by any
act, except the deathwatch of the wounded in Lincoln's war.[32]

The fate of Whitmanian policy brings to mind the observation
that words in poetry are only as effective as the institutions in
which they have meaning. More particularly, "bad faith" attaches
to open form in that it anticipates, by the radical nature of its
truth, no institution in which its words can have effect, no world
in which its text is transmitted, and yet no presence of the self-
authorized person it liberates except the image or eidolon of the
poem. Correlatively, we note from the fate of Lincolnian policy,
which is our history: that the language of closed form is empowered
because it is of the same structure as human institutions; but that
such institutions, or for that matter such poems (Yeats's for
example), are only as moral as the grammar of their construction,
and powerless to mediate by secular means the irrepressible conflict
of legitimacies which is the principle of their life.

Are there then, as between Whitman and Lincoln, two policies of union or only one? There is, on the showing of this argument, only one—with this qualification: A faithful response to Whitman's originality will be a continual critique, in view of a policy toward institutions, of the structures of representation, in the light of the revelation of personhood unmistakably presented in Lincoln's language and countenance—the archetype of the doomed companion laboring in history, whom we now know and hope to love. The open road is the one line that is not imaginary.

NOTES

1. The argument of this paper is extensively indebted to James Buechler, "Abraham Lincoln, American Literature, and the Affirmation of Union" (1955), a Harvard Honors essay.

2. See Arthur Bestor, "The American Civil War as a Constitutional Crisis," in Lawrence M. Friedman and Harry N. Scheiber, *American Law and the Constitutional Order* (Cambridge: Harvard University Press, 1978), p. 234:

> But the abstractness of Constitutional issues has nothing to do, one way or the other, with the role they may happen to play at a moment of crisis. Thanks to the structure of the American Constitutional system itself, the abstruse issue of slavery in the territories was required to carry the burden of well-nigh all the emotional drives, well-nigh all the political and economic tensions, and well-nigh all the moral perplexities that resulted from the existence in the United States of an archaic system of labor and an intolerable policy of racial subjection.

3. The analysis of Lincoln's meanings that follows is not psychological in method. I have, however, greatly benefited from the findings of Dwight G. Anderson, *Abraham Lincoln, The Quest for Immortality* (New York: Alfred A. Knopf, 1982); also, George B. Forgie, *Patricide in the House Divided* (New York: W. W. Norton, 1979), and Charles B. Strozier, *Lincoln's Quest for Union* (New York: Basic Books, 1982).

4. The destruction by the Revolution of the older "prestige order," based on inherited class or status, was accompanied by the development of an "indigenous class structure . . . based upon property." See Jackson Turner Main, *The Social Structure of Revolutionary America* (Princeton: Princeton University Press, 1965), pp. 282, 283. The loss of feudal status-criteria, and the loss also of the model of the hypostatic union (the union of persons in

the Trinity), were correlative shocks contributing to the crisis. Emerson and Whitman attempted to recuperate the former development by reconstructing on a secular basis the empowerments lost as a consequence of the latter.

5. See John T. Irwin, "Self-Evidence and Self-Reference: Nietzsche and Tragedy, Whitman and Opera" in *New Literary History* 9, no. 1 (Autumn 1979):177–92. I fully agree with his notion of the "endlessly oscillating grounding" of self and text in Whitman, but not with his assimilation of Whitman's song to Schopenhauer's music.

6. In a conversation with the Reverend J. P. Gulliver in 1860, Lincoln specified two biographical moments in which his style was formed. As a child, he says:

> I used to get irritated when anybody talked to me in a way I could not understand. I don't think I ever got angry at anything else in my life. I was not satisfied until I had repeated it over and over, until I had put it in language plain enough, as I thought, for any boy I knew to comprehend. This was a kind of passion with me. . . . I am never easy now, when I am handling a thought, till I have bounded it North, and bounded it South, and bounded it East, and bounded it West.

The other moment he describes as the discovery of a means to make *demonstration* result, as Webster's dictionary promised, in "certain proof." He supplied the means by secluding himself in his father's house "til I could give any proposition in the six books of Euclid at sight." Gulliver's report was published in the New York *Independent,* 1 September 1864, rpt. in James Mellon, *The Face of Lincoln* (New York: Viking Press, 1979). Lincoln's source for the "house divided" image as a logical contradiction is Tom Paine's *Common Sense,* 1:8 of *The Complete Writings,* ed. Philip Foner (New York: Citadel Press, 1945).

7. The centrality in Lincoln's mind, and the minds of his audiences, of the hermeneutic proposition—"the intention of the law-giver is the law"—is attested by its place in "The First Inaugural." Roy P. Basler et al., *The Collected Works of Abraham Lincoln* (New Brunswick, N.J.: Rutgers University Press, 1954), 4:263; hereafter cited as Basler.

Much of the Lincoln-Douglas debates, and other central arguments of Lincoln, notably "The Cooper Institute Address," are efforts to infer from indirect indications the intentions of the fathers who become archetypes of the hidden meaning-intending will of the singular person. Lincoln's God is also such a person. Divergence of interpretive inference is one of the obstacles to unanimity which, as I shall suggest, Whitman undertakes to abolish: "Have you felt so proud to get at the meaning of poems? / Stop this day and night with me and you shall possess the origin of all poems." "Song of Myself," 11.32, 33 in Sculley Bradley and Harold Blodget, *Walt Whitman: Leaves of Grass* (New York: W. W. Norton, 1973); hereafter cited as Bradley.

8. Marianne Moore's "Lincoln and the Art of the Word" in *A Marianne Moore Reader* (New York: Viking Press, 1965) characterizes him as a "Euclid of the heart." The standard essay on Lincoln as a writer is Roy P. Basler, "Lincoln's Developmet as a Writer" in *A Touchstone for Greatness* (Westport, Conn.: Greenwood Press, 1973). See also, Edmund Wilson, *Patriotic Gore* (New York: Oxford University Press, 1962), pp. 119ff.

9. Lincoln's identification of the deontological distinction between right and wrong with the rhetorical authority of "logic" can be seen in the following reply to Douglas at Alton (Basler 3:315): "He says he 'don't care whether it [slavery] is voted up or voted down' in the territories. . . . Any man can say that who does not see anything wrong with slavery, but no man can logically say he don't care whether a wrong is voted up or voted down. He may say he don't care whether an indifferent thing is voted up or down, but he must logically have a choice between a right thing and a wrong thing."

10. F. O. Matthiessen, *From the Heart of Europe* (New York: Oxford University Press, 1948), p. 90.

11. For Whitman on abolition, see Whitman's essays in *The Brooklyn Daily Eagle* in 1846 and 1847, reprinted in Cleveland Rodgers and John Black, *The Gathering of Forces* (New York: G. P. Putnam's Sons, 1920) 1:179–238. Note also Whitman's essays in the same volume on union. Whitman and Lincoln held the same political views, except that Whitman's attitude toward government and political parties displayed his aversion to units of social organization other than the individual and the whole. For the development of the Transcendental writers of the period toward the acceptance of abolition, see Daniel Aaron, *The Unwritten War* (New York: Alred A. Knopf, 1973).

12. Basler, 4:264.

13. "I therefore declare that, in view of the Constitution and the laws, the Union is unbroken; and, to the extent of my ability, I shall take care, as the Constitution itself expressly enjoins me, that the laws of the Union be faithfully executed in all the States" (Basler, 4:265).

14. Taney in Dred Scott makes plain the primary function of the Constitution as a regulative document which creates by secular means rights-bearing human beings, according to the principle of difference: "The words 'people of the United States' and 'citizens' are synonomous terms, and mean the same thing. . . . It is true, every person, and every class of persons, who were at the time of the adoption of the Constitution recognized as citizens in the several States, became also citizens of this new political body; but none other; it was formed by them, and for them and their posterity, but for no one else" in Henry Steele Commager, *Documents of American History* (New York: Appleton-Century-Crofts, 1949), pp. 339–45.

15. This was a conscious and practical matter. E. Merton Coulter (*The Confederate States of America, 1861-1865* [Baton Rouge: Louisiana State University Press, 1950], p. 10) cites a Georgia editor (*Atlanta Southern Confederacy*, 25 October 1862) who says of slavery that it made "the poor man respectable." It gave the poor "an elevated position in society that they would not otherwise have." For the specific legal requirement of respect by slaves see the *Code Noir* of Louisiana, cited in John Codman Hurd, *The Law of Freedom and Bondage* (New York: Negro Universities Press, 1962) 2:157, 158. More generally, "Slavery was seen as a model of dependence and self-surrender. For Plato, Aristotle, and Augustine this meant that it was a necessary part of a world that required moral order and discipline; it was the base on which rested an intricate and hierarchical pattern of authority" (David Brion Davis, *The Problem of Slavery in Western Culture* [Ithaca: Cornell University Press, 1966], p. 90; hereafter cited as Davis).

16. Emory Holloway, *The Uncollected Poetry and Prose of Walt Whitman* (Garden City, N.Y.: Doubleday, Page & Co., 1921), 2:69; hereafter cited as Holloway. For the functional analogy between body/matter/slave, and soul/spirit/master, see Davis, p. 304.

17. Hooloway, 2:65.

18. See "Fragment on Free Labor" (Basler 3:462), and "Address before the Wisconsin State Agricultural Society, Milwaukee, Wisconsin," 30 September 1859 (*ibid*, pp. 471ff.).

19. Edward Sapir, *Language: an Introduction to the Study of Speech* (New York: Harcourt Brace, 1949), p. 224; D. H. Lawrence, *Studies in Classical American Literature* (New York: Viking Press, 1964), p. 170. For Cesare Pavese, see Gay Wilson Allen, *The New Walt Whitman Handbook* (New York: New York University Press, 1975), p. 317.

20. In "Democratic Vistas" at p. 981, *Walt Whitman: Complete Poetry and Collected Prose* (New York: Library of America, 1982).

21. "The Eighteenth Presidency" in Clifton Joseph Furness, *Walt Whitman's Workshop* (Cambridge: Harvard University Press, 1928), p. 109.

22. Cf. 15.171 of "When Lilacs Last . . .": "And I saw askant the armies." The "crossing" moment, as in "Calvary Crossing a Ford," or the crossing of bodies in #5 of "Song of Myself," signifies for Whitman immediacy of access, unqualified by space or time. So, also, in "Crossing Brooklyn Ferry": "I see you face to face."

23. Basler, 5:535.

24. Ibid., p. 537.

25. On honor and dishonor as a zero-sum transaction see the "Epilogue" to Gregory Nagy, *Comparative Studies in Greek and Indic Meter* (Cambridge: Harvard University Press, 1974), p. 261.

26. Bradley, p. 714, 11.123–24.

27. The expression is William James's. James's "radical empiricism" is fundamentally explanatory of Whitman's epistemology.

To be radical, an empiricism must neither admit into its constructions any element that is not directly experienced, nor exclude from them any element that is not directly experienced. For such a philosophy, *the relations that connect experiences must themselves be experienced relations, and any kind of relation experienced must be accounted as "real" as anything else in the system.* . . . *Radical empiricism,* as I understand it, *does full justice to conjunctive relations,* without however treating them as rationalism always tends to treat them as being true in some supernal way, as if the unity of things and their variety belonged to different orders of truth and vitality altogether.

William James, *Essays in Radical Empiricism and a Pluralistic Universe* (New York: E. P. Dutton, 1971) pp. 25, 26.

28. Whitman's equivocation of the difference of sign and signified, word and thing, body and soul, "I" and "you" expresses an intention to rid conjunctive transactions (whether seeing, loving, speaking, or political bonding) of all representational mediations. This is the reason of his use of Lucretian optics (as in "Crossing Brooklyn Ferry"), his interest in phrenology, his dislike of political parties, poetic diction, mythology, and so on.

29. "Celebration" in Whitman (as in "I celebrate myself") invokes the meaning of pluralization which inheres in all cognates of Latin *celebrare*. Pluralization as a solution to the bad faith of speaking at all (where silence signifies fraternal union, and speech interrupts that union) is vividly expressed by George Fox in *A Battle-door for Teachers and Professors to Learn Singular and Plural:* "All languages are to me no more than dust, who was before Languages were, and am redeemed out of Languages into the power where all men shall agree" cited by Richard Bauman in "Speaking in the Light: The Role of the Quaker Minister" in Richard Bauman and Joel Sherzer, *Explorations in the Ethnography of Speaking* (Cambridge: Cambridge University Press, 1974), p. 146.

30. Basler, 4:90.

31. Basler, 5:537.

32. My discussion of Whitman is intended to show that a serious political poetry (like a serious policy of any kind) is not merely an advocacy, but an addition to the given repertory of conjunctive relationships such that "literary" judgment about the poetry's success or failure constitutes an assessment (or problematic") of the coming-to-pass, as an actual state of affairs, of the life which is its "subject." In this sense, a poetic structure is a political policy. Whitman identified for modernism, and for our time as well as I believe, the heuristic primacy of the structural features of poetry.

Library of Congress Cataloging in Publication Data
Main entry under title:

The American Renaissance reconsidered.

    (Selected papers from the English Institute; 1982–83,
new ser., no. 9)
    1. American literature–19th century–History and
criticism–Addresses, essays, lectures. I. Michaels,
Walter Benn. II. Pease, Donald E. III. Series:
Selected papers from the English Institute; new ser.,
no. 9.
PS201.A476 1984   810'.9   84-47940
ISBN 0-8018-2542-3
ISBN 0-8018-3937-8 (pbk)